The
Trombonist's
Handbook

Reginald H. Fink

The author studied with the late Emory B. Remington (*The Chief*), graduated from the Eastman School of Music and received his Ph.D. from the University of Oklahoma. He has been principal trombonist of the Oklahoma City Symphony Orchestra and a member of the Ithaca Brass Quintet. Among the other ensembles with which he has played are the orchestras of Pittsburgh, Buffalo and Rochester.

As a respected teacher, his students have achieved acclaim as members of leading symphony orchestras and major Armed Service bands. In addition, his students hold positions in respected schools and universities.

In recent years, Dr. Fink has become well known for his educational publications which are being used throughout the world. He has served on the faculties of Oklahoma City University, West Virginia University, Ithaca College and The Ohio University, teaching in the areas of performance, music education, acoustics and research. His in depth understanding of many areas of knowledge has contributed to the comprehensiveness of this detailed text.

The Trombonist's Handbook

A Complete Guide to Playing and Teaching the Trombone

by Reginald H. Fink

Accura Music   Athens, Ohio 45701

ISBN: 0-918194-01-6

Library of Congress Catalog Card Number: LC 76-55601

Cover Design: Paul Bradford

Lithographed in the United States of America by Edwards Bros., Inc., Ann Arbor, Michigan

Dedication

to my wife, *Lorraine*
and my children, *Carl Peter* and *Kristine Rebecca*

Acknowledgements

Thanking everyone for their help, inspiration and encouragement is nearly impossible, but I must attempt to mention a few who contributed either to my development as a musician and teacher or who encouraged this writing. To my first teacher, my father, A. Reginald Fink, and to my other trombone teachers, the late Dallas Minnich, the late Martin L. Keller and the late Emory B. Remington (*The Chief*), my deep appreciation for their help and patience. Also to all the teachers, conductors and colleagues with whom I have worked, my thanks for their generous sharing of musical insights.

My thanks also to Prof. William R. Brophy of The Ohio University and Ms. Rebecca Reynolds for encouraging me to complete this work; Mr. Paul Bradford for his cover design; Ms. Patricia Black for her editorial help; and Ms. Eva Bell for her assistance with the typing.

Thanks also to Carl Fischer, Inc. for permission to reprint excerpts from *Studies in Legato*, and to C. G. Conn, Ltd. and Warren E. Collins, Inc. for the photographs they provided.

Finally, to my students, who over the years brought me a wide variety of performance problems, who cooperated with their solution and who thus contributed in a unique way to the advice given in this book, my appreciation.

Reginald H. Fink

Table of Contents

Table of Illustrations

Preface

You will find that each teacher has a different approach even though they are all working towards the same goal. As you continue to study, the differences will multiply. It would be a serious mistake to believe that one teacher is completely right and that all other teachers are entirely wrong. A certain approach may suit a particular student better than another approach, but very seldom is an approach wrong for everyone.

In this book, I will recount several correct ways of learning to play the trombone. Over the past 25 years of teaching I have found these to be good procedures. I have dropped many procedures in which I used to believe. I have found that other procedures are especially useful though I originally rejected them. Therefore, I can recommend these procedures only for the present. They are not the final word.

I will criticize certain methods which I consider to be either physically or mentally dangerous. I will also criticize some false assumptions about the physiology of the body, even though these may be good *ways of thinking*, though physically impossible. For instance, some think the diaphragm tenses to support the breath even though tension in the diaphragm causes a downward motion and is a function of inhalation. When air is exhaled, the tension of the diaphragm is released and it is not possible to push the air out with the diaphragm.

Bring a positive mental attitude to the reading of this book. The most important difference between a good player and a mediocre player is the attitude they have about themselves, about playing trombone, and about practicing. The better player is not always the most talented, nor the most diligent. He simply thinks positively and makes logical and efficient use of his practice time. The mediocre player may have more talent and may practice more, yet he does not get results. He is a loser. This loser takes the correct technique and wastes hours proving to himself that he cannot do it.

All the procedures listed in the book are valid and efficient. I can endorse each of them as an excellent method for learning to play the trombone. On the other hand, just as there is no perfect golf swing, there is no trombonist with a perfect approach. You should not worry if you do not use quite the proper technique. The sound that comes from your bell is what is important.

I owe many of the ideas in this book to the late Emory B. Remington, a great friend and teacher. The suggestions are also the result of years of professional playing, long hours of practice, and innumerable private and class trombone lessons. I hope that with this writing that I am able to help others achieve better musical performances with less effort. If this is true, I will have been repaid for my efforts.

Reginald H. Fink

Chapter 1
Handling the Trombone

Opening the Case

Improper and hurried opening of the case can damage the trombone. Shaped cases carry the slide attached to the lid. The slide will be twisted out of alignment if the case lid is opened with the slightest twist.

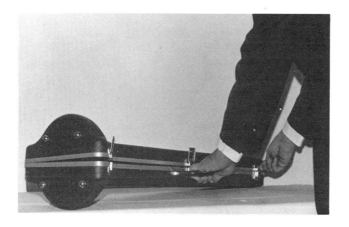

Fig. 1   Incorrect Way of Opening the Trombone Case

Caution: Open trombone-shaped cases with a calm, unhurried action with one hand on *each* of the clasps. **DO NOT** open the case with one hand placed at the end of the lid while the other hand holds the handle or the bottom of the case.

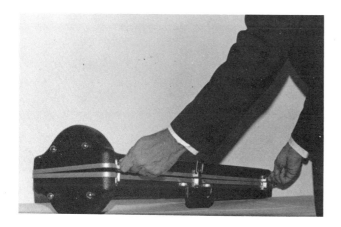

Fig. 2   Correct Way of Opening the Trombone Case

Handling the Trombone

The slide can be damaged if you grasp the two slides together.

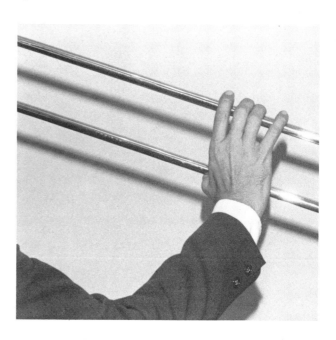

Fig. 3   Incorrect Way of Grasping the Trombone Slide

Grasp the slide by the braces. Assume that the slide lock is not locked and grasp both braces together. Do not bump the tubing of the slide against furniture or the rim of the bell when assembling it.

Assembling the Trombone

1. Place the case on the floor (not in your lap) and open it carefully. Do not twist the lid of the case.

2. Release *all* clasps. Now the parts can be picked up as needed without having to release a clasp while juggling another part of the trombone.

3. Pick up the bell section with your left hand.

4. Pick up the slide section with your right hand by taking hold of both braces.

5. Push the tapered end of the slide section into the bell section receiver with a twisting action. Adjust the

1

sections so that the slide and bell sections are at an angle of not more than 90°. Tighten the bell lock. **NOTE:** It is very easy to nick the outside slide with the rim of the bell during this operation. Be careful!

6. Twist the mouthpiece into the slide section. **DO** **NOT** hit the mouthpiece with the heel of your hand to seat it.

The procedure listed above is only one way of organizing the routine into small steps. Modify it as necessary.

Chapter 2
Hand Grips and Playing Position

Hand Grips

Left Hand

Wrap the middle, ring and little fingers with the palm of the hand around the upper slide brace. The palm and these three fingers do most of the work of supporting the **ENTIRE** weight of the trombone.

Fig. 4   Correct Left Hand Grip

Place the index finger against the side of the lead pipe a little below where the mouthpiece enters the instrument. Place the thumb around the bell brace or on the F attachment lever.

You should be able to hold the instrument parallel to the floor with this three-finger grip. Your forearm and wrist muscles will develop strength with a few days of serious practice.

If your left-hand grip is weak, you will try to support the weight of the instrument by hunching your left shoulder, tilting your head or by twisting your neck. These actions restrict your breathing, tighten your throat and twist your embouchure.

Do not use your right hand to help support the instrument. This slows the slide technique, bounces the instrument when shifting positions and makes legato playing uneven.

THE ABILITY OF THE LEFT HAND TO SUPPORT THE ENTIRE WEIGHT OF THE INSTRUMENT WITH EASE IS IMPORTANT TO THE DEVELOPMENT OF THE EMBOUCHURE, THE BREATHING AND THE SLIDE TECHNIQUE.

Right Hand

While looking into the palm of your hand, place the first joint of the index and middle fingers at the bottom of the slide brace.

Fig. 5   Correct Right Hand Grip

Place your thumb on the other side of the bottom of the slide brace. The brace should touch the side of the thumb near its tip.

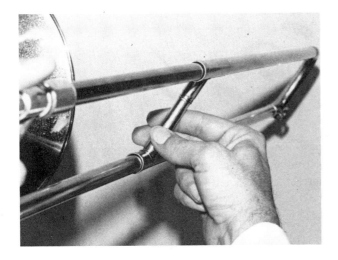

Fig. 6   Correct Right Hand Grip from Player's View

Curl your ring and little fingers into the palm of your hand. These fingers are not used in the manipulation of the slide.

Alternate Righthand Method

With the palm of your hand facing the floor, place the first joint of the index and middle fingers at the bottom of the slide brace with both fingers touching the top of the lower slide. The side of your index finger is placed against the bottom of the slide brace.

Place the end of your thumb on the other side of the bottom of the slide brace. (This is the same as the other method).

Comparison of the Two Righthand Grips

Both grips are recommended by competent players and teachers. There are nearly as many who recommend one method as the other. I prefer the first method because it allows the fingers of the hand to flex more easily and it adds a whip action to the motion and final positioning of the slide. Besides, the wrist flexes more easily in this direction. More movement is possible through flexion and hyperextension than through abduction and adduction. (See Fig. 7 and Fig. 8).

Those who recommend the second method insist that the positioning of the slide is more accurate and some claim that it is more rapid.

Playing Posture

All of the normal requirements of good posture apply to the trombone. You must sit and stand erectly with balance and relaxation.

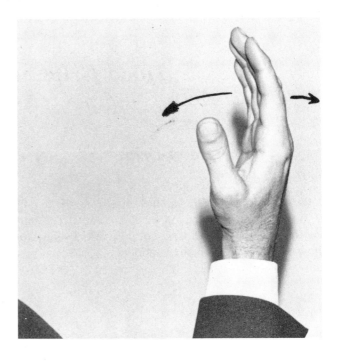

Fig. 7   Flexion and Hyperextension

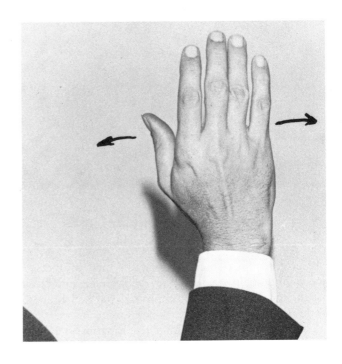

Fig. 8   Abduction and Adduction

You also have some posture problems that are unique to trombonists.

Bring the trombone to your face, do not push your head forward and stretch your neck to meet it. Many embouchure and tone-production problems can be traced to tension in the upper chest and neck which may be caused by stretching the neck or holding the head in an unusual position. Another part of the problem may be caused by your inability to support the weight of the instrument with your left hand. Still another reason may be the extreme marching band posture that requires you to play the trombone while holding it parallel to the ground. Since most trombonists tend to angle the instrument slightly downward, most players must make a physical adjustment to accomodate this marching band requirement. Lean back from the waist to avoid stretching your neck or thrusting your chin forward if you must hold the trombone out straight.

The tubing of the bell section of the trombone will touch your collar or your neck. This adds additional stability to the instrument. The left arm should be held slightly away from your chest and your left shoulder should be relaxed. **DO NOT** hunch your left shoulder or hold your left elbow against your chest to support the weight. The instrument cannot be supported by resting it against your face, your left shoulder or while your arm is propped on your chest.

Sit on the left side of the music stand, if at all possible. In this position, your bell is to the left of the music, the tone projects past the stand, the bell does not obstruct your view of the music and the slide is less likely to hit the upright support of the stand. Those who must sit on the right side (or in the middle when there are three playing from the same stand) have to adjust so that they can see the music and yet avoid hitting the stand with their slides. Many players develop problems with their embouchures and postures by having to sit on the right side of the stand all of the time. The only way to avoid this is to buy extra music.

Do not twist your posture by using improper slide technique. If you hold your right shoulder still when reaching for sixth or seventh position, the arm may not extend far enough. Do not allow the trombone to swing to your right so that the shoulder can be used to extend the reach of the right arm. Swinging the instrument to the right eventually will twist the embouchure and the posture. Always hold your trombone straight when reaching for the extended positions and *hunch* your right shoulder *forward* to give your right arm the needed reach.

Body posture while playing the trombone is relaxed and erect. Do not hold your elbows away from your chest in an exaggerated manner, but do not let them touch your rib cage either. Most of the problems connected with posture are caused by a weak left hand grip, a rigid marching band posture, the crowding of three players to one music stand, or the incorrect extension of the slide for the sixth and seventh positions.

Chapter 3
Care and Maintenance

Lubricating the Slide

The slide can be lubricated with slide oil, cold cream or one of the commercially prepared slide creams. Most advanced trombonists prefer to use cold cream or one of the slide creams. The creams are inexpensive and work smoothly for a long time without care. As a rule, oil must be added more often than cream to keep the slide working smoothly.

Lubricating the Slide with Cold Cream

1. Remove the outside slide and lay it in a safe place.

2. Hold one of the inside slides with one hand and with the other hand wipe it with a lint-free cloth or lint-free toilet paper.

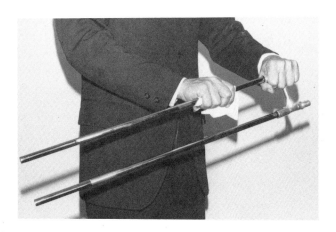

Fig. 9 Wiping the Slide

Do not use specially softened paper or facial tissues which have lint. Be careful not to bend or push the slide when wiping it. Hold the tissue around the slide with your thumb and fingers and wipe down the slide with a pulling action. Never wipe by pushing up the slide. Not only will the pushing bend the slide, but some of the old dirty lubricant will be pushed up into the slide receivers. It will soon work loose and foul the new lubricant.

To avoid bending the slides out of parallel, always hold the same slide with both hands. **NEVER** hold one slide while wiping the other.

3. Daub the cold cream on the slide at several places

then smooth it out. Rub it over the entire surface of the slide, but do not allow it to be pushed into the slide receiver. Again, handle only one slide at a time. **DO NOT** hold one slide while working with the other.

4. Wipe the slide with a tissue as you did in Step 2, but do not use as much pressure. Use only enough pressure to remove the excess cream. The slide should have only a greasy film of cold cream on it after you have wiped it. If the white of the cream can be seen, there is too much remaining on the slide.

5. Spray the entire slide with water.

6. Carefully slip the inside slides into the outside slides. Do this slowly at first because it is very easy to catch and twist the slides when replacing the outside slide.

7. Spray the slide with water from time to time to renew the slipperiness.

Alternate Method

Some players prefer to apply the cream to the boot or stocking of the slide only. In time, the lubricant transfers to the entire surface of the slide. The effect seems to be the same as having placed the cold cream on the inside slide in the first place.

Problems

The cream gets gummy when mixed with oil. When the cream is first applied to a slide that has previously been oiled, the slide action is usually poor. The slide will have to be cleaned and lubricated every few minutes until all of the oil has been removed.

Most people when first learning to lubricate the slide put on too much cold cream and do not wipe enough of it off. If you have put too much cold cream on the slide, the slide will not work well even after wiping the slide correctly because there is an accumulation of cream on the inside of the outside slide. To remove the excess, either wipe the slide frequently until the excess has transferred to the inside slide and been wiped away, or run a cleaning cloth on a rod into the outside slide. (The use of the cleaning rod is explained later in this chapter).

Cleaning the Trombone

There are at least four good reasons for cleaning the trombone regularly. Dirt, old lubricants and organic material collect in the instrument and the growth of bacteria and fungus is rapid in the warm humid atmosphere of the trombone.

If this material is not removed, it:

1. becomes a health hazard
2. narrows the bore of the trombone
3. aids the corrosion and deterioration of the metal
4. fouls the moving parts

Cleaning the Mouthpiece

The throat and backbore section of the mouthpiece is the first point to become dirty. This section is one of the most critical portions of the instrument. The dirt is near your mouth and is a hazard to your health. The bore is small at this point and a little dirt will greatly change the bore dimensions, altering the response, intonation and tone quality of the trombone.

The mouthpiece should be scrubbed regularly with either a mouthpiece brush (available at music stores) or a swab made from a pipe cleaner. Scrubbing is not necessary if you habitually run water through the mouthpiece every few days.

Fig. 10   Mouthpiece Brush

Cleaning the Inside of the Inside Slide

The inside slide can be cleaned by washing it with water or by scrubbing it with a brush that is mounted on a metal spring snake. The quickest and easiest method, though, is to wipe the inside of the slide with a long cloth swab (one inch wide and at least two inches longer than the slide). Attach the swab to a sturdy

non-kinking string (high test fishing line or rotary valve string) and a small fishing sinker. **IMPORTANT:** The cloth must be longer than the slide so that if the string breaks the swab can be grasped and pulled from the trombone.

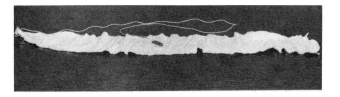

Fig. 11   Slide Swab

Drop the sinker and the line through one of the slides and then, while holding on to the slide, pull the swab through. Great care must be taken to avoid bending the slides out of parallel when using a swab. **NEVER** hold the brace or the opposite slide. Place the force of the pulling only on the slide that is being cleaned.

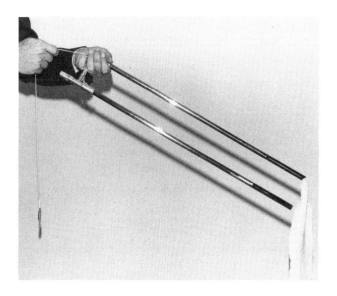

Fig. 12   Swabbing the Inside of the Inside Slide

Repeat on the other slide.

Dirt will not build up if the slide is swabbed every few weeks. Also, swabbing is far more convenient than taking the trombone to a bath tub or shower. Furthermore, the bore dimensions are kept the same if the swab is used every few weeks rather than cleaning a large amount of dirt from the bore every six months or so.

Cleaning the Outside of the Inside Slide

The inside slide usually only needs to be wiped and lubricated regularly. If chronic slide trouble develops, it is possible that the receivers have accumulated dirt. This dirt leaves the receiver and works its way down the slide and fouls the action. It is then necessary to scrub the receiver with a small brush or a pipe cleaner. Remove the springs if the receiver is equipped with them. They can be reached with a crochet hook and pulled out. They are not attached. After the receiver is cleaned, the springs are reinstalled by simply pushing them back into the receiver. If the slide trouble persists, check the inside of the outside slide for dirt and dried lubricant.

Cleaning the Inside of the Outside Slide

It is not necessary to clean the outside slide as often as the mouthpiece or the inside of the inside slide. The dirt is usually dried lubricant and brass corrosion and does not need to be cleaned more than every six months. A cleaning rod is needed to wipe the inside of the outside slide. The swab described above is used to wrap the rod so that it will not scratch the inside of the slide.

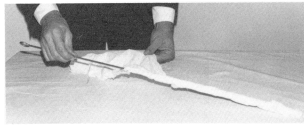

Fig. 13   Wrapping the Cleaning Rod

A few inches of the swab should be pulled through the hole at the end of the cleaning rod and the remainder of the swab is wrapped around the rod. Dip the end of the cleaning rod in kerosene and then push the rod up and down the slide, using a rotating motion.

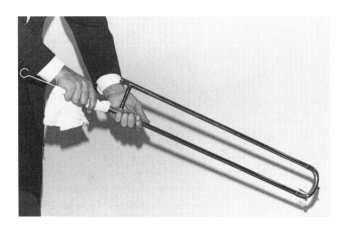

Fig. 14   Cleaning the Inside of the Outside Slide

Handle the slide carefully and hold the slide that is being cleaned with the other hand. The slides may be twisted out of parallel if the slide is held by the brace or the other slide.

Water and a snake-type brush must be used to clean the crook of the outside slide. This cleaning job will not have to be done often if the inside of the inside slide is kept clean with the swab.

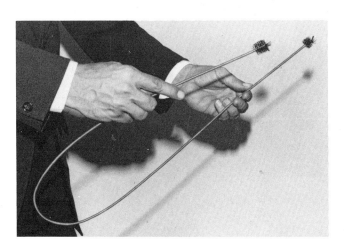

Fig. 15   Snake-Type Brush

Cleaning the Bell Section

The bell section seldom needs to be cleaned. Occasionally a swab can be pulled through the small section (after removing the tuning slide), but unless the inside of the inside slide has not been cleaned for a long time, you will not find any dirt in the bell.

Cleaning the F Attachment

The F attachment section rarely needs to be cleaned. Check it for dirt only when the valve has had to be dismantled for restringing. It is impractical and unnecessary to take the valve apart to see whether there is dirt in the F attachment tubing. If the inside of the inside slide is kept clean, very little dirt and organic material will collect in the F attachment tubing. (Instructions for dismantling the F attachment valve are in Chapter 8, F Attachments).

Chapter 4
Embouchure

Embouchure Formation

The formation of the embouchure for trombone playing is very important. Care should be taken from the very beginning so that correct habits are set during the first few moments of playing.

In general, the embouchure is formed as if you were pronouncing the letter *M*. When saying the *M*, the teeth are separated and the lower jaw is brought down and out so that the front teeth are opposed to each other, as when preparing to bite celery with the front incisors. Your lips are tensed and rolled in slightly—more than they would be if just pronouncing the *M* in normal conversation. Finally, the corners of the mouth are tucked in against your teeth as if you are trying not to smile.

Pronouncing an *M* will not automatically produce a correct embouchure. HOW the *M* is pronounced is more important. The muscles of the face are set in a combination pucker and smile which stops the puffing of the cheeks and forms the corners of the embouchure. In short, the embouchure has a strong and determined set which looks like "the brass player's face." (Farkas, *The Art of Brass Playing*, p. 19)

Many older method books tell you to smile and stretch the lips like strings over the front teeth, (Clark), and others tell you to pucker the lips (Schlossberg). Either method if carried to the extreme creates problems. The stretching of the muscles makes them thin and makes them vulnerable to damage from mouthpiece pressure. To change registers you almost have to slide the smiling lips over the rim of the mouthpiece. Puckered lips can muffle the vibration and the tone just chokes off when you attempt to play higher or louder. Analyse the tendencies of your embouchure and stop either extreme before it becomes a habit. In most cases, the smiling muscles of the cheeks are stronger than the puckering muscles of the lips, and you must emphasize puckering for embouchure control. Sometimes the pucker is stronger than the smile and then you must make a constant effort to smile. In the ideal embouchure the mouth corners move neither to the center nor to the sides when you change registers.

I teach my young students to form an embouchure by saying *M* and then making a "putt-ing" sound with their lips. This sound is difficult to describe in print, but develops from contracting the lips into a center point (as one would squeeze a drinking straw). Then the lips are released outwards from this center point with a fricative *P* sound. The release of the lips is controlled so that the lips buzz a few times before the sound stops. The sound may be written *MP****. There are no vowel sounds for this noise and the support comes from the air in the mouth. It is not supported from the air in the chest. This lip action seems natural to a nine-year-old, and is one of the many sounds that a baby makes as he experiments with his lips while learning to speak. When I *show* the student how to make the sound I also show him the firm face, the spreading of the jaws **AND** the focusing of the vibration of the lips in the center without talking about embouchure. With this beginning, the player does not even think of letting his lips flap loosely. After a few pronounciations of *MP****, I ask him to buzz his lips at this center point without the mouthpiece. Now he has to exhale air from his chest through his lips, but he is not asked to use his tongue. The written form of this buzzing sound without tongue would be *MP*P*P*P*P**. After this, I help the student place the mouthpiece on his embouchure and work on the first notes.

It takes far less time to go through this procedure with a student than it takes to read the above. It takes fewer than 60 seconds of the first lesson, but in that time several good habits are started: holding the jaw firmly with the teeth apart, rolling the lips slightly, setting the corners of the embouchure and concentrating the buzz in the center portion of the lips.

Mouthpiece Placement

The mouthpiece is placed on the embouchure—the embouchure is not formed on the mouthpiece.

After the *M* embouchure is formed, the mouthpiece is placed midway between the corners of the mouth and as high on the upper lip as is comfortably possible.

Fig. 16 High placement of the Mouthpiece on the Embouchure

10

Many old method books recommend a half and half or even a one-third upper and two-thirds lower lip placement.

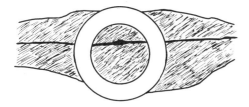

Fig. 17   Low Placement of the Mouthpiece on the Embouchure

Most modern professional players place their mouthpieces so that there is more upper lip than lower lip in the mouthpiece. Only players with severe underbites use more lower lip than upper as a rule.

The size of the trombone mouthpiece influences its placement and the opening of the jaws. At first, you may form an embouchure which will not give you a large even surface for the seating of the mouthpiece. After a few trials, you will learn how far to spread the jaws so that the lips will make an air-tight seal with the mouthpiece. You will make this jaw spread as part of your embouchure formation and after a few weeks of careful practice, you will be able to form an embouchure and place the mouthpiece without adjusting the spread of your jaws.

Mouthpiece Angle

The mouthpiece tends to slant slightly downwards, because the upper rim of the mouthpiece usually rests on or above the bump on the gums at the base of the upper teeth. The teeth may be perfectly aligned, but the bump on the gums pushes the rim of the mouthpiece forward.

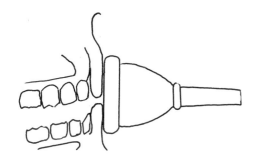

Fig. 18   Correct Alignment of the Teeth

Some teachers insist that the lower jaw be brought forward until the mouthpiece (and the instrument) will meet the embouchure at a 90° angle. In other words, they insist that you sit and stand erectly with the trombone held parallel to the ground. For most trombone players this 90° angle is **WRONG.** The jutting of the lower jaw (to which the base of the tongue is attached) forces you either to tongue between the teeth, or curl your tongue to be able to tongue behind the upper teeth.

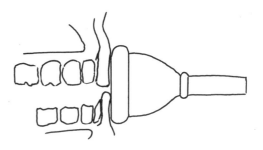

Fig. 19   Incorrect Alignment of the Teeth

For the marching band, where trombones must be held parallel to the ground, it is better for your embouchure if you do not push your jaw forward, but lean your head and chest back instead. Leaning back does not distort the embouchure, but does force you to play with your head and chest at an angle which can place an unnatural strain on your neck and your breathing. You should not point your instrument at the ground (as a furrow digger), but should allow the instrument to slope downward at a 20° to 30° angle to the ground. This angle is not the same for all players and in a marching band some will have to lean their heads back and some will have to lean very slightly forward in order to have the trombone slides aligned. The 30° angle to the ground position should be a good compromise position. Only the underbite players can achieve a parallel position without strain or embouchure distortion.

Direction of the Air Stream

The bump on the gums makes the embouchure appear to recede even though the teeth may be properly aligned. Examine the photographs of the trombonists in Farkas, *The Art of Brass Playing.* Also take special note of the embouchures of older players whose playing has endured and matured through the years. (At a recent national workshop for trombonists, whose ages ranged from 18 to 79, only a few of the 142 embouchures did not recede. The large majority had some degree of recession.)

With the usual receding embouchure, the air stream tends to leave the lips in a slightly downstream angle. The underbite player is the exception to this rule. The underbite player tends to be an upstream player. Though photographic studies and various other tests tend to prove that some players do not play downstream, I recommend that for teaching and playing purposes that you think downstream. I suggest that you mentally aim the air stream at the lower part of the mouthpiece cup, somewhere near the throat of the mouthpiece, rather than attempt to direct the airstream directly at the throat of the mouthpiece. (This is confirmed by Reinhardt, *Pivot System* and disagreed with by Farkas, *The Art of Brass Playing*.)

Aperture of the Embouchure

The shape of the aperture of your embouchure is important. The aperture should be as round as possible. To change the shape of an elliptical aperture to a round one, pucker in and open the jaws still further. Holding the lips in a stretched manner, with a long elliptical aperture, tends to make the tone airy and buzzy. The tone is usually improved immediately and quite noticeably when the player thinks of rounding his embouchure and rounding the aperture of the buzzing portion of the lips.

Using the Mouthpiece Visualizer

The placement of the mouthpiece on the embouchure and the size and shape of the aperture of the embouchure can be checked with a mouthpiece visualizer. Visualizers are purchased or can be made by welding a rod to the rim of a mouthpiece.

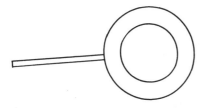

Fig. 20   Mouthpiece Visualizer

Visualizers are quite useful for checking the position of the normal set of the mouthpiece, but they may not give you the correct impression of a buzz or an aperture. The visualizer does not give you the same resistance as the instrument. Avoid making adjustments on the visualizer to prove a point. In other words, work with a mouthpiece visualizer, but do it sparingly and objectively.

Vibration of the Lips

Whether both lips or only one lip of the embouchure vibrates has been an ongoing argument for several years. Also, some say that the lips touch when buzzing the mouthpiece in the same way as when playing the instrument, while others say that buzzing is artificial and that the lips vibrate near each other but do not necessarily touch when playing the instrument with the best possible tone (like the puff theory of vocal production).

Lloyd Leno's recent high speed photographic study proves that both lips do vibrate, they touch each other during this vibration and they vibrate at the same frequency as the pitch that is being played. Even so, it is advantageous for many people to focus their attention on only the upper lip when trying to shape an aperture or deepen the tone. For those who are having difficulty producing a full tone, particularly when tonguing rapidly, it is useful to think that the aperture is open and motionless. For those who are having difficulty making precise attacks, it is better for them to think of the lips being moist and touching during the attack. Therefore, what you think about is more important than what really happens physically. In Chapter 6, Attacks and Releases, the emphasis is on what you think about rather than what you actually do. This is not to degrade scientific research in these areas. Leno and others have made excellent contributions to the knowledge of performance, but, on the other hand, the use of a mental picture which research proves is physically impossible should not be rejected.

Weight Distribution of the Mouthpiece

Though you should use as little mouthpiece pressure as possible, it is helpful to think of resting the weight of the mouthpiece on the lower lip. (This applies to downstream players). With the weight on the lower lip, the lower lip takes the brunt of any pressure used and releases the upper lip to contract and relax for the pitch changes without too much interference from the mouthpiece. When you are first learning to play, it is quite helpful if the mouthpiece weight is pivoted from one lip to the other: shifting the weight to the lower lip when ascending and to the upper lip when descending. Pivoting is useful even when working on elementary middle-register lip slurs. For the more advanced player, the concept of pivoting the mouthpiece weight is helpful in both the extreme upper and lower registers.

Upstream players will pivot in the opposite direction as downstream players. That is, if you are an upstream player you will pivot up to ascend and down to descend. For a more complete description of this change in mouthpiece weight distribution, see Reinhardt, *Pivot System.*

Remember two things about pivoting. One, it must be slight and is not a change of embouchure. The lower jaw may move slightly, but the basic mouthpiece placement on the lips remains the same. The mouthpiece does not slide on the lips. Two, this system does not work if you have tired lips, poor breath control, tight throat or heavy mouthpiece pressure. Many find that pivoting the weight is helpful when first learning or reviewing the smoothness of a register change, but that it fails them under pressure when they need it most. In other words, the pivoting should be used as a way of thinking or as a device for changing register and not as a substitute for proper technique (breath control, endurance, embouchure control, *etc.*).

Mouthpiece Pressure

Use only enough mouthpiece pressure to make an airtight seal between the lips and the mouthpiece. At one time, many teachers recommended a no pressure system of playing, but later they found that some pressure is necessary. It may also be necessary to use slightly more pressure in the upper register when the pressure of the air stream may be higher than in the middle register. It may also be necessary to use slightly more mouthpiece pressure to keep the lips from slipping out of the mouthpiece when playing very loudly in the low register. Your general rule should be: Use as little mouthpiece pressure as possible and this usually means that you should use less pressure than you are using at present. Most players tend to develop the muscles of their left arms rather than the muscles of their embouchures and thoraces.

Building the habit of light mouthpiece pressure or breaking the habit of excessive mouthpiece pressure must be done over a long period of time. You must consciously pull the mouthpiece away from your embouchure when warming up. You must continue to pull the mouthpiece away while playing any etude which does not tax you to your capacity. Playing without excessive pressure takes a great deal of mental effort and you must think about it all the time. The teacher should constantly remind his student while he is playing to use less pressure. Simply agreeing to use less pressure is not enough. You must play with less pressure nearly all the time, if the habit is to be established.

Even after minimum pressure has been established, you will have to check this habit from time to time, and spend more time trying to play with even less pressure.

Playing Other Brass Instruments

You can perform on several instruments with different mouthpieces, but the size of the mouthpiece is crucial. Do not play on a mouthpiece that is *nearly* the same size as your regular trombone mouthpiece. Your regular mouthpiece breaks down the fat particles in the lip muscle where it rests on your embouchure. In time there is a slight groove in the lip muscles, and this groove enables you to find the spot on your embouchure when you set the mouthpiece. Two distinctly different mouthpieces will develop two distinctly different lip grooves. Two fairly similar mouthpieces will develop one wide groove and then neither mouthpiece will be able to find an exact spot on which to rest. Once the mouthpiece cannot rest on a definite spot, serious embouchure problems begin.

This is not to discourage you from playing other instruments, in fact some professionals and all instrumental music teachers must play other instruments. Many music education students do not like to take courses in minor instruments because they feel that they will hurt their embouchures. When they do take such courses they tend to practice the minor instruments as little as possible. This negative approach can be harmful to the embouchure of both the trombone and the other instruments. You can learn a great deal about trombone playing by practicing other instruments if this practice is logical and spread over a reasonable period of time.

It is my experience that you can spend up to 45 minutes per day practicing other wind or brass instruments without developing any problems. In fact, your trombone playing will benefit from this practice. The embouchure muscles will develop strength and endurance if the practice is normal and not hurried. I do recommend that you follow your trombone practice with the practice of the minor instruments rather than try to practice trombone after working on another instrument. Most trouble begins when the minor instrument is practiced too much in a short period of time before an exam on that instrument. Avoid this. Practice the minor instruments regularly and do not increase your practice time as an exam approaches. Place this practice *after* the regular trombone playing of the day.

Your trombone embouchure will be strengthened by practice on clarinet, oboe, bassoon, trumpet and French horn. A correct clarinet embouchure demands firm corners of the mouth and a flat unpuffed lower lip. The oboe embouchure develops the embouchure's pucker and aids the development of your high register. The bassoon embouchure develops the center-focused, rounded low-pressure aperture in the center of the lips. The trumpet develops the control of the roll and firmness of the lips. The French horn develops control of the center of the lips as does the trumpet and encourages you to relax in the center of the embouchure while holding the cheeks under control.

Embouchure control is related to the control of the throat and oral cavities, and this tone control through throat control is further learned by practicing clarinet, bassoon, French horn, baritone and tuba. The low-air-pressure breath control needed for trombone is also developed by work on flute, baritone, tuba and French horn.

In addition to embouchure development, some instruments sharpen your responses. They also aid the development of rapid note reading. The late Walter Beeler, former conductor of the Ithaca College Band, believed that all trombonists should learn to play baritone, even if they never perform on it, so that they develop more rapid reading and more rapid responses. This mental quickening can also be developed with the woodwind instruments.

Don't forget the concepts of musical style and tone that can be learned through the study of minor instruments. These concepts, though not directly applicable to your trombone playing, will broaden your musical thinking and make you a more sophisticated musician.

Embouchure trouble will develop *only* if the practice of the other instruments precedes the trombone practice or if it is done infrequently and excessively. If the work on minor instruments is done with logic and forethought, you will benefit from it.

Wet Lip or Dry Lip

Whether a wet lip or a dry lip is the best embouchure cannot be discussed in a few lines. Briefly, I believe that there are many advantages to the wet lip; I do not recommend that any trombonist use a dry lip.

A dry lip can become a crutch for the player with a weak embouchure. As he tires, he slightly moistens his lips and the mouthpiece, then drys them until they are slightly tacky. He then sticks his embouchure onto the mouthpiece. Momentarily, the mouthpiece helps him hold his embouchure in place.

Continuing to use a dry lip not only promotes a weak embouchure, but also causes problems when the mouthpiece gets stuck slightly off center. The mouthpiece can be slipped into place on a wet lip, if the first spot was not quite correct. With a dry set, you must either stop and reset the mouthpiece or play on the wrong embouchure.

The constant wiping by a dry lip player has two more disadvantages. One, waving the wiping cloth is distracting to the audience, or worse, may push the conductor to the point of firing you. Two, you are constantly wiping away the epidermis (the protective layer of skin) and oil from the lips. You are also placing all sorts of bacteria, viruses and foreign matter on the now sensitive lip skin. The wiping helps to promote irritation and infection.

Playing with a wet lip increases the flexibility of the lip. The lips can slide over the rim of the mouthpiece when changing registers. Further, wet lips do not have to be wiped constantly and you can play without waving a cloth around or without putting the latest available germs and dirt on your lip and mouthpiece. (For a more detailed discussion see Farkas, "Wet Lip Vs. Dry Lip," in *The Art of Brass Playing*.)

Chapter 5
Developing the Tone

Hear a Good Tone

A good tone depends on: One, a concept of a good tone; and two, the relaxation of the body so that the muscles of tone production can work efficiently. To learn to hear a good tone, you must listen to the playing of your teacher, listen to the best local trombonists and listen to recordings of professional orchestras and bands on the best high fidelity sound equipment. Learning to hear a tone does not happen in a minute, an hour or a few days. It is a way of listening which develops over a long period of time.

Relax

Relaxation must be developed so that the muscles that produce the tone can work efficiently. Learning to do this also takes a long time. At first, you were just concerned with getting the note, but as your tone placement becomes secure, you must try to get the same results with less effort. As long as many of your muscles are kept tense, you will be unable to develop a sensitiveness in the muscles you use to produce the tone. Relaxation means only that you use the muscles needed and no more. Relaxation does not mean being flabby or sloppy. It is a controlled letting go which increases the efficiency and sensitivity of your muscles.

As relaxation develops, you should become more sensitive to the feeling in your lips and your oral cavity. You should work to develop a *mezzo forte (mf)* tone that flows as easily as the way you talk in a normal conversational tone. At first you need to use more effort than you use for talking. You must consciously breathe much deeper and *blow* with a steady pressure, but in time the habit of breathing and blowing will become natural. Do not work to get the same feel that you had when you first learned to play. Since your body is getting used to the exertion, you will not feel the work as intensely as time passes.

Later, as you learn to control your body with more precision and your relaxation is developing, *fortissimo (ff)* and *pianissimo (pp)* can be played without strain or inefficient exertion. Trombonists who can sustain a *fortissimo* or *pianissimo* for long periods have not only built up strength and endurance, but have relaxed all of the other muscles of their bodies so that no energy is wasted. The working muscles of the breath and embouchure are not cancelled by a contraction of a muscle which is opposite the working muscle. *Fortissimos* are played with the same ease as you would use when talking to someone across an open field. The breath action is forceful, but not forced; the throat action is placed, but not choked. *Pianissimos* are played with a steady, controlled breath action. Imagine that you are blowing to bend the flame of a candle without blowing out the candle.

The need for a relaxed approach when producing a tone, whether *pp, mf,* or *ff,* cannot be overemphasized. A relaxed approach must be given constant attention. Many advanced students seem to waste more energy than professionals use to produce a tone. (For a further discussion of tone problems as related to breathing see Chapter 18—Breath Control.)

Common Problems

The common causes of a poor tone are the constriction of the mouth caused by closing the jaw, the tensing of the tongue, the choking of the throat and the use of the tongue to release the note.

Closed Jaw

A common cause of poor tone is the closed jaw; yet, this is easily corrected. You simply think "Open the mouth," "Drop the jaw slightly" or any similar idea that will separate your teeth more and enlarge your mouth cavity.

Stiff Tongue

To relax the tongue, lower the back of your tongue by saying *Too, Taw,* or *Toe* and hold the back of your tongue in this lowered position while moving only the tip of the tongue. Since the back of the tongue is connected to the front of the tongue, you will tend to move the entire tongue while playing. Though the base of the tongue may really move, the idea of holding the base of the tongue down and motionless is an excellent method of improving a poor tone. The front portion and tip of the tongue must move with the ease and relaxation of conversational speech. The tongue is pointed, flexed and controlled, and not allowed to thicken or move slowly. The action will be rapid, but not tense. (A further explanation of proper tongue action is found in Chapter 6—Attacks and Releases.)

Tight Throat

Relax and open a choked throat by using the same vowels that you used to lower the base of your tongue—*oo, aw* or *oe.* Also, breathe as if you are trying to fog a window. Trying to lower your Adam's apple when playing is also an excellent idea. Edward Kleinhammer suggests that you "relax the cough muscle."

It is difficult to separate the tensions of the jaw, tongue or throat. If the tone is poor, any one or a combination of these factors may be the cause. Since the jaw, tongue and throat are connected, and the tension from one part spreads to adjacent parts, you should consider your jaw, tongue and throat as one unit.

Rather than concentrate on any one factor, check all of the above factors one after the other while working to open your tone.

Tongue Release

Cutting off the note with a tongue release, using the tongue as a valve, is another very common cause of poor tone quality in trombonists. The corrections for this problem are discussed in the next chapter—Attacks and Releases.

Excessive Mouthpiece Pressure

Excessive mouthpiece pressure can hurt the development of a good tone. (See Chapter 4, Embouchure, for a discussion of mouthpiece pressure.)

Tone and Breath Support

A common and temporarily successful remedy for a poor tone is to increase the amount of breath support. For beginning and young students, more support is recommended. The elementary student usually neither inhales enough nor blows enough air to sustain a tone. As a general rule for advanced students, more breath support is **NOT RECOMMENDED** for tone improvement. Although more breath support usually results in dramatic and immediate improvement, the long term effects are damaging. At first, the increased support *overrides* the tension of the jaw, mouth and throat. More air gets through these restricted air passages and the tone improves. In time, however, the tension in the mouth usually increases and even more support will be necessary to force the breath through. Increasing breath support only adds to the tensions and is only a crutch which momentarily improves the tone. If your

face flushes or the blood vessels in the neck and forehead bulge when playing in the middle register, you are using too much breath support. For proper support, all restrictions of the air flow must be relaxed. Rather than increase support, relax your throat and tongue. Breath support should be used, but not abused.

The Anatomy of a Trombone Tone

In an experiment with rubber lips and an air pressure tank, Robert Weast was able to determine what lip tension and what air pressure was needed to produce a note on a brass instrument. He could set the lips at a certain tension and then adjust the air pressure until he got a certain note. He then plotted this point on a graph.

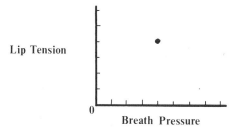

He found more than one point to be plotted, and that by decreasing the lip tension and increasing the breath pressure he got the same note as before. Thus, within certain limits, he could plot several combinations of lip tension and breath pressure for the note B flat. There was not just one point on the graph, but several points which could be connected with a straight line.

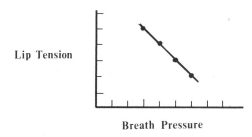

Weast also noted that the same lip tension could be used for playing several different notes by varying the air pressure.

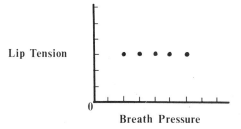

Conversely, changing the lip tension meant several different notes could be played with the same breath pressure.

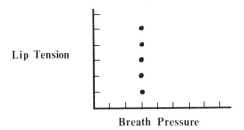

When all these choices are plotted on a graph, with each line representing one note, the graph of the various lip tensions and breath pressures looks like this:

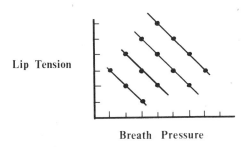

Though Dr. Weast has been criticized for an experiment which does not involve human production of tones, his work is an excellent way of thinking about tone production. Remove one of the notes (lines) from the graph above and place it upright with the top being the point at which a great deal of lip tension is used with very little breath pressure and the bottom of the line is the point which is a combination of very little lip tension and a great deal of breath pressure.

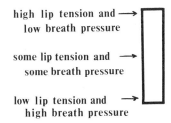

Though there are several possible combinations available, there is probably one combination of lip and breath that will give the best tone. A balanced combination of lip tension and breath pressure which is near the middle point of the line will result in a centered tone. The tone produced on the trombone varies from a quality which is very pinched and quite buzzy (all

lip tension and little breath pressure) through the best one (some lip tension and some breath pressure) to a smokey dull tone (little lip tension and a great deal of breath pressure).

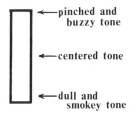

The pinched tone at the top of the drawing is like the tone of a young player who is not breathing and supporting the tone. The dull smokey sound at the bottom of the drawing is like the tone of the Dixie land tail-gate trombone player who plays this way either because he wants that type of sound or because he has lost his lip and can only produce a tone by blowing large quantities of air.

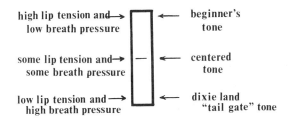

Fig. 21 Anatomy of a Trombone Tone—Quality Variation

Except for the players with strong lungs and weak lips, most trombonists tend to play above the center of the tone by using more lip tension than is necessary. I have found that many serious students have worked to place the tone in the center, and still are using more lip tension than necessary.

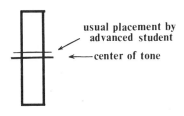

Fig. 22 Anatomy of a Trombone Tone—Advanced Students

The tone placement can be checked with a stroboscope since there is a difference in pitch as well as a difference in tone. (The pitch is sharper as more lip tension is used and flatter as the lip tension is relaxed).

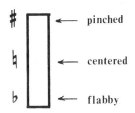

Fig. 23 Anatomy of a Trombone Tone—Pitch Level

In many ensembles everyone plays sharp and the group thinks that to play flat is to play out of tune. The serious player tends to play sharp along with everyone else. Later he joins a group that plays at A = 440 Hz and he must pull his tuning slide out several inches to get down to the pitch. As a general rule, if a modern professional quality trombone must be pulled out more than an inch to reach A = 440 at normal room temperature (72°F.), the trombonist is probably placing the pitch above the center of the tone.

Lowering the Tone Center

To lower the pitch, place the tone in the center, and improve, deepen and darken the tone quality, follow these steps:

1. Warm up in a normal manner.

2. Tune the trombone with a stroboscope to A = 440.

3. Play several notes, check the intonation with the stroboscope, and establish a firm aural image of the proper pitch.

4. Reset the tuning slide so that it is extended only about one half of an inch.

5. Play the tuning notes in tune with the stroboscope, by allowing the pitch to sag. Relax the lips, jaw, tongue and throat. **DO NOT** lip the pitch down. **DO NOT** blow the pitch down. Simply let the pitch go down. Check your throat adjustment and learn to control the pitch with a change in throat setting while relaxing your embouchure and jaw.

6. Recheck your new concept of pitch and tone with a stroboscope at least every week until it is an established habit. Recheck every few days at first so that you break your old habit of thinking "Flat is out of tune and sharp is good." Remember that by chance half of the out-of-tune notes in this world are sharp.

In some ensembles all of the notes are sharp with some being sharper than others.

Lowering the tone center is only one way of opening a tight tone quality. It can be used only when you have control of your embouchure. **IMPORTANT:** Your embouchure is to be relaxed, but the lips must not be allowed to become flabby. The jaw, tongue, throat and breathing are relaxed and the breath flow slightly increased until the pitch falls to the proper level. The key to the whole approach is relaxation. Your throat is important for the placement of the pitch and tone. Thinking only about the relaxation of the embouchure is a mistake. Trumpet players think of *lipping* a note down when it is too high. This idea is poor because it suggests work and less work is what is desired. It is better to think "Relax the lips," "Lower the back of the tongue," or "Enlarge the shape of the throat." The lips must be kept rolled partially, however, and must not be allowed to collapse too far outward or the tone will become grainy and airy. You should think of *throating* the pitch down, through a relaxed enlargement of the back of the mouth.

Lip Slurs for Tone Improvement

There are many warm-up routines and many lip training exercises that use lip slurs. Although there are many possible combinations, all lip slurs are made from one or the other of two types of slurs——ascending or descending.

The benefits of practicing lip slurs are gained not by some magical set of up and down slurs, but from the way in which the exercises are practiced. How the lip slurs are played is far more important than what order or variety of lip slurs is used. Most student trombonists try to imitate the rapid lip slurs of the advanced player and forget tone, smoothness and relaxation. Trying to play lip slurs faster without relaxation causes the tone to choke up. The whole tone production system becomes more tense and flexibility decreases rather than increases. Lip slurs must be played with tone, ease and smoothness. The speed and facility of lip slurs will increase without difficulty once relaxation has been achieved.

Practicing Lip Slurs

Slowly before Rapidly

At first, lip slurs should be played slowly and with precision. The slur must change pitch to the next note exactly on time, without a noticeable change in volume or tone color and without a noise or slight break in the slur. Until relaxation and control are mastered, increasing the speed will only produce more tension and establish poor habits.

Evenly before Rapidly

The rhythm and the volume level must be even. Do not attempt to force the speed of a slur until the control of the changes are relaxed and precise. Do not let a series of alternating notes, such as

become uneven with either the upper or the lower note being shorter or louder than the other note, *i.e.*

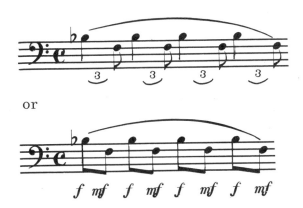

or

Always Center the Pitch

Lip slurs have a way of making you tense and unless you take care they will tighten your tone production. For example, the following lip slur

should be diagramed:

Many players do not lower the pitch all the way to the center of the tone of the lower note and then overshoot the center of the pitch when they slur up. Their slur would be diagramed:

Do not be so concerned with the slur that the lowering to the second note is tentative (and sharp). Do not worry about slurring back to the upper note. Do not give the upper note an extra push which will send the pitch to the sharp side. In the above exercise, always descend a perfectly tuned interval of a fourth to a full and round tone and then return *exactly* to the tone and pitch on which the exercise was begun. Listen carefully to the tone, stay relaxed and check the pitch with a stroboscope. When playing more complex lip slurs, such as:

keep all the notes in the center of the tone and pitch. A diagram of the correct slurring would be:

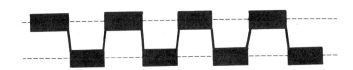

Don't let the pitch slowly rise as the exercise progresses like this:

Even advanced players will sometimes allow the pitch to rise and the tone to close slightly. On a slur such as:

they will overshoot the center of the pitch on the way up and never come down to the center of the pitch as they come down. This incorrect performance is diagramed:

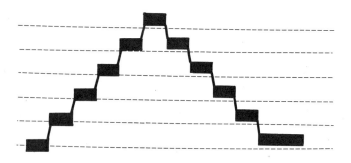

Make the tone and pitch of the descending notes true and open. On the slur above, pay particular attention to the last two notes. Many stop paying attention to relaxation when they know that they will successfully complete the slur. Do not let the pitch of the easy notes rise. Place the pitch properly on every note of all lip slur exercises.

Do Not Use a False Embouchure

Just being able to make the slur is not the same as playing the slur with a correct embouchure. Lip slurs are used to help blend the various registers of the instrument together without making any unnatural adjustment of the embouchure. If you slip the embouchure on the mouthpiece or use an unusual pivot of the jaw to make the slur, your production will be blocked from developing smooth register changes. Use an embouchure that is normal for a middle register note. Then develop smooth transitions and subtle pivoting from this normal embouchure.

Some players approach all notes from an upper register embouchure setting. They then think of all other notes as being low notes. To slur up, they think of returning to their normal setting. They view all their notes as being below their normal setting and have less difficulty with ascending slurs. They do not think "Slur up"; they think "Return to normal." This approach is recommended, provided the embouchure does not shift or slip during the slur.

Learn to Slur Down before Slurring Up

It is easier to slur down than up. The tone, smoothness and ease of a descending slur is usually better than an ascending slur. Some elementary method books ask that lip slurs be played ascending first. In other words, they ask the student to slur up to an unfamiliar setting. To be sure of getting the upper note, the player overcompensates and the slur is squeezed or choked or the air stream is bumpy. It is far better to descend first and then *return* to the beginning pitch (ascend). The settings for the upper note have then been tested and the return to this setting is only a matter of memory (not guesswork). In elementary work, a preliminary note should be added to a printed exercise,

becomes

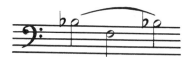

so that the confidence and relaxation of the tone production is assured. Later, when the setting of the upper note is secure and the approach can be made without worry, the preliminary note is omitted.

Develop the Feel of the High Register Notes Before Attempting to Slur to Them.

Developing the feel (the setting) for upper notes is the same idea as the previous paragraph, but applies to advanced players in upper register etudes and advanced legato studies. For instance, in *Studies in Legato*, a troublesome slur from

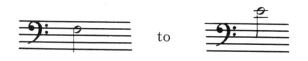

should be practiced

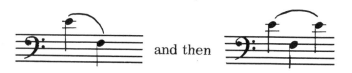

Finally, when all insecurity has been removed, the slur may be played as written. Your state of mind is very important and when slurring to a higher note it is undesirable to think UP to the note. UP is filled with fear and strain. Instead, think RETURN. Return to a note that you played sometime before and for which you know the settings. Do not force your tone production as you slur up; only tense enough to return to the proper high-register setting.

Avoid Making the Same Mistake Twice.

If you repeat a mistake like failing to make the next note, playing a slur with too much roughness, having a silence between two notes of a slur, *etc.*, it is beginning to become a habit. Repeatedly attempting to play a slur correctly and making the same mistake again is a bad habit which will produce more bad habits. When a mistake is made, change your approach for the second try. Though your correction may not work either, at least you did not repeat your first mistake. On your third try, modify the approach again. Sooner or later you will find the correct response and you will have avoided the setting of an incorrect response. Once correct, the phrase should be repeated several times to set it. When the correct response has been set, you are less likely to make a mistake at that point and if you do, the mistake will be an accident not a habit.

Long Tones—Pro and Con

Some types of long-tone exercises are part of every warm-up or lip training routine. Almost anyone recommends some long tones as a way to develop tone, breath control and endurance.

You should remember, however, that the lip-building and warm-up routines of the major teachers use long tones as only a small part of the total program. Most of the work is done with lip slurs, intervals and legato studies. The long tones in the late Emory B. Remington's exercises are held for a few seconds each and take less than five minutes' time to perform. Schlossberg has only one page of long tones in a rather large book of exercises for the development of the embouchure.

Though it is necessary to learn to control sustained notes, they should not be practiced too much. Daydreaming is one of the easiest and most harmful habits to develop in all lip-building routines, and boring long-tone practice is apt to promote poor concentration. Lip slurs, legato studies and vocalises will improve the tone, the control, the breath capacity and the endurance just as well as long tones will, but they will also build technique and musicianship. Besides,

legato studies are more interesting to practice and hold your attention better than long tones.

Tension can easily creep into the playing of long tones and this tension is either not noticed or is accepted by habit. In legato studies, the tension is instantly detected when the slurs become more difficult. As soon as the tension is noticed you should take steps immediately to relax it before it becomes a habit.

Tone development through long-tone practice should not be neglected, but must be limited to a short period of time. The lips must not be strained and the breathing must not become tense. For additional development of the tone, breathe control and endurance, use vocalises and legato studies.

Musical Performance

Tone should be developed through musical performance rather than exercises, lip slurs and long tones. Producing an excellent tone must become a relevant part of playing musically and the more music that can be placed in the practice routine, the better. This does not mean that the practice routine is divided into two parts, exercises and music. Instead, music or a musical style is to be included in all but the very fundamental exercises. Even lip slurs, scales and the pattern exercises of Slama, Blume, Kopprasch, *etc.* should be phrased and played with as much musical drive as possible.

Easy songs should also be played with special attention to the musical sound. These tunes, many of which you can play from memory, should be transposed to remote keys so that the tone quality of all the notes on the instrument are blended. Certain keys use notes that are in extended positions. The tone should be developed so that no matter what the key, the tone is consistent on all notes. (An excellent article on this approach to tone development is Bernard Goldberg's *Tone Development through Interpretation: A Tribute to Maitre Marcel Moyse for His 80th Birthday.* Elkhart, Ind.: Armstrong Flute Co., n. d.)

In addition, opera arias and advanced vocalises should be played with attention to tone, vibrato, dynamics and phrasing. Do not think that this musical work is to be done with a soft legato style only. Opera arias demand full *bravura* playing at times and your tone must be *fortissimo*, without forcing, during the climaxes.

Divide the time you spend on detached playing between *leggiero* and *pesante* style. Both styles can be applied to most of the standard etude books, particularly the *Clef Studies* and the *26 Sequences* of V. Blazhevich. Perform these etudes in an orchestral style in which ALL notes are played with a full tone, yet with a drive and connection to the phrase. Many players fail to develop the full dynamic range because they practice these etudes in a comfortable style only.

Many people play all short notes with less than their best tone. Actually you must play the shorter notes louder than the long notes so that they sound equal to the audience. Unless the short notes are emphasized, they will be lost in the sound of the ensemble. Drive these louder short notes so that they do not become heavy and drag the movement of the phrase.

The ultimate goal is to play with such musicianship (which includes a beautiful tone) that listeners hear only the music and are not conscious of your tone. Thus the circle is complete. Musical performance develops tone and the tone develops musical performance.

Chapter 6
Attacks and Releases

Trombonists are usually taught to begin a note by saying "T." The tongue begins the stroke from a spot somewhere behind the upper teeth between the bottom of the upper teeth and the gum line.

I recommend that you place your tongue on the same spot that your tongue touches when you talk. Pronounce the words *Talk, Today* or *Together.* These should give you the most natural and most habitual location for your tongue action. Pronounce the words naturally with the speed and ease of your normal conversation. Do not slow, labor or accent the syllables.

The tongue action with the trombone attack seems to be less explosive than the trumpet attack and the syllable may change from T to D on the lower pitches and softer dynamics. Whether you use T or D, the tongue *action* is always quick and relaxed. It is pulled away from the contact point with a rapid and confident movement.

Some people blame the tongue for many or all of their attack problems. On the contrary, the tongue only determines when the note will begin. Most bad attacks are caused by incorrect settings of the embouchure or throat or incorrect breath control.

Model

The ideal attack, tone control and release may be diagramed as:

The attack is a sharp click at the same volume as the tone which follows. The tone is steady and the release tapers as the breath flow stops. No correction is necessary.

Problem No. 1

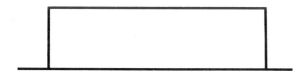

This is a diagram of the most common error. The attack is correct and the tone is steady, but the release is made by cutting the breath flow with the tongue, using the tongue as a valve TO END the note. To break this bad habit: Stop blowing when you want the note to stop, inhale slightly when you want the note to stop, fake an inhalation when you want the note to stop, or say "*ah*" at the end of the note, *i.e.* "*Tu-ah.*" Use the techniques above when detaching notes at a slow speed. When establishing the new habit in more rapid tonguing, you stop the breath with a breath action as when you laugh "*ha-ha-ha-ha-ha*" at a very rapid speed. Now place a *T* at the beginning of each syllable, "*tah-tah-tah-tah-tah.*" With very rapid tonguing there are two ways of ending a note. One, the release is actually made with the throat, but this technique should develop naturally (never attempt to learn a throat release). The second and recommended method does not stop the breath and you simply articulate a series of *Ts* on a continuous flow of air. The notes sound detached because there is a taper to the notes as the tongue strikes for the next note. This taper makes the notes sound as though they have been detached. With this approach, the tongue cannot stop when the *T* is pronounced. The tongue comes forward, strikes and leaves the teeth in one motion.

Although some commercial trumpet players use a tongue release for effect, all "legitimate" players release without tongue. Using the tongue to release a note on the trombone hurts the tone quality. A tongue release would be used only when the note is marked *sec* (dry).

Problem No. 2

This is another common problem, especially when playing softly or under great stress. The tone is correct, once it has begun, and the release is correct, but the attack is airy. The air sounds for awhile before the tone begins. It is possible that your lips are not wet enough or your lips are not being held close enough to each other. Wet the lips and be sure that they are nearly touching.

An airy attack can be caused by moving your jaw when making the attack or hunting the correct setting of the note after the attack has been made. Don't chew the note, and be prepared for the sound of the note before the attack. Practice this exercise to correct this unwanted chewing action.

Before playing each note, remember the feel of the note before when it did finally sound and then duplicate that feel when attacking. Hold your jaw, base of your tongue and your throat into the setting of the note and keep them there from the time of the release until the next attack is attempted.

Sometimes the tongue action causes airy attacks. The tongue tends to slow down when playing softly or when you are worried about the entrance. The slow tongue rations the air to the embouchure. For a moment after the attack, the air is not flowing enough to sustain a note. Once the tongue gets all the way out of the air stream and the oral cavity is open far enough for the air pressure to flow properly, the note will speak. Draw the tongue quickly. Pull the tongue away from the teeth with a relaxed, rapid and positive action.

The improper setting of the throat, base of the tongue and lip settings can cause a slight "ftt" of air between the attack and the tone of the note. Practice the exercise above and also buzz the desired pitch on the mouthpiece. You may find that you miss the note by a great distance on your first attempts to buzz the pitch on the mouthpiece because your embouchure was so poorly set that the resonance of the trombone could not develop on the desired pitch. Once your buzz is exactly on the correct pitch, your attack will probably be correct, **PROVIDED** that the slide is set at the proper spot.

Inaccurate placement of the slide is the most frequently overlooked cause of missed attacks. The correct note is being made by the lips and throat, but the instrument is not in resonance with that pitch. Instead the trombone is set for a slightly different note. On some notes, particularly high G and high F sharp, the misplacement of the slide by as little as a quarter of an inch can cause the attack to be blurred, distorted or airy.

In summary, the airy attack can be caused by dry lips, lips too far apart, incorrect throat adjustment, jaw movement, inaccurate lip buzz, slow tonguing or inaccurate slide placement. To develop accuracy, moisten your lips, touch your lips together, hold your jaw still, feel the note in your throat, buzz the correct note, tongue quickly and place the slide at exactly the correct spot.

Problem No. 3

This is a diagram of a note that has a good tone and release, but has a poor attack. The attack is too soft or too blunt. Either the attack is too subtle or it is not being backed with air immediately. To strengthen the attack say a sharper and more explosive "Tah." Also move the point of contact of the tongue to a lower position on the upper teeth. The breath must begin immediately after the attack with a good flow of air. Tongue and blow, or blow with the attack, are ways of solving the problem.

Problem No. 4

The attack is dirty, fuzzy or has a definite *crunch*. Either the lips, the throat, the tip of the tongue or the base of the tongue is set wrong. Do not tongue between your teeth or let the tongue touch your lips. Your tongue may be moving too slowly or the tongue action may be too explosive. Tongue quickly, tongue quickly and lightly or tongue from a spot a little higher in the mouth. Some players squeeze their lips together when the attack is made. If they kept their lips squeezed, anyone could tell what the trouble was, but they relax their lips to their proper tension immediately *after* the attack. This way they get a good tone even though the attack was bad. Practice the exercise for No. 2 to get rid of the preset tension of the embouchure.

As the half notes are repeated, find the settings for the best tone and hold these settings when making the attack.

Mouthpiece buzzing helps establish the tone placement. If the lips are too tense at the beginning of the note, the mouthpiece buzz will probably slide from a higher pitch into the correct pitch. Practice mouthpiece buzzing until the note begins exactly on pitch.

Problem No. 5

This is a diagram of an explosive attack with a weak tone. Either the tongue is too hard or there is not enough tone. If the amount of tone is increased, the attack will be correct.

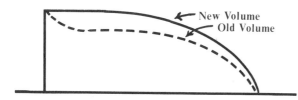

This slap-tonguing develops when you incorrectly try to play louder. The heavy attack makes the note louder for only a moment. But as soon as the air from the attack is used, the tone diminishes to an inadequate level. To balance the attack, blow more air immediately after the attack.

On the other hand, the volume may be correct and the attack is simply **TOO HEAVY**. Some players attack by tonguing between their teeth or by touching their lips with their tongues. They should tongue behind their teeth.

Also, the tongue may be spitting rather than cleanly pronouncing the syllable, *Tu*. The tongue should draw down or draw quickly away from the upper teeth. The tongue neither propels the air, nor spits. Finally, the syllable *Tu* may still be too heavy for an attack even when pronounced correctly. If so, tongue from a spot that is higher on the upper teeth or use a *Du* syllable. The *Du* is pronounced just as quickly as a *Tu*, but it is slightly less explosive. Use a quick *Du* syllable to soften the attack, especially in the lower register.

Problem No. 6

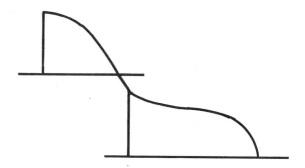

This is a diagram of a correct attack, except that the note begins on the overtone above the desired pitch and then slips to the correct pitch OR the note begins correctly and then slips to the overtone below the desired pitch.

When the pitch is too high at first it may be an extreme example of problem No. 5, in which the attack is so explosive that it catches the upper overtone before the tone begins on the proper pitch. The solution: Attack more softly.

There may be too much preparation and too much breath support for the note. This happens when a large breath is taken and the elasticity of the lungs is allowed to squeeze out too much air with the attack. Don't puff and don't over support. Rather hold back the breath at the instant of the attack.

When the beginning pitch is correct and then drops to a lower overtone, the breath pressure is not sufficient to sustain the pitch. At the beginning of the note, the lungs and breathing apparatus can develop quite a large amount of pressure because they are stretched. Their natural elasticity may momentarily provide the correct breath pressure. Once some of the air has left the chest cavity, there is no longer enough natural elasticity to sustain the pressure and you must supply more pressure through support. In order to sustain the correct pitch, more effort must be applied as the air in the lungs is exhausted. The solution: Increase the breath effort as the note is held.

Problem No. 7

The attack and release are correct, but the tone is wobbling or quivering (either in pitch or in volume).

The problem occurs on all brass instruments, but the solution is different on each. With high resistance instruments, the breath pressure can be increased without danger, but with the relatively low resistance of the trombone, an increase in breath pressure causes other problems. If the breath pressure is increased, you may increase your lip tension and, although the tone may straighten out, your tone quality will become thin and tight. On low-resistance instruments, it is better to relax your lips and let the pitch level fall to its proper level. A colleague of mine recommends that you try to feel the air stream coming back up the lead pipe of the instrument, particularly when faced with the tremor in the tone because of *nervousness*. In any case, more support is seldom the solution to the problem. Blow a steady stream of air, relax the lips—let the tone settle down into its center or feel the air stream returning back from the lead pipe into the mouth. (For further information on using relaxation to allow the tone to settle to a lower pitch, see Chapter 5, Developing Tone).

Problem No. 8

This note is correct until the end when it slowly falls flat and looses tone quality. This is common with players who are attempting to break their old habit of cutting the tone with the tongue. As they try to stop the tone by stopping the breath, the tone falls. Their release action is correct, but it is too slow. Stop breathing sooner or pretend that there will be a quick inhalation at the end of the note.

Some experienced players allow the tone to fall when they fail to pay attention. They have stopped listening to the pitch and tone and begin to daydream. Pay attention to the pitch, the breath flow and the lip aperture until the note has been completed.

Problem No. 9

This final example diagrams the tone which is correct until the release. The release pinches off and probably goes sharp at the same time. Advanced players with strong embouchures may pinch the lips or close the throat as they release. The solution: Don't pinch the note off with the lips, don't pinch the note off with the throat, retain an open lip aperture and throat cavity when releasing.

Chapter 7

Legato Playing

The slide makes it possible for the trombonist to execute one of the smoothest legatos of all the orchestral instruments. It also creates difficulties with legato playing if not handled properly.

Basic Techniques

Three basic techniques are needed to master legato control. One, blow with a steady stream of air; two, move the slide rapidly (at the last possible moment) to the new position, and three, tongue lightly as the slide arrives at the new position.

Four legato quarter notes should use an air stream that is as even as an air stream for a whole note. Although this is easy to understand, most beginning players still do not sustain their breath when changing notes. Their first legato playing probably resulted in *glissandos*, because their slide technique was faulty. Then rather than correct their slide technique, they changed the flow of their breath between notes to avoid the *glissando*.

A trumpet player can change from one note to another with a rapid movement of the valves. The trombonist must move from one position to the next just as rapidly, but usually moves too slowly. When asked to move faster, he moves sooner, but not faster. To obtain the proper slide speed, you must *wait* until the last possible moment before moving to the new position, and then make this movement with the fastest possible speed.

To move rapidly, the slide must be in excellent working condition. The slide that is dented, out of line or not lubricated properly will not be good enough for legato playing. Try as you may, you just will not be able to move the slide with the speed that is necessary. To check the working order of the slide, hold the instrument perpendicular to the floor. Unlock the slide and let it *rest* on the right hand. Do not hold on to it. Now lift the trombone quickly with the left hand. If the slide leaves the right hand, even for a moment, it needs attention. If, after cleaning and a reapplication of lubricant, the slide still will not remain at rest on the right hand, have the instrument repaired *immediately*. (For detailed cleaning and lubricating instructions, see Chapter 3, Care of the Instrument). Note: The above test does not prove that the slide is in excellent condition, it only indicates whether it is *good enough* for legato playing.

Finally, the tongue must articulate with a soft brush-like stroke exactly as the slide arrives on the next note. Different teachers suggest different tongue syllables. Many teachers suggest that the tongue say *D*. This *D* is attached to what ever vowel is being used and becomes *Dah, Due, Dow, Daw, Day, Dee, etc.* Others find that an *L* stroke of the tongue is better. The syllable is then *Lah, Lue, Loe, Law, Lay, Lee, etc.* Jaroslav Cimera, former Chicago radio staff trombonist, was noted for his smooth legato and he suggested that an *R* be used. This *R* was not like an English *R*, but was one flip of the tongue of a rolled Italian *R*. The *R* is attached to the vowel sound being used (*Ru, Roe, Rah, Ree, etc.*).

When learning to use *D* legato tonguing, beginners usually strike the tongue against the gums with too heavy a stroke. When using an *L* or the flip of a rolled Italian *R*, the stroke of the tongue tends to be too soft to be heard. I first ask the beginning student to use a brushing stroke of the tongue as when saying the *TH* in *The, They, Though,* and *Thou.*

First Exercises

The first exercises should develop a consistent and automatic brushing action of the tongue. Begin in the middle register where you have no other tone production problems to hamper the learning of this new habit. Allow plenty of time for your mind to guide and control the tongue action. Use half notes at first. Proceed from the middle register to the lower register, and from the middle register to the upper register.

Preliminary Exercises
from
Studies in Legato for Trombone by Reginald H. Fink

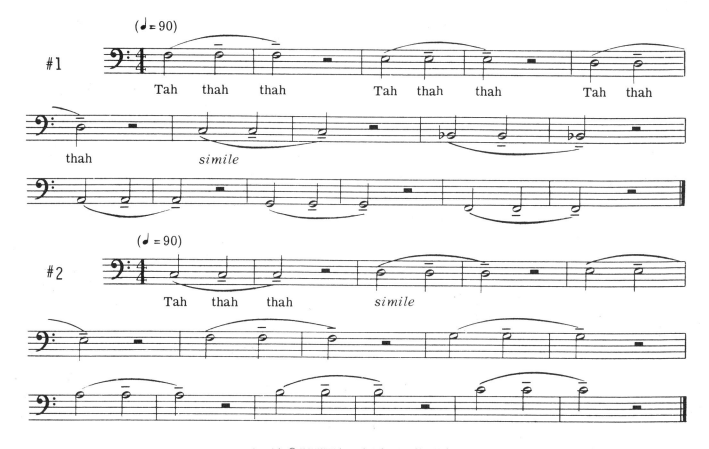

(Used by permission of Carl Fischer, Inc., New York)

As the stroking of the tongue becomes natural, relaxed
and consistent, use the same type of exercise, but tongue
at quarter-note speed.

Preliminary Exercises
from
Studies in Legato for Trombone by Reginald H. Fink

(Used by permission of Carl Fischer, Inc., New York)

The coordination work with the slide can begin only after the tongue can make the legato stroke automatically. Return to an exercise using half notes, and practice connecting two adjacent positions. Use a steady breath, a rapid last-moment slide movement and a legato tongue just as the slide arrives in the new position.

Preliminary Exercises
from
Studies in Legato for Trombone by Reginald H. Fink

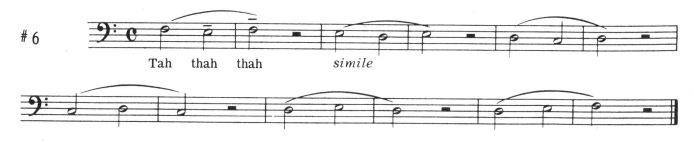

6

Tah   thah   thah   *simile*

(Used by permission of Carl Fischer, Inc., New York)

More difficult exercises with slide movements using shifts of two, three and four positions are learned next. Finally entire exercises moving in quarter and eighth notes should be mastered. (See Reginald H. Fink, *Studies in Legato for Trombone,* Carl Fischer, Inc., 1967, 1969 Preliminary Exercises, pp. 3-6.)

Other Articulations

As your skill develops, the tongue stroke is altered to give the correct sound. On repeated notes the stroke must be heavier than on changing notes, and it is usually necessary to use a heavier stroke of the tongue when playing either louder or lower. Learn the *D, L* and *R* syllables after the *TH* stroke has been perfected. Additional exercises are unnecessary; these softer and stronger strokes of the tongue are developed as the music demands. For instance, when ascending a legato scale, slowly blend the consonant from *TH* to *L* to *R*. When descending, move from *R* to *L* to *TH* to *D* to *T*. Exactly which are the sharpest strokes is debatable, but I believe that the consonants when arranged from softest to strongest are *R, L, TH, D, T.* Exactly which consonant is used is unimportant. What sound is produced is important. You should choose the consonant that will produce the proper sound.

In extremely low register work, the tongue stroke must be rather heavy, and some players use a *T* consonant. This *T* is the same tongue stroke that is used when playing in a detached style, but the breath flow is sustained and the end of one note blends into the beginning of the next.

Natural Slurs

Some books use a great deal of space explaining and teaching the difference between natural slurring and legato slurring. With natural slurring, no tongue is used. You can change from one overtone partial to another without a *glissando.*

Natural Slurs

Legato Slurs

The legato slurs occur when you do not change notes of the overtone series, and a legato tongue must be used to help avoid a *glissando.*

Legato Slurs

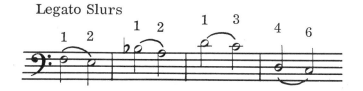

There is a slight difference in sound between legato slurs and natural slurs, and for consistent tone production, I suggest that you use a very slight legato tongue on all slurs, whether they are natural or not. The slight legato tongue will also aid your security and precision. The legato tongue will help you maintain a constant tone and syncronize the slide movement with the lip, mouth and throat changes that occur when slurring from one note to the next.

I suggest that you use natural legato in only two instances: one, when warming-up and two, when playing certain technical passages. Natural slurring forces you to make precise adjustments with your embouchure, mouth, throat and airstream. You do not have the tongue to help you focus and place the note. With addition of the legato tongue in performance, your control is then that much more precise. Certain passages were designed by a trombonist to be played with natural slurs (*e.g.*, the Arthur Pryor solos). Other passages need a few natural slurs to give the repeating tongue a momentary break so that the speed can be maintained (*e.g.* the bottom portion of the second page of the first movement of the Gordon Jacob, *Concerto for Trombone*). Without the momentary break, the tongue action stiffens and slows down. In technical passages such as the Jacob, *Concerto*, alternate positions must be used on the legato slurs so that they can be played as natural slurs.

Finally, the legato tongue should be both so light and so precise that it not only aids the security, but is almost as inaudible as the natural slur.

Chapter 8
F Attachments

Adding an F attachment to a tenor trombone does not make it a bass trombone. Many first and second trombonists in major symphony orchestras have F attachments on their large bore tenor trombones and even small-bore student model F attachment trombones are available. The difference between a tenor trombone with an F attachment and a bass trombone depends on the size of the bore and darkness of the tone quality. (See the explanation found later in this chapter.)

The F attachment, which is equal to the length of tubing used to reach sixth position, does not lower the instrument a perfect fourth. The F attachment does lower a first position B flat a perfect fourth, but it will only lower a sixth position F a major third. Thus, as the slide is extended, the F attachment produces less of a pitch difference. When the F attachment is engaged, the trombone has rather than the usual seven positions not quite six full positions.

Slide Positions

The approximate spacing of the slide positions is as follows:

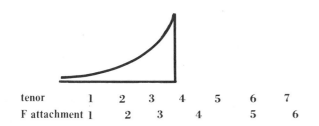

Fig. 24 Comparison of Tenor Trombone Positions with F Attachment Trombone Positions

Do not think of two systems of slide positions. Relate the F attachment positions to the normal positions of the trombone, *i.e.*, E flat is not in F attachment third position, but is in a flat third position; a D flat is not in F attachment fifth position, but is in sixth position.

The following chart relates the F attachment notes to normal tenor trombone slide positions.

Fig. 25 Relationship of the F Attachment Pitches to the Positions on a Tenor Trombone

Technical Advantages

The F attachment trombone has many technical advantages. First trombone parts having many Cs and Bs, and low Fs and Es are not unusual. On a straight trombone, it is not easy to play a pattern that includes B flats, Cs, As, and Bs. None of these low notes have any alternate positions and there is no way to make the sequence of positions in the following excerpt any easier.

Fig. 26 Slide Positions Without an F Attachment

With an F attachment, the passage is quite simple. Note: There is a standard procedure for indicating the use of the F attachment which was begun by Allen Ostrander and followed by Fink, Gillis and Fote. A note on the F attachment is marked with a V (valve). Notes marked with Arabic numerals are to be played without the F attachment. These authors assume that the player can find the note on the valve and that the indication V is all that is necessary.

Fig. 27 Slide Positions With an F Attachment

The C is played using the valve with the slide placed in first position and the B is played using the valve

32

with the slide placed in a flat second position.

The use of the F attachment for low Fs and Es is similar.

These examples are not the only uses of the valve. Don't neglect the others. The most commonly over-looked pattern is a series of notes which includes a D flat. The following pattern occurs in tonal music in the keys of four or five flats.

At first the F attachment trombonist may perform it this way:

Fig. 28   Incorrect Use of the F Attachment

Notice though that when it is played this way there is a five-position shift between the C on the valve and the D flat in fifth position.

The passage should be performed by playing the B flat with the valve and playing the C in sixth position.

Fig. 29   Correct Use of the F Attachment

The longest shift is fewer than three positions—from flat third position for the B flat to C in sixth position. Using the valve for B flat is quite convenient in high speed patterns.

Rules for Using the F Attachment

The following are general rules for using the F attachment valve.

Rule 1.

Do not overuse the valve for Cs, Bs, Fs and Es.

INCORRECT   INCORRECT

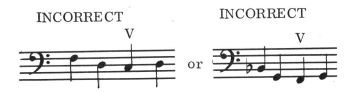

Rule 2.

Do not neglect the use of the valve for B flats and As.

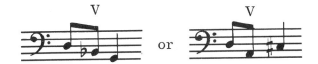

Rule 3.

Use the valve for Cs, Bs, Fs and Es if moving to *and* from other notes in first, second and third positions.

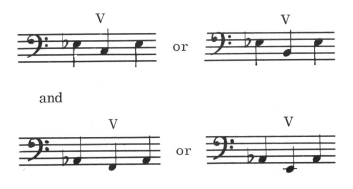

Rule 4.

Cs and Fs may (or should) be played in sixth position, if moving to and from other notes in fourth position.

Rule 5.

If the pattern includes a fifth position note, the Cs and Fs will not be played on the valve. Instead, play Cs and Fs in sixth position.

INCORRECT

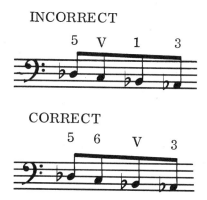

CORRECT

Rule 6.

Use the valve to play the B flat in a G flat major arpeggio.

Rule 7.

Use the valve to play the A in an F sharp minor arpeggio.

These rules are only a few of the possibilities for efficient use of the valve. Also, there are instances when the correct use of the valve may feel uncomfortable to the professional player and he will choose another, more comfortable way even though it causes his slide to move farther. Besides, the tone quality is not full on the second overtone below the B flat and you should avoid playing certain notes on the valve that occur on a strong pulse or are part of an exposed passage.

Never use the valve for the performance of the higher partials. The upper register tone quality of the valve is muffled, the intonation insecure and in legato passages there is an audible slap as the valve is engaged.

To further understand the use of the valve, you should study the patterns in the Ostrander, Fink and Gillis method books listed in the bibliography later in the book.

Bass Trombones

Any trombone which has an additional section of tubing mounted in the bell section which lowers the first position pitch a perfect fourth is considered an F attachment trombone. Historically, a bass trombone was pitched with its fundamental in F and looked like an extended version of a straight tenor trombone. The extreme positions had to be reached with a handle.

The invention of the rotary valve made it possible to build an instrument which was a combination of the tenor and bass trombone. The instrument is the length of the tenor trombone and has the additional tubing of the bass trombone installed in the bell section. Originally these instruments were referred to as tenor-bass trombones, but now are simply labeled bass trombones. These instruments retain the **TONE QUALITY** of the original bass trombones.

The bass trombone has a bell diameter of at least nine and one-half inches and has a bore diameter of approximately .562 inches. Instruments which are smaller than this, having a bell diameter of eight and one-half inches and a bore of .547 inches, must be considered large-bore tenor trombones with F attachments. These smaller instruments are played by the first and second trombonists in American symphony orchestras. Although these trombones have the same range as the bass trombone and have a more penetrating pedal tone register, they cannot equal the large sonorous quality of a bass trombone. You can use a large bore tenor trombone with a large mouthpiece to play the bass trombone part in medium and even large bands and orchestras, but in professional groups with the higher dynamic levels, the large-bore tenor trombone becomes raspy and cutting when playing the bass trombone part.

Low B Naturals

The F attachment does not make the trombone completely chromatic to the low-pedal B flat. A low B natural is not available on either a bass trombone or a tenor trombone with an F attachment.

During this century, more and more composers and arrangers have been writing low B naturals for the bass trombone and the players have developed several methods of producing that pitch.

Until recently, it was common to obtain low B naturals by pulling the F attachment slide out about a foot and pitching the attachment in E. The slide positions for the E attachment are:

Fig. 30 Relationship of the E Attachment Pitches to the Positions on a Tenor Trombone

The disadvantage of an E attachment is that you no longer can play a C and an F on the valve. Also, you must play with the upmost concentration or else you automatically try to play a note where you normally play it on the F attachment. In rapid passages, you may make errors unless you have spent a great deal of time practicing with the attachment pitched in E.

To avoid having to pitch the attachment in E, learn to lip the pitch of the low C down to a low B. This is easier if you have a bass trombone equipped with a rather large mouthpiece. By learning to play a low B natural by lipping a low C one half tone lower, you still retain all of the notes of the F attachment in their usual positions.

You should also learn to fake the B natural in a flatted third position using the valve. Acoustically this is theoretically not possible, but many players can develop this note and find it quite useful. The tone quality of this fake B natural is not full and it can only be used in rapid passages or unexposed ensemble playing.

I recommend that the single valve bass trombone player learn to play a B natural both by lipping the low C down and by faking the note in a flatted third position. Playing the B in a flatted seventh position is necessary for the execution of the solo *glissando* in the Bartok, *Concerto for Orchestra*.

Playing the B natural in a flatted third position is useful when playing a rapid chromatic scale up from or down into the pedal register.

Double Valves

F-E Attachment

Another way to solve the low B natural problem is to use a trombone with a double valve. The first valve is the usual F attachment, while the second valve is attached to the F attachment and lowers the attachment to E. Thus with one valve the standard F attachment technique is used and by pulling the lever to both valves, a low B natural can be played in a flat seventh position. There are also some technical advantages with the E valve. (See Ostrander). The E valve is arranged so that it is operated with the F valve. The extra tubing cannot be used unless the F attachment has been engaged also.

F-E Flat Attachment

Within the last decade, many players have been pulling or extending the E slide so that it is pitched in E flat. Not only does it make it easier to reach the B natural (it is now in sixth position instead of flat seventh position), but it gives you many more technical advantages. The rules for using the E flat valve are too numerous to list, but all leaps of a minor third or larger in the register below the staff are possibilities. For example, with only an F attachment, it is cumbersome to play a B flat *arpeggio*.

If you use the F valve for the F, there is more than a four-position shift between the F and the D:

If you use the F valve to play the B flat in a flatted third position, you shorten the distance of the longest shift to slightly under three positions, but have to begin the phrase with the B flat on the valve and you could get a better tone if you played the B flat in first position.

With a second valve tuned to E flat, you play the B flat in the best location, first position without the valve; the F is played normally, using the F attachment; and the D is played with the slide in a flatted second position, using both valves.

Although it is possible to play the other arpeggios below the staff with a single F attachment:

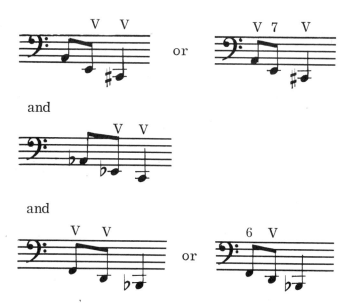

Fig. 31   Slide Positions Using the F Attachment Only

Less slide movement is needed if a combination of the two valves, F and E flat, is used:

Fig. 32   Slide Positions Using the F-E Flat Attachment

F-D Attachment

The D attachment has been developed during the past few years and is an extension of the E flat valve. The D valve adds an additional minor third to the F attachment (in first position only). The location of the notes on the D valve depends on the tuning of the valve slides. Their approximate locations are:

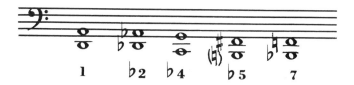

Fig. 33   Relationship of the D Attachment Pitches to the Positions on a Tenor Trombone

There are more technical advantages with the D valve than with the E flat valve. Leaps of a minor third or larger, possible but unhandy on an F attachment, are easier with an E flat valve, and are still easier on the D valve:

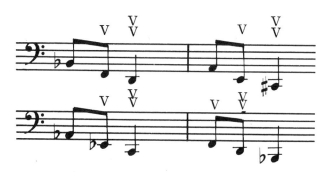

Fig. 34   Slide Positions Using the F-D Attachment

The chromatic scale on an F-D valved bass trombone would be played:

F and G Attachment

On a trombone with an F and G attachment, either attachment lever can be operated independently of the other. The F attachment lever is operated by the left thumb. The G attachment lever is operated by the left ring finger. If both attachment levers are engaged, the trombone is in D.

The notes on the G attachment are:

Fig. 35 Relationship of the G Attachment Pitches to the Positions on a Tenor Trombone

There are many technical advantages to a G attachment. Listing them is beyond the scope of this book, but a couple of obvious uses involve quick changes from first position B flat to a fourth or fifth position note, *i.e.*

Tuning the F Attachment

Both the F attachment and the D attachment valve slides can be tuned to the intonation of the main body of the trombone. As a rule, the valve slides are extended somewhat at all times, and seldom is it proper to play with the slides pushed in all the way. Usually the more the main tuning slide is pulled out, the more the attachment slides must be pulled. How the attachments are tuned is the choice of the individual.

Some players tune their F attachments so that the middle Fs are in unison:

Tuning the F attachment this way is not always desirable because the low F on many instruments is flat and to play it in tune you must compress the slide receiver springs. Some prefer to tune their F attachments so that the low F will form an intune interval of a perfect fourth with the low B flat.

This tuning is satisfactory for tenor trombonists, but bass trombonists find that the low Cs on the valve are very sharp even when the hand slide is extended to the point where it is about to fall off the inside slides.

Some single valve bass trombonists extend their F attachments as far as practical so that the low C on the valve is nearly in tune. They tune their third position E flats in octaves without moving the hand slide:

This tuning is so flat that the low F on the valve must be played with the slide completely compressing the springs in the slide receiver and even then it may be necessary to lip the tuning up to the proper pitch. Besides, this tuning may not have extended the valve slide quite far enough to be able to play the low C in tune, especially in places where the tuning is quite critical, for instance, in the trombone choral of the Brahms, *Symphony No. 1.*

For the beginner, I recommend that the valve slide be tuned so the low F forms a perfect fifth with the low B flat. In time, as you become more comfortable with the tone production on the F attachment, you can extend the valve slide so that the middle Fs are in tune at the unison. Only if you begin to specialize on bass trombone parts where low Cs are common would you need to extend the valve slide any further.

Once the F attachment has been tuned, the second valve slide can be adjusted. (The second valve slide cannot be tuned before the F attachment slide is tuned because every change in the F attachment slide changes the tuning of the second valve slide also). The second valve is usually tuned as flat as possible so that the low B natural is easy to reach. The E flat valve is tuned so that the E flat is played when the hand slide is compressing the springs in the receiver all the way.

Those with a D valve also tune flat so that the D is played by completely compressing the springs. With this tuning it is then nearly possible to play a B flat in flatted seventh position. Although the B flat in long seventh position may not have the tone of a pedal B flat in first position, it makes the technique of the figure

easier than attempting

Left Thumb Action

Many players use an incorrect left thumb action when they first begin playing a trombone with an F or F-D attachment. Either because they have a weak left hand grip or because they are not accustomed to the additional weight of a trombone with an attachment, they are unable to support the instrument properly with a grip that uses only the fingers of the left hand and leaves the thumb free to manipulate the valve. Any attempt to support the instrument with the left thumb will slow the dexterity of the action and make it so cumbersome and jerky that you may continually break valve strings. The finger grip of the left hand must be strengthend so that it supports the entire weight of the instrument even when the slide is extended.

The thumb placement on the valve lever is important. Do not wrap your thumb around or hook your entire thumb over the valve lever. A rather large muscle in the hand then controls the valve action. The motion is gross and not precise or agile. This gross motion also may break the valve string. A point slightly behind the tip of the thumb should touch the lever. Now the finer muscles of the thumb itself can flex to move the valve lever and the thumb action is rapid, precise and delicate.

F Attachment Valve Maintenance

Oiling the Valve

Most rotary valves do not touch the sides of the valve casing. Thus it is seldom necessary to oil the rotor of the valve directly. During the breaking-in period there may be a few high spots on the rotor or casing that have not been worn down. Then the rotor may be oiled by allowing a few drops to run down the main pipe into the valve or by putting a few drops into the F attachment pipe that leads directly into the valve.

The points that *must* be oiled are the bearings on the shafts that suspend the valve in the casing. Remove the valve cap to reach one of the bearings. Place a few drops of oil on the valve shaft where it comes through the valve back head.

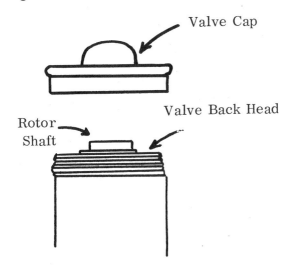

The bearing on the other side is more difficult to reach. Follow these steps: One, Remove the valve cap;

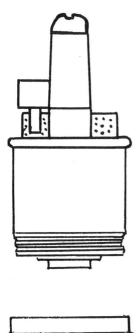

Two, Loosen the stop arm retaining screw a few revolutions;

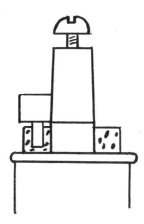

Three, Tap the screw until it is flush with the stop arm hub, (the valve back head will have become dislodged by this time also). Use a raw hide mallet, a plastic headed hammer, or a mouthpiece wrapped in a handkerchief so that the screw is not marred;

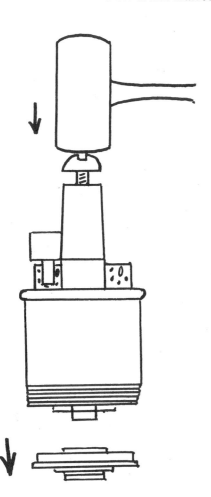

Four, Pull up the rotor stop arm so that the rotor shaft is exposed;

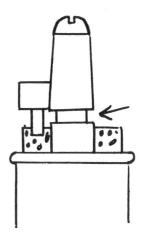

Five, Oil the rotor shaft; and finally, Six, Push the stop arm down on the shaft, replace the back head bearing, install the valve cap and tighten the stop arm retaining screw.

To avoid loosening the stop arm screw to oil the bearing, simply drop oil in the space between the stop arm and the valve housing and let the oil work its way down the valve shaft into the bearing.

Special rotary valve oil can be bought, but many trombonists use clarinet key oil, valve oil or slide oil. Without oil the wear on the bearings is rapid and in a short time the valve will become noisy. Without oil the bearing becomes elliptical and the rotor shaft begins to slap back and forth in the out-of-round hole. Regular oiling of the bearings of the rotary valve will greatly increase the life of the bearing and postpone the problems of a noisy or binding valve.

Silencing Noisy Valves

Rotary valves will make a clanking sound when opened or closed, if the cork stops have worn and the stop arm hits the metal of the stop. If new cork stops are needed, see the section below: Installing New Valve Corks.

If the corks are satisfactory, the noise is then caused by worn bearings. First, oil the rotor bearings. If the clanking persists, check the tension of the valve string. Valve strings stretch and often the clank of a valve can be removed by simply increasing the tension of the valve string, or balancing the tension of the string so that the string is not loose at the end of one of the strokes of the valve lever. For further details, see the section below: Restringing a Rotary Valve.

Finally, reoil the bearings of the rotor shafts using

a heavier oil such as household oil or sewing machine oil. Some trombonists prefer to use gun oil. Only one or two drops of this oil is placed on each bearing, and a small can of oil will last for several years. How much oil is used depends on the wear of the bearings and if the valve action becomes sluggish, you will have to add a few drops of valve oil to the bearing to dilute the heavier oil.

Many trombonists become accustomed to the clank of their valves and are unaware as it gradually becomes noisier. Unlike such trombonists, conductors will not tolerate the clank of a valve and the professional trombonist maintains his valve so that it is never heard in action.

Installing New Valve Corks

Each rotary valve has two cork or rubber bumpers which are hit by the stop arm as the valve is opened or closed. In time these corks wear, become compressed, or crack and fall out. If the cork wears down or falls out, there will be a clanking sound as the stop arm hits the metal which held the cork. You can hear that you need new corks.

If the corks are only compressed or worn, the valve may seem to be working properly, but without checking the valve back head, you cannot be sure. The valve back head and the rotor shaft have one or two scratch marks on them to aid in the alignment. They can be seen by removing the valve cap. The marks should appear:

When the valve lever is pressed, the valve shaft will rotate within the valve back head and the marks should appear:

Some valves have different markings or rotate in the opposite direction but the principle is the same. The markings on the shaft should align with the marks on

the valve head cap, provided the valve head cap mark aligns with the mark on the valve casing.

On newly corked instruments, the marks on the rotor do not quite travel all the way to the mark on the valve back head. The repairman or instrument builder adjusted the corks this way on purpose so that as the corks are played in the rotor arm will not travel too far. After instruments have been used for awhile, the corks will become compressed and allow the stop arm to travel just far enough. Later, they will travel too far.

When the rotor passes the markings, the holes in the rotor are not aligning themselves properly with the valve ports. The trombone responds as though it has a leak (which it does). The corks must be replaced.

Rotary valve corks are sold in cylindrical pieces, and you can cut about three corks from each piece. To install a cork which appears to be far too large for the tiny metal holder, grip the cork with a pair of needle nosed pliers, compress it and force the cork into the metal claws. No glue or cement is necessary. When the pressure of the pliers is released, the cork expands in the holder for a firm fit. Push the cork until it touches the bottom of the metal holder. Cut off the excess cork with a sharp knife or razor blade. Save the excess for the next time. Now check the alignment of the marks on the rotor shaft and the valve back head, and trim the corks with a razor blade until the stop arm *almost* travels far enough for the marks to align. Remember that some excess cork should be left so that in time as the cork is compressed, the marks will only align with and not travel past the marks.

Neopreme rubber can be used instead of cork and the above procedure remains the same no matter what material is used.

Disassembling the Valve

The valve seldom needs to be completely disassembled. Unless the valve and the tubing ducts around it are dirty and cannot be cleaned by running water through the valve, you will never have to dismantle it. If the valve must be disassembled, the string is removed; the valve cap is removed; the stop arm screw is loosened, tapped with a plastic hammer until the rotor is loose, and then removed, and then the valve comes apart. As all the technical manuals say—"Reverse the order to reassemble."

Restringing the Valve

Rather than wait for the valve string to break, while hoping that it will not, you should become familiar with the stringing of a rotary valve before the string breaks. Study the stringing pattern so that you can duplicate the pattern WITHOUT a model to follow (there is no model after the string has broken).

To string a rotary valve:

1. Take a five inch piece of braided linen fishing line (Cuttyhunk Linen 25 lb. Wet Test) and knot one end several times. Braided nylon fishing line can be used, but nylon tends to break rather than fray, and will not give you as much warning that the string is about to break. Use monofilament fishing line only in an emergency and change to a braided linen as soon as possible. Monofilament line breaks very easily when weakened by a metal burr or some other sharp edge and should not be used to string a rotary valve unless it is absolutely the only string available.

2. Thread the string through the hole in the side of the valve extension lever.

4. Hold the valve extension lever in position with the left hand and also hold the string in place on the set screw with your left thumb, and thread the string under itself and on around the stop arm hub.

3. Loosen the string set screw a few turns, pass the string over the stop arm hub and around the threaded part of the string set screw.

5. Tighten the set screw so that the string is held in place.

6. Pass the free end of the string over the string that is already in place and thread it through the hole next to the set screw on the valve extension lever.

Some players position their levers so that the string passes *under* the secured string. Otherwise the string rubs against itself when the valve is operated. Until the stringing is completed you will not be able to tell whether the string should pass over or under the secured string.

7. Loosen the set screw on the valve extension lever

and pass the string around the threads of the screw and under itself.

8. Tighten the set screw on the valve extension lever. Leave enough string so that it can be gripped should the restringing have to be repeated and cut off the excess.

9. Now check the adjustment of the string. Move the valve extension lever and notice whether it is in a comfortable position. Also check the string tension. If the valve lever is not positioned correctly, loosen the screw on the stop arm hub and slide the string until the position is correct. After the lever is positioned correctly, loosen the screw on the extension lever and adjust the string so that it is firm but not tight. Note: Now that the stop arm set screw is tightened, only half of the string can be adjusted by loosening the extension arm screw, so you may have to loosen the stop arm set screw again, in fact several times, until the valve lever opens and closes the valve without any binding of the string or without any looseness in the string.

At first the stringing of the valve is a nerve-wracking job which will take several minutes. An experienced player can restring and adjust his valve in a few minutes. String operated valves have the advantages of being quiet and extremely dependable if they are properly maintained. They have the added advantage of being adjustable without the need of an instrument repair man. If you are a new owner of an F attachment, you should learn to restring and adjust your valve without delay. You will then have no problems when it must be restrung and adjusted.

Chapter 9
Selection of Trombones and Mouthpieces

Many factors will influence your choice of a trombone and a mouthpiece. I will not try to make specific recommendations for you, but I will attempt to mention as many considerations as possible and leave the final decision to you and your teacher.

Bore and Bell Size

There has been a noticeable trend to larger instruments. Not long ago, trombones had both smaller bores and smaller bells than are now popular in the United States. In the late 1940s, the trombone was considered large if it had a seven and one-half inch bell and a bore of .500″. Not until the mid-1950s were larger instruments produced in quantity on a production line basis. Trombones with an eight and one-half inch bell and a bore of .547″ are now in production by the major companies of the world and tend to be the standard size for the principal trombonist both in major American symphony orchestras and in university orchestras and bands.

The concept of tone quality in the United States has changed and the sound of the larger trombone is preferred. At one time, large bore instruments were thought to be too large for general playing. It was also believed that only professional full-time adult players could fill them. Although jazz and commercial work trombonists still prefer a smaller instrument, many of the younger players are setting a trend toward the use of larger instruments even in these fields. The argument that a student cannot fill a large trombone was never true, when you remember that a junior high school player can fill a tuba.

Tuning Slide Location

During the first part of this century, when trombones were manufactured with two pieces of tubing for the bell section (one for the high pitch and one for the *new* low pitch, A = 440), the tuning slide was placed in the slide section of the instrument. In time the tuning slide was placed in the bell section again. With the tuning slide in the bell section, the slide can be lightened, but the dimensions of the bore of the bell section are distorted. Theoretically, the trombone should be cylindrical for the first portion of its bore and conical for the final part. The tuning slide in the bell makes it necessary for the tubing to be cylindrical in two sections rather than allow the tubing to continuously flair all the way through the bell section. Until recently, this acoustical problem was ignored in favor of the lighter slide. Recently, some instruments have been produced with the tuning in the slide and a bell section which is completely conical. Whether this is a trend that will develop can only be judged with the passage of time.

Metals and Plating

Most trombones are presently made with brass bells, although there are those who prefer a sterling silver or a nickel-silver bell. The ingredients of brass can be mixed with several different proportions and among some symphony orchestra players, the dark or red brass is preferred for its darker tone. The plating of instruments with silver is becoming rare and no longer are instruments plated with gold except on special order. Professional trombonists have argued for a long time about whether the plating, the lacquering or the playing of the instrument affect the tone. It is generally agreed that heavy plating does tend to deaden the tone. Plating can be applied in a thinner layer than lacquer and theoretically such an instrument has a more live response than a lacquered instrument. How lacquer or the number of coats of lacquer will affect the tone is still highly debated. Whether the actual playing of the instrument may crystalize the metal along certain vibrational patterns in the brass is yet to be proven by scientific research, but some players are so convinced that the way a trombone is played does influence its response that they limit the playing that they allow anyone else to do on their instrument.

Slide Receivers

Many trombones only have felt or cork bumpers in the slide receivers. Others have springs mounted in the slide receivers and these springs absorb the shock as the slide arrives in first position. Thus the shock is not transferred through the mouthpiece to the lips and teeth. More important, the springs, when they are not compressed, mark the location of first position. If the note in first position is slightly flat (as with the D above the staff and certain first position F attachment notes), you can compensate for the flatness and compress the springs. Thus, you can actually play notes slightly higher than first position. Some players without springs in their receivers, tune sharp and then play first position not quite touching the cork of the receiver. This makes the placement of a normal first position rather indefinite. I prefer to use springs to solve first position intonation problems.

Attachments

Before valves were invented in the first half of the 19th century, a bass trombone was pitched in F. It was shaped like the present day tenor trombone, but with longer dimensions. A handle was usually attached to the slide so that the player could reach the extreme positions. With the invention of the rotary valve, the additional tubing of the bass trombone could be mounted on a large tenor trombone and added to or subtracted from the tubing of the tenor trombone with the movement of the thumb. To be correct, the modern bass trombone should be called a tenor-bass trombone, since its fundamental overtone series is B flat like the tenor trombone. Only when the rotary valve connects the additional tubing is the trombone pitched in F like a bass trombone. With the disappearance of true bass trombones, the tenor-bass trombone has become known as the bass trombone, although there are still some bass trombones pitched in G or F in use in Europe today.

The F attachment does not necessarily make the instrument a bass trombone. Adding an F attachment to a tenor trombone, particularly a smaller bore trombone, does give you some technical advantages, but a bass trombone is usually considered a bass trombone when it has a bell of nine and one-half inches or larger and a bore of at least .562". The tenor trombones with F attachments can play in the same range as a bass trombone, but because of their tone quality should be considered tenor trombones with F attachments. The uses of and the technical advantages of the F attachment are explained in Chapter 8.

When purchasing an instrument with an F attachment, several points must be considered.

Thumb Lever Placement

Some levers are located below the bell joint brace and you must use only the four fingers of your left hand to hold the trombone. At first this feels awkward since you have been used to placing your thumb around the bell joint brace to help hold the trombone steady. Other levers are located so that your thumb must reach around the bell joint brace to push the valve lever. This makes it easier and more comfortable to hold the instrument but severly limits your thumb motion. I prefer the freedom of thumb action which can be obtained from a valve lever that is located away from the bell joint brace.

Valve Linkage

It is common to connect the valve lever to the valve rotor with a linen or nylon string. With string linkage, the string tension and the placement of the valve lever can be raised or lowered by adjusting the string. There is occasionally a problem when the string breaks. On other trombones, a metal ball and socket joint at the end of the valve lever connects the valve rotor. This ball and socket linkage does not break like the string, but the position of the thumb lever cannot be adjusted easily. Besides they tend to rattle and become noisy with use. Some of the ball and socket joints are spring-loaded so that the action in the joint is held firmly as wear occurs. Some ball and socket joints must be greased with Vaseline or packed with cotton wadding to silence their action. Caution must be used when greasing this valve linkage, because the grease or packing tends to slow the action of the valve.

A third type of linkage uses a nylon bar to connect the lever with the rotor. These do not become noisy with wear, but they can bind the action of the valve. As a personal preference, I believe that the string connection provides the fastest valve action, is the most easily maintained by the trombonist himself and is the most reliable. Although the string can break, I have been able to avoid this problem in concerts and rehearsals by regularly examining the string and changing it at the first sign of wear. With proper preventive maintenance you can expect 100 percent reliability from a valve with string linkage.

Valve Lever Travel

There is a wide variation between the design of the valve levers of the various models of trombones. Some levers must be pushed for nearly one inch to engage the F attachment. Others have a travel of only a small fraction of an inch. Short lever travel increases the speed and clarity of the valve action. With levers having a longer travel, the effort needed to engage the valve is easier. Although the valve with the longer travel may feel easier and better at first, I prefer the speed of the lever with the shorter travel. The muscle of the thumb will quickly develop so that the shorter travel will be preferred.

Multiple Levers

Although once experimental, many new models of bass trombones have two valves. (For an explanation of these valves and their advantages, see Chapter 8—F

Attachments). There are four common arrangements of levers to operate two valves. One, the valve levers are mounted side by side, much like the adjacent keys on a saxophone. Two, the levers are mounted one above the other, so that one lever is pushed when the thumb is partially flexed and both levers are pushed when the thumb is flexed further. Three, the two rotors are connected to a single thumb lever, so that when the lever is pushed in one direction one valve is opened, and when it is pushed in another direction the second valve is opened also. Four, the second valve lever is positioned on the other side of the bell joint where it can be operated by the ring finger of the left hand.

All of the two-valve arrangements have certain disadvantages at their present stage of development. When the levers are mounted side by side, the thumb must be able to roll or slide from one valve lever (the F attachment) to the second valve lever (which engages both valves) with a smooth motion which will not break a legato slur. Also the thumb, once positioned on the second valve lever, must be able to roll or slide back to the first valve lever without breaking a slur. With some trombones, this rolling or sliding of the thumb between the valve levers cannot be done without twisting the hand into unusual positions. Some players have solved this problem by fashioning a small half crescent thumb saddle and having it mounted between the two levers. Thus they can operate one or both valves by rocking the direction of the thumb pressure. Mounting the valve levers one above the other makes legato playing easy, provided the valve levers are positioned comfortably for the particular player's hand. Some arrangements require that the thumb also curl around the bell joint brace and this can be quite uncomfortable for some players. For other players, the levers would have to be bent for them to be able to operate the levers with smoothness and ease. One lever which operates two valves is just becoming available commercially at this writing and it could offer many advantages if the travel of the lever is not too long and the linkage can be made reliable and silent. Two separate valve levers, one for the thumb and one for the left ring finger, may provide the best solution, but some people find the positioning of the levers quite uncomfortable and in addition they have difficulty holding a heavy bass trombone with the remaining three fingers.

Alto Trombones

The trombone section of an early 19th century orchestra contained one alto, one tenor and one bass trombone. The principal or first trombonist played alto trombone. Not until later in the 19th century did composers stop writing the first trombone part in the alto clef. Recently there has been renewed interest in playing the works originally written for alto trombone on an alto trombone and the serious trombonist may consider the purchase of such an instrument.

Alto trombones are pitched in two keys, E flat or F. The alto in E flat seems to be the more popular choice at the present time. Only half of the slide positions are the same as notes on tenor trombone on either instrument, so the slide technique of the alto in E flat is no easier to learn than the alto in F. The alto trombone must be practiced regularly and the positions memorized as if beginning again if you are to be secure when performing on it.

The modern alto trombone has a bell with an exponential flare and though it still has a light tone and cannot be forced, it produces far more sound than the funnel-shaped bells of the alto trombones of the Baroque period. This exponential flare of the modern instrument gives it increased volume like the improved woodwinds. Although a purist would erroneously note that the stringed instruments in an orchestra are very old, these instruments have been reworked to give them more volume. They have been given longer necks, larger bass bars and now use wound strings with increased tension rather than the original gut and silk strings. Thus the stringed instruments are playing louder than they did originally and the increased flare of the alto trombone bell is appropriate in modern symphony orchestras.

Baroque Trombones

Models of Baroque trombones are being manufactured on a small scale and many individuals and universities are purchasing these instruments for the performance of Baroque music. The funnel-shaped Baroque bell reduces the volume and alters the harmonic overtone series of the tone so that the basic tone quality is more mellow or less brilliant. It is easier to perform Baroque compositions with voices with the proper blend and balance by using Baroque trombones than by using modern instruments with exponentially flared bells.

Do not buy a Baroque trombone without checking its pitch. The trombone may be an exact copy of a certain old instrument, but in that particular country at that time the pitch level may have been as much as a whole tone above or below our present A = 440. It is better to purchase an instrument which is in tune, rather than buy an instrument that is noted because it is an authentic copy.

Playing a Baroque tenor trombone is not too difficult for a modern trombonist. Although the tone is muted and mellow, the slide positions and pitch placements are familiar. Playing an E flat alto or an F bass Baroque trombone is confusing because you must learn a new set of slide positions. In cases where the trombonists cannot dedicate the time and energy to learning to play the Baroque trombones, the performance may be more successful if the conductor allowed them to use their own modern instruments. The volume of modern instruments can be reduced to Baroque volume in several ways. The players can be seated to the side or behind the vocal group, rather than in front. They can be seated on carpet and behind a heavy curtain which would extend from the floor to a height of two and one-half to three feet. Finally, they could be asked to use felt hats (See Chapter 10, Mutes). Although a performance of this type would not use the authentic instruments, the sound and the total effect would possibly be just as authentic and the intonation and technique would be far superior to the original or the recreated performance using Baroque trombones.

Mouthpieces

There has been a trend for trombonists to use larger and larger mouthpieces. What used to be a large professional model mouthpiece a few decades ago has become the ideal student model today. At first, the trombone should be fitted with a mouthpiece that is slightly smaller than one inch in diameter. In time you may wish to change to a mouthpiece that has a diameter which slightly exceeds one inch.

Changing to a larger mouthpiece, if handled properly, can increase your volume, the richness and depth of your tone and your flexibility, but do not change to a larger mouthpiece unless you are ready for such a change. In time, any loss of register or endurance will be regained.

When changing to a larger mouthpiece you should not experiment for a few days with it, then change to another for a few more days and then change again. The change should be made as if it is a permanent change and no further changes (either to a larger or smaller mouthpiece) should be made until the first change has been established for a month or so. Each mouthpiece you change to should only be slightly different from your last mouthpiece. You should not choose a mouthpiece that is drastically different than the one you are used to just because a well-known professional trombonist uses such a mouthpiece. It is foolish for a new bass trombonist to buy the largest mouthpiece available. In time you may need such a mouthpiece but you should change mouthpieces every year or so to get to this larger mouthpiece with changes that do not develop bad habits and overtenseness which stunt your progress permanently.

You should not avoid larger mouthpieces however.

Many performers use mouthpieces that are too small because they are comfortable and because they are small enough to let them force and pinch notes. An excellent way of solving some tone production problems is to move to a larger mouthpiece. This removes the crutch from your embouchure. With the larger mouthpiece, you must produce correctly or get no tone at all.

There are five major points to consider when buying a mouthpiece:

Rim

The rim of your first mouthpiece should be moderately wide, have a somewhat flat surface and have a moderate interior edge. As you progress you may prefer a rim that is more rounded and less wide. This second mouthpiece will not be as comfortable as the first, but it will increase your flexibility because it will not restrict the movement of your lips and the rim will tend to cut into your embouchure if you use too much pressure. A more rounded edge, although it is said to take the edge off of the attack, will keep you from relying too much on the grip you can get on your lips with a broader rimmed mouthpiece. The more rounded edge encourages you to place the mouthpiece on the embouchure correctly. With mouthpieces with a sharp bite, you are tempted to give the mouthpiece a twist as it comes into contact with your lips. This twisted stretch of the lips will momentarily form an embouchure, even though the embouchure will disappear as soon as the mouthpiece looses its grip. It is better to choose a mouthpiece with a rim which does not allow cheating and encourages you to develop a correct embouchure.

Cup Diameter

Your first mouthpiece should have a diameter of slightly less than one inch. A mouthpiece of this size will make it possible for you to develop a full tone in the lower register yet retain a moderate amount of control and brilliance in the middle and upper registers. As your embouchure develops, you should change to a mouthpiece that is one inch in diameter or larger. As with the change in rim size and shape, a change to a larger diameter has both advantages and disadvantages. The larger diameter allows you to place more red of the lip in vibration in the mouthpiece and you can develop a larger and deeper tone. The additional room also increases your flexibility. The disadvantages include a loss of some upper register and a loss of some endurance. If the embouchure is normal and you are producing the tone correctly, you will regain your endurance and upper register in a few weeks. If you have a weak embouchure or incorrect tone production habits, do not attempt to "buy" a bigger tone and more flexibility by purchasing a larger mouthpiece. You must produce the tone correctly on the larger mouthpiece or you will develop several new bad habits.

As a teacher, I have changed some of my students to a larger mouthpiece in order to remove the crutch of the old mouthpiece and force them to produce the tone correctly. This procedure is only recommended as an extreme measure when other methods have failed. A student should change to a larger mouthpiece under supervision by a teacher.

Cup Depth

Many student trombones are presently being equipped with mouthpieces which have the appropriate depth. Many of these mouthpieces are modeled after the Bach 12C or the Bach 7C. It is difficult to measure the depth of the cup with your finger or a pencil, because the diameter of the throat or orifice influences the depth measurement and this depth measurement does not consider the *shape* of the walls of the cup. As the dimensions of the cup are increased, the side walls are usually extended downwards further at first. Thus the bottom of the cup has a more noticeable bowl or acorn shape. As the depth of the cup is enlarged further, the bottom of the bowl is cut in more of a funnel-shape and the throat is enlarged. With the largest mouthpieces, this funnel shape tends to extend all the way from the rim to the throat and the throat is now placed deeper than the throat of a normal cup.

A mouthpiece with a deeper cup has the same advantages as a mouthpiece with a larger diameter. It is easier to produce a darker larger tone in the low register, the tone is less brilliant in the middle and upper registers and the flexibility is increased. The disadvantages include the loss of endurance and a loss of high register. Again, the disadvantages are overcome in a few weeks if you have a strong embouchure and correct tone-production habits.

Throat-Shoulder and Orifice

The hole in the bottom of the mouthpiece is commonly called the throat, but in recent research by the Conn Corporation these dimensions have been divided into two measurements, the shoulder (the curvature of the transition from the cup to the throat) and the orifice (the size of the throat bore itself). Enlarging the throat influences the tone production in the same way as the enlargement of the diameter or the cup of the mouthpiece. Increased tone, volume and flexibility, and loss of endurance and high register occur with the increase in size.

Backbore

How rapidly the bore of the mouthpiece flares from the throat into the instrument is a factor that is often neglected in determining the suitability of a mouthpiece. The faster the flare, the more open the mouthpiece becomes and the advantages of a faster flare are the same as those obtained from a larger diameter, a larger cup and a larger throat.

Altering Mouthpiece Dimensions

You should not attempt to rework the dimensions of a mouthpiece to achieve a certain effect. Reworking one dimension without making appropriate enlargements of the other dimensions may destroy the proportions. No scientific research has been done on trombone mouthpieces, but some has been completed on trumpet mouthpieces (See Jody C. Hall, *The Proper Selection of Cup Mouthpieces*, Elkhart, Ind.: C. G. Conn, Inc., 1963). For the moment it may be assumed that the effects of dimension alterations are the same for both and that a radical change of one dimension could cause extreme intonation problems.

Platings

Trombone mouthpieces are usually plated with silver, but some players prefer a gold plating. Those who prefer gold claim that the feel of the mouthpiece is softer and smoother. No matter which you choose, you must be sure that the brass of the mouthpiece is kept covered with some type of plating. The brass of a mouthpiece that has lost its plating can irritate the skin of the embouchure and cause it to break out in a rash or pimples.

Detachable Rims

A professional player's embouchure becomes very sensitive to the exact shape of the rim of his mouthpiece. Some players notice quite a difference between their personal mouthpiece and another mouthpiece that is supposed to be exactly the same. Other players need to be able to change mouthpieces to be able to play other instruments—bass trombone and euphonium— which may require a different shank or a different cup depth. By using a detachable rim, you can play on several mouthpieces with varying cup depths, throats, backbores and shanks without disturbing the set of the embouchure.

Lucite and Nylon

Some players prefer to use a nylon mouthpiece or a brass mouthpiece with a lucite rim for outdoor work. It is difficult to keep a metal mouthpiece warm during cold outdoor work and the cold mouthpiece damages the skin of their embouchures. Nylon mouthpieces can be machined to any shape, but only a limited selection of sizes are now available commercially. Another manufacturer produces detachable lucite rims for an extensive variety of mouthpieces. The lucite rim can be replaced with a metal rim for indoor work. Most players do not like the feel of the plastic for indoor work, and use the plastic one only when outside.

Choosing a Mouthpiece

Mouthpieces must be chosen with care. If you want to move to a larger mouthpiece which is a radical change from your regular mouthpiece, you should make several small changes over a period of time rather than attempt to change in one step. Don't be reluctant to change, but do not change without careful thought and consultation with your teacher.

Chapter 10
Mutes

Many kinds of mutes have been developed for trombones. Almost every kind of mute that has been produced for trumpets has also been made in a larger size for the trombone, but there is a noticeable difference in tone quality when some trumpet mutes are enlarged and used by trombones. Trumpet and trombone straight mutes have a matching tone quality. Some cup mutes for trumpet and trombone will produce the same tone quality. Other types of mutes do not match and can be used as solo mutes or as individual section mutes only. Further research may develop other types of trombone mutes which match the tone of trumpet mutes, but there is one other problem. The trumpet player can carry a large collection of mutes in his case, but the trombonist would need a large shopping bag to carry his mutes. It is very inconvenient for a trombonist to carry more than one or two mutes at a time.

Straight Mute—Fiber

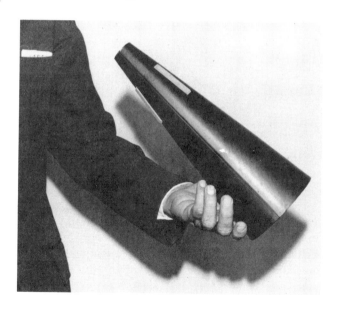

Fig. 36   Straight Mute—Fiber

Before the recent improvement of metal straight mutes, the most common mute was the straight mute made from fiber board or cardboard. These mutes have a wooden end and a body which is formed either from laminated fiber board or cardboard. Excellent quality

mutes are available in a variety of sizes so that a mute can be selected that will both fit the bell of the trombone and not cause unusual intonation problems. Fiber mutes do not add as much cutting edge to the tone as a metal mute does when played *fortissimo*, but they can be played softly without a penetrating buzz. With a fiber mute, you can *diminuendo* nearly to silence, whereas a metal straight mute tends to retain an edge at soft dynamic levels. The fiber mute is used when the muting direction is: Mute, *Con Sordino* (or *con sord.*), *avec sordino* or *dämpfer*. Occasionally the instructions will specifically ask for fiber mute or fiber straight mute.

Straight Mute—Metal

Fig. 37   Straight Mute—Metal

Excellent quality, spun aluminum, straight mutes have been developed for trombones in the past decade. The presently available models usually raise the pitch of the larger trombones (they are not quite large enough for a trombone with an eight and one-half inch bell), but the mutes of the other brass instruments tend to make them sharp also, so as a section, the intonation remains relatively the same. When muting, the tuning slide should be pulled out a fraction of an inch to keep the pitch level the same as the open instrument. The pitch can be lowered by gluing thicker corks on the mute, but this lets more sound past the outside of the mute and the tone quality is changed. Another method of lowering the pitch of the mute is to tape or glue a cardboard or plastic tube in the end of the mute. The further the tube is extended, the lower the pitch. After the best tube length is found, the excess inside the mute is trimmed off and discarded. The tube is then taped or glued in place.

The metal straight mute is used when the muting direction is: Mute, *Con Sordino* (or *con sord.*), *avec sordino* or *dämpfer*. Occasionally the instructions will specifically ask for metal mute or metal straight mute.

The tone quality of fiber and metal straight mutes do not blend and the section should use either fiber or metal. The principal of the section or the conductor would decide which type to use for particular compositions.

Cup Mute

Fig. 38   Cup Mute

Cup mutes, though used a great deal in jazz and commercial work, are not commonly used in symphony orchestra and concert band work. Cup mutes that both fit the bell of a large trombone and also have good intonation and the proper tone color are difficult to find. The only way to adjust a mute with a fixed cup is to add corks or file the corks. Filing the corks makes the cup fit closer to the bell, but then the mute fits deeper and the tone is restricted from passing the corks at the upper end of the mute. Adding corks moves the cup away from the bell, but also allows more tone

to pass the corks. Thus, the tone color and intonation of the mute are being varied at the same time. Purchase a mute with an adjustable cup if possible so that you can adjust the coverage of the bell without changing the corks. If the corks must be adjusted to alter the pitch or to allow more or less tone to pass the corks, the cup can be readjusted without difficulty. The cup is adjusted to suit the style of the music. In section work, the cup is usually opened about an inch. In some amplified solo work, the cup is closed nearly against the bell for a dark, muffled tone.

Wa-Wa or Harmon Mute

Fig. 39   Wa-Wa or Harmon Mute

The Wa-Wa or Harmon mute, which is fairly common in trumpet literature, does not retain the same tone color when enlarged and used in trombones. The characteristic trumpet tone in a Harmon mute has a penetration and a shimmer, which a trombone Harmon mute does not achieve. Present models of trombone Harmon mutes develop more resonance in the lower partials of the tone. The trombonist seldom needs a Harmon mute in present jazz and commercial work, and rarely needs one for symphonic orchestra work. An example of its comic effect is found in Lucien Cailliet's *Pop Goes the Weasel* and for the jazz effect in Gershwin's *Rhapsody in Blue*. Both of these examples are solos and use the mute fully assembled. The trumpeters dismantle or adjust their Harmon mutes to vary the tone color. Usually the "cookie cutter" is removed from the stem.

Fig. 40   Wa-Wa or Harmon Mute with "Cookie Cutter" Removed

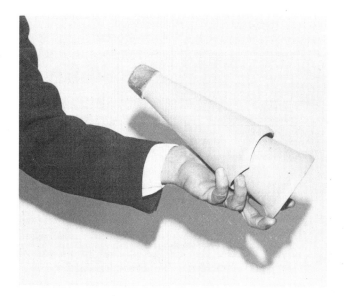

Fig. 41   Solotone or Mega Mute

This cookie cutter is replaced only for the Wa-Wa effect when the hand alternately blocks and opens this hole. Other tone colors are gotten by extending the stem or removing the stem completely.

When music written or arranged between the beginning of this century and the 1940s asks for Harmon mute or Wa-Wa mute, the mute is to be used fully assembled. A + over the note indicates that the fingers of your hand cover the cookie cutter and an 0 indicates that the hole is open. Where the Wa-Wa effect is not to be used, the orifice of the mute is not covered, and the 0s or +s are not marked. In general, arrangements made since the 1950s will assume that the cookie cutter has been removed. The direction: Harmon mute or Wa-Wa mute expects the mute to be played with the stem in and the cookie cutter removed. Other changes are indicated by the arranger, *i.e.* Harmon mute, stem half extended; Harmon mute stem fully extended, or Harmon mute, no stem.

Solotone Mute

During the first half of this century, there was a great deal of experimentation with all varieties of mutes. One type of mute that favors trombones more than trumpets is the Solotone mute. The tone passes through the mute in the same way as it passes through a Harmon mute. The cork on the mute forms a complete seal and none of the tone of the instrument passes between the sides of the mute and the bell of the instrument. All of the tone must enter and pass through the mute. The tone is diminished and reinforced in the first

chamber and leaves this chamber via the cardboard tube which is permanently mounted. (The Harmon mute has a tube which is movable and removable, but the Solotone mute has the tube fixed in place.) The tone is centered and focused by the megaphone-shaped cone as it leaves the tube.

The Solotone mute is used in the trombone parts of the dance band music of the first half of this century. The use of the Solotone is far more common than the use of the Harmon mute for trombones. It is usually used as a solo mute. I only know of one use in the symphony orchestra repertoire: the trombone solo in a small orchestra arrangement of the third movement "On the Trail" of the *Grand Canyon Suite*, by Ferde Grofé and this is designated *Megaphone*. The conductor usually prefers to have the solo played open.

Plunger

Although mute makers sell a plunger, which is simply a six-inch bowl with a small handle, many trombonists purchase and use a rubber toilet plunger. The wash basin plungers are too small for trombone (they are better suited for trumpets) and the special plungers of modern design are not appropriate either. The simple six-inch diameter plunger is best. It can either be held by the rubber socket where the handle used to be attached or it is turned inside-out to better fit the shape of the hand. The plunger is moved by the left hand while the instrument is supported by the left wrist on the edge of the bell. The left shoulder is also hunched to keep the upper part of the bell section from slipping.

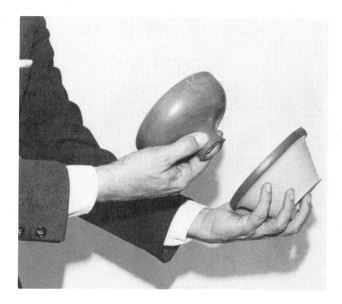

Fig. 42   Two Types of Plungers

Fig. 43   Hat, Metal Hat or Derby

Using the plunger is tiring (and at times damaging) to the embouchure since the instrument is usually leaned against the embouchure also. In addition, you cannot operate the F attachment when using a plunger (a fact often forgotten by the arrangers and composers). The part is marked in English only—Plunger. The bell is to be covered when there is a + over the note and uncovered when there is an 0 over the note. A + and an 0 together indicate that the note is to begin closed and then be opened immediately. In some cases, contemporary composers will write a + on the first note of a phrase. Then with a broken line over several notes, finally indicate that the last note is open. The phrase is to begin closed and the bell is to be opened gradually as the phrase is played. The reverse, 0 – – – – – – – – – – – +, would indicate that the phrase is to begin open and gradually close as the phrase is played.

Hat, Metal Hat or Derby

The metal hat is shaped like a derby. It is slightly elliptical, measures six and one-half by eight inches on the inside, and is about four inches deep. It is mounted on a stand so that you can turn quickly and play into it without having to stop and pick it up. Some prefer to place a handkerchief in the hat to dampen the resonant edge that the metal gives to the tone. On occasion, the hat is removed from the stand, held in the hand and used like a plunger. When the changes from open to closed are rapid and successive, it is easier to hold the hat. A passage that is to be played in the hat will be marked: in hat, in metal hat, in derby.

Derby is found only in early big band arrangements. Deep hat means that the bell of the instrument is held as close to the hat as possible. A trumpeter can play in deep hat by placing the bell of the instrument in the hat, but since a trombonist's bell is larger than the hat, he can only play very close to the hat.

Bucket

Bucket mutes are commonly used by trumpets but seldom used by trombones. The bucket is usually lined with soft material and has three spring clamps which grasp the bell and hold the bucket an inch or so away from the bell. Originally, buckets were made to fit trombones with seven or seven and one-half inch bells. They are used so rarely today that it is difficult to find a bucket that will fit an eight or eight and one-half inch trombone bell. The sound of a bucket can be imitated by playing into a metal hat that has some soft material in it. The designation in the music is in English only: Bucket.

Felt Hat

The felt hat is used more by trumpeters than trombonists, and is usually homemade. It is made by removing the band from an old felt hat and by cutting a slice a few inches long about one inch parallel to the edge. The hat is hung over the front of the bell with the rim of the bell sticking through the slit. In general, the felt hat is used for simply dampening the tone of a robust player who is performing in a small club or is playing with a small jazz ensemble.

Quasi Horn

The direction, quasi horn, may only indicate that you are to play without vibrato and by using extended alternate slide positions. In other cases, the arranger wants you to place your hand in the bell, so that your tone is slightly spread and muffled. You are coloring the tone with a slightly cupped hand, just as a French hornist does with his hand in his bell. The hand in the bell partially blocks the bell and removes some of the upper partials from the tone. The hand is either held flat against the bottom of the bell, allowing the tone to pass over the back of the hand, or the knuckles of the fingers are bent and rested against the upper side of the bell so that the tone passes through the fingers.

Fig. 45   Alternate Hand Position for *Quasi Horn*

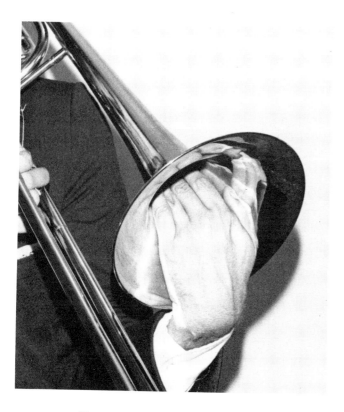

Fig. 44   Hand Position for *Quasi Horn*

The trombonist has less use for mutes than the trumpeters, and for the most part can play most of his orchestra and band music with a straight mute. Only rarely will these parts call for a cup mute. For jazz and commercial work, both a straight and a cup are needed, but other mutes are used only rarely. Instead of a plunger or hat, you can get by by using your hand or the cup from your cup mute.

When purchasing a mute, always buy a recommended mute that is known to fit your particular instrument. Undersized mutes in large instruments force the pitch sharp, stuff up the tone and block some low register notes completely. An oversized mute will not produce the correct tone quality and may fall out at the wrong moment. Filing the corks may make the mute fit better, but the mute may fit too close to the bell and muffle the tone quality.

Chapter 11
How to Practice

A Practice Routine—One Hour

How much a person should practice and how the practice time is divided among warm-ups, scales, lip trainers, etudes and solos varies with the individual AND THE TEACHER. Therefore, the following practice plan is suggested as a model. The plan should be changed to meet your needs.

Warming the Instrument

Before playing the first tone, the trombone must be warmed to playing temperature. Check the lubrication of the slide and the operation of the rotary valve, and then warm the instrument **AND THE MOUTHPIECE** to playing temperature. In cold weather the instrument can be warmed by placing it *near* a heat vent. Caution: do not place it too close or the lacquer will be blistered. Warm the mouthpiece by holding it in your hand or by running warm water through it. Next, you should slowly blow several lungsfull of warm moist air into the *lead pipe* of the instrument. After the trombone is warm, you can begin your actual warm up. Only in mild weather is it possible to warm the instrument with the mouthpiece in place. A cold mouthpiece not only warms slowly to the heat of the lips and breath, but it chills the muscles of the embouchure. Also, the warm air looses some of its heat as it expands while passing through the throat and backbore of the mouthpiece. (The faster you blow the air stream, the *cooler* this stream is as it enters the instrument.)

Warming the instrument before beginning the lip warm-ups is very important, and until the air in the instrument is as warm and humid as it is in performances, the air column will not be acoustically stable. Attempting to warm-up on a partially cold instrument is like trying to play someone else's instrument. As the humidity and the temperature rise in the instrument, the tone, the pitch, and the resistance change. Thus, the person who trys to warm-up on a cold horn ruins his security with an instrument that is acoustically different from one minute to the next.

Arthur Amsden recommends, "Don't fail to pour water through your cornet before beginning the day's work; never mind WHY, just DO IT and note the benefit of this simple device." (These don'ts in the preface of *Amsden's Celebrated Practice Duets*, Oskaloosa, Iowa: C. L. Barnhouse, Inc., 1936 have been omitted in later editions). Although he said, "never mind WHY," I assume that not only does the water wash the instrument, but that it raises the relative humidity of the air column to nearly 100 percent, the normal humidity of normal performance. With Amsden's procedure, you will begin to practice with an instrument that is acoustically the same every day. It is messy to run water through a trombone everyday, and I prefer to use other methods of cleaning the instrument (see Chapter 3), but getting the relative humidity to 100 percent is acoustically important. Thus warming the trombone over a hot air vent is not enough. In cold weather, warm the horn near a hot air vent and then raise the relative humidity by blowing your breath into the lead pipe.

The few minutes used to warm and humidify the instrument before attempting to warm-up the lips, greatly aids the establishment of consistent tone production habits.

Warm-Up

The warm-up of the instrument is not to be counted as part of the practice hour, and the hour of practice will take more than 60 minutes. The actual playing of warm-up exercises should take about 10 minutes and I would recommend the exercises of Emory B. Remington or the early pages of Max Schlossberg. (Your scale and arpeggio practice should take another eight to 12 minutes.)

If you are not too advanced, these warm-up exercises are really not warm-ups, but are lip trainers. A warm-up exercise is something that is easy for you and warms and relaxes the muscles of the embouchure. A lip trainer is an exercise that places a stress on your muscles and is tensing and exhausting to your embouchure. Therefore, what is a lip trainer to a beginner will become a warm-up as you become stronger and more proficient. Thus, if your lips are not strong enough, the warm-up will be cut to a few minutes.

Scales and Arpeggios

Your scale and arpeggio practice should take another eight to 12 minutes. The scales and arpeggios should be reviewed in an orderly sequence, so that over a period of two and not more than three days, you review all of the scales. At first, when scales and arpeggios are being learned, you should review all the scales you know everyday, while the remainder of the time is spent learning one new scale and arpeggio. In either case, spend eight to 12 minutes a day practicing scales and arpeggios. (For further details see Chapter 13, Scales and Arpeggios).

Use a metronome when warming up and reviewing scales, so that you maintain a steady speed. Do not defeat the purpose of the exercises by playing them slower or faster than they should be played. For the scales, the metronome can be used to push the tempo ever so slightly. Also, use the metronome to measure rest periods. Many players spend too much time resting or preparing to play the next exercise. They pace the floor, lubricate the slide, flap the lips, squeeze the embouchure with their fingers and do many other things that delay the beginning of the next exercise. Rest and relaxation are important, but for many it becomes a time-consuming bad habit which wastes time and kills the momentum of the warm-up procedure. Do not turn the metronome off between exercises. Let it run. The ticking during the break will remind you to begin soon again.

Etudes

When the warm-up and scale review has been completed, begin to learn new material. The new etudes should be attacked while your mind and lip are still fresh. Whether you begin with legato exercises or staccato exercises is your choice. Neither type of exercise should be a problem since the scales were reviewed in both staccato and legato style.

Some players prefer to practice the easier exercises first and then work on to the newer more difficult ones, and I use this method myself. There is a positive reinforcement, a feeling of well-being and accomplishment, as the old exercises are played again and the improvement is noted. With this positive mental attitude, I then begin to work on the newer and more difficult exercises. This approach to learning the etudes and pieces is particularly useful when the exercises are assigned in the same order as they appear in the book. Thus, after a review of the etudes which are most certainly to be heard at the next lesson, you proceed to the later exercises. On a day when things are going well, you may move on into exercises that will not be called for for a week or two, but in the meantime the brain has gotten an idea of the new etude and the process of incubation is underway. Incubation is a psychological term for the development of the

solution to a problem in the brain is not consciously thinking about the Do not attempt to expose your mind t and pieces. Attempting incubation on a lot of material is a waste of time and may plant some bad habits (they also incubate). You should read ahead only to the etudes that are to be learned in the next two to four weeks.

Solos

The pieces are usually reserved for the end of the practice period. Only if the piece is physically taxing would there be any reason to practice it earlier in the period.

Warm-Down

Finally, the last 30 seconds to a minute or more of the period should be spent warming-down. This warming-down relaxes the lips and allows the blood to flush the acids from the muscles of the embouchure. Playing the first few easy warm-up exercises at a *mp* and then playing a few soft, fairly long pedal tones are excellent warming-down exercises. If the lips are warmed-down, they will be less tense and stiff the next time you play. Warming-down for a minute or two is time well spent.

Summary

One Hour (without interruption)
    (:05)—Warm and humidify the trombone. Warm the mouthpiece.
    :10—Warm-Up (Lip Trainers)—Emory B. Remington, *Warm-Up Exercises* (Rochester Music Publishers) or Max Schlossberg, *Daily Drills and Technical Studies for Trombone* (Baron)
:08 to :12—Scales and Arpeggios
:13 to :17—Studies or Etudes in a detached style.
    :15—Studies or Etudes in a legato style.
    :10—Solo (or additional work on legato or detached etudes)
    (:01)—Warm-Down

One and One Half Hours (without interruption)
Same as above with additional time used for studies and etudes.

Two Hours (without interruption)
Same as above with additional time used for studies, etudes and solo.

Time in ( )s is not included in the hour.

Practice Efficiency

How people learn and what conditions make learning easier and faster have been under study by psychologists for a long time. Several learning theories have been developed in the past 100 years. But when studying learning theory, there is a frustration because one deals only with theories and not laws. Even so, you do not have to accept only one learning theory and reject all others, when trying to establish a practice routine. There are parts of many learning theories that can be applied to the learning of the physical, mental and psychological skills necessary for playing a trombone. For further information on learning, study any one of the many published learning theory books. Hill, Winfred F., *Learning: A Survey of Psychological Interpretations*, San Francisco: Chandler Publishing Co., 1963, is a particularly concise and easily understood survey of learning theory.

Starting and Stopping

The primary problem of a practice routine is to decide when to *start* and when to *stop*. In other words, how much time should be given to each individual problem and in what order to attack the problems, is the decision every trombonist must make. The beginning student should practice for short periods and possibly several times a day. The younger student is weak and cannot pay attention for long periods and if the practice period exceeds his attention span, he will not learn anymore and he may unlearn some things. Besides, the muscles of the lips and cheeks do not warn you that they are overtaxed or stiff, like the muscles of the arms or legs. Everyone knows how stiff arms or legs can be after that first spring day's game of softball or touch football. The day after sensation in the lips is nothing like the day after stiffness in the arms and legs. The lip muscles simply do not work, but you get no sensation of pain unless the lips are badly bruised and swollen.

To practice efficiently, you must have the courage to *start* and begin working on the solution to a problem. You must be persistent and continue to work on the problem for a reasonable length of time. Finally, even though the problem isn't solved, you must have sense enough to *stop* before you develop bad habits or damage your lip. After awhile or in the next practice period, you must *start* on the problem again, work for awhile, then *stop* before damage occurs.

Varying the Emphasis

You should vary your practice routine so that you remain mentally alert and physically rested. If you are concentrating on a certain type of playing, then other types of playing should be sandwiched into this routine. For example, if you are working on high register legato playing, the rest periods of a minute or two, spaced every 5 or 10 minutes, could consist of low register lip slurs, middle register *mp* detached exercises or softly sustained pedal tones.

Extending the Practice

Advanced players should know of the benefits of an extended practice session. Occasionally, a practice session should be extended beyond the normal time limits in an attempt to find a solution to a certain problem which you have not been able to solve with normal routines. During the extra long work, even when becoming mentally and physically tired, you may achieve a breakthrough. In other words, the fatigue can contribute to your giving up an old habit. The fatigue relaxes you physically and mentally, and it forces you into a slightly different approach. This slightly different approach may be the key to the solution of the problem. It is recommended that these extended practice sessions be used *only on rare occasions*. Extend the session only if it will cause no physical damage. This type of practice, if attempted too often for too long, will frustrate you, generally depress you and do more damage than good.

Reminiscence

The concept of reminiscence has been used by athletes for quite some time, but only recently has it been advocated in music performance. Though there are several theories of reminiscence, in general it is known that during the break between practice sessions something happens which helps the performance two or three days later. It is not known whether bad habits are forgotten more rapidly than good ones, or whether the unconscious mental limitations you have set for yourself have been forgotten, but it is known that after a break of two or three days the performance is better than it has ever been before. There is presently a high-note trumpet method being marketed that uses a theory of reminiscence. It has the performer do the high register exercises *every other* day only. On alternate days other skills are developed. (No method suggests that a person practice or perform only every other day.)

Many performers use the idea of reminiscence by performing and practicing only six days of the week. The day off either aids the forgetting of bad habits or allows the good habit to develop, and although there are some disadvantages to taking a day off, there are many physical, mental and emotional benefits also.

Occasionally, perhaps annually, reminiscence can be observed after an extended break of a week or more. After the break, you must return to the routine of practice and performance with care, or you will damage yourself while developing a few new bad habits. The build-up after long layoffs must be done in slow progressive steps, and long layoffs are only suggested for performers who are advanced and have just completed an intensive season of performances.

Mental Rehearsal

Mental rehearsal is especially recommended when physical fatigue and nervousness are a problem. Mental rehearsal allows you to extend the practice session beyond your limits of physical endurance. It is also a convenient way to practice when you cannot play the instrument. If the music, etude or scale is memorized, it is even possible to practice while walking, riding a bicycle or attending a boring lecture. Nervousness can be calmed by both mentally reviewing the music and by thinking about the location and conditions of the coming performance. Maxwell Maltz, in *Psycho-Cybernetics* recommends that a mental review of everything about a certain location, including the odor of the room, the sound of the audience, *etc.*, can prepare you for a more successful and less tense performance.

Setting a Routine

The practice routine of every successful player is unique. Every good player finds the best combination of the various types of etudes and exercises. His routine is usually quite set and unvarying, and it gives him not only a set way of improving his technic but gives him a sense of security. He is secure because his routine assures him of success. Many mediocre players change their routines so often that it is impossible for them to develop any emotional or physical security. They constantly search for the routine which will solve all their problems immediately and never settle on one system long enough to get the benefits of that system. Whatever routine you chose, it should be adhered to and not varied without good reason. If you are looking for a routine, I suggest that you begin with the routine at the beginning of this chapter and then slowly evolve a better routine that is more suited to your needs. Change your routine with cautious experimentation and the advice of established performers and teachers. Do not extend your warm-up routine unless absolutely necessary. Some fall into the habit of warming-up for 30 to 45 minutes to loosen up their lip. They should look for the cause of the stiffness and eliminate the cause rather than spend a lot of time each day getting rid of the stiffness. In time, you will develop a routine which is the most efficient for you. Then it should be kept for a long period of time before it is played with or changed any more. Trying something new stops the development of many potentially fine performers.

Summary

Five procedures can be used to increase your practice efficiency. One. Practice in short sessions so that neither the lip muscles or the mind become unduly fatigued. Two. Practice in a very long session on occasion to try to discover an easier and better way of playing. Three. Do not work on certain exercises on certain days, or don't practice at all on one day of the week, so that some learning can be accomplished by reminiscence. Four. Mentally rehearse particular etudes or solos to increase your learning and your consistency without tiring your embouchure, and Five. Use special practice routines with caution and stay with a set routine most of the time to build security.

Chapter 12
Slide Technique

Hand Grips

The slide technique depends on a relaxed righthand grip and a lefthand grip which will support most of the weight of the trombone. The right hand only moves the slide to the proper location. If the instrument is supported by the right hand, the instrument will bounce every time the right hand moves and your lip will be bruised and maybe the attack will be broken. The slide *must* be in proper working order. It must be lubricated, aligned and free from dents. A slide that sticks will force your right hand to do too much work, make it difficult for the left hand to hold the instrument still and make you use too much mouthpiece pressure. If the slide binds as it is being pulled up, the embouchure is pressed unless your left hand pushes away. If the slide binds as it is being pushed out, the mouthpiece will be pulled away from the lips unless your left hand pulls back. In either case, your left hand does not properly counteract the pushing and pulling of the slide, and to be sure that the mouthpiece is kept against the embouchure, you use extra pressure.

Precise Placement

The exact placement of the slide is determined by the ear, but you can use your eye and the feel of the arm to help you. The slide should remain in your field of vision so that exact placement can be aided with a slight glance. Although beginning method books warn against touching the bell with your fingers, many fine players do touch the bell or slide receiver to set the exact placement of second, third and fourth positions. This is only a crutch and is suggested only when the exact placement of a sustained note must be assured beyond all doubt. It cannot be done when playing rapidly.

To develop exact slide placement, aurally and visually check the position of the slide while playing:

movement to the next note is begun. Exercises like the one above should be practiced until the motion is precise and exact even in the most rapid passages.

Timing

There are many possible combinations of slide positions, and each one causes different intonation problems. The most common problem occurs when the slide has to change speeds between notes, such as:

The change between B flat and A is a relatively short distance, and is less than half of the distance between A and G. (For the spacing of the slide positions see the measurements at the bottom of page 79.) When playing the first figure rapidly it is common to begin to shorten the distance between G and A and lengthen the distance between A and B flat. In the second figure, the distance between B flat and A flat is almost twice the distance of A flat to G, and as it is played rapidly, the distances are made more equal. In both figures the A tends to become *half flat*.

Listing all the possible combinations in which the slide changes speed between notes is not necessary. Any combination of three notes is a potential problem. You should take care when playing rapidly that the intermediate notes between slide direction changes are

Although the placement may be precise at the slower speeds, the right hand will be slow and lazy with the rapid movement. The hand will begin to cheat by not quite moving all the way to the position before the

not placed just anywhere between these changing points. Place the notes as exactly as if they were being played at a much slower tempo. To play in tune, the slide movement must change speed between almost every note. The proper timing of the slide speed is the basis of good intonation in rapid passages.

Staccato Passages

If you watched the slide of an excellent player through a sound-proof window, it might appear that he was playing legato when he was really playing staccato. The slide movement for staccato passages tends to be smooth, without jerks and almost without stops. The wrist and hand motions are relaxed and flexing when the slide movement is reversed. In very rapid passages, the wrist and hand will begin to move in the opposite direction as the slide rests on a position. Then with a crack the whip motion of the fingers and wrist, the slide is moved off rapidly to the next note. Finally, the wrist and fingers act as a shock absorber as the next position is reached, slowing down the movement of the slide, and cushioning the slide against the bump that would occur when the right arm stops moving.

A competent performer has a slide action that is relaxed and looks easy. The movements of the right arm, wrist and the fingers are smooth and coordinated. The action is not tight, rigid or jerky, but it is also not sloppy or slow.

To develop a precise yet relaxed slide control, you must first train the right arm to *feel* the distances between positions. First, *glissando* from first to seventh position and return:

Now staccato tongue the chromatic scale down and back. Retain the same easy motion of the arm and smoothly time the slide so that it passes the note just at exactly the correct moment.

At first there will be intonation problems since the arm is not paced properly and does not exactly pass each note at the proper time. The *glissando* should be practiced some more and then the staccato passage attempted again. Alternating the work on both exercises

will develop both smoothness and precision of the arm motion.

To develop the controlled whip action of the fingers and wrist, the following exercise should be performed while holding the right elbow immobile against the chest. Use the flexibility of the wrist and fingers to move the slide.

The forearm is placed about half way between the two positions so that the wrist and fingers can reach both positions by flexing and extending. The exercise should be repeated on several pairs of notes, and the interval should be expanded to a minor third (first to fourth position and return). A lot of practice with the elbow held immobile is not necessary. Once the flexibility of the wrist and fingers has been obtained, the exercise is no longer needed. Once the crack the whip action of the fingers and wrist has been developed, combine it with the smooth precise flow of the right arm.

Legato Passages

You will play *glissandos* if the slide is moved with a smooth action when playing legato. When playing staccato, the slide can move between positions when there is silence, but in legato playing there are no intentional silences and the slide movement must be as rapid as possible. The slide must remain on each note as long as possible and then be moved rapidly to the next note at the last possible instant. If you watched a legato passage through a soundproof window it would appear that the performer was playing in quite a jerky style. In other words, the slide action looks smooth and languid if the playing is staccato and it looks rather quick and somewhat jerky when playing legato.

When perfected, the slide technique for legato work is not as rigid and jerky as it would first appear. Although the slide does move at the fastest comfortable speed (arriving at the note just in time), the motion has a controlled relaxation which is created by the flexing of the wrist and fingers. The wrist and fingers lead the movement of the slide and absorb the shock of stopping the slide in legato work just as they did in staccato work. The difference is that the flexing of the hand to move and stop the slide is faster and more exaggerated in legato work than when playing staccato.

Rapid legato slide technique is based on precise arm movements and a relaxed righthand grip. Develop this technique by gradually increasing the speed of your legato scales and your legato etudes. Volume II, of the *Melodious Etudes* of Bordogni as edited by Rochut, are excellent studies for the rapid, precise *and relaxed* positioning of the slide.

Chapter 13
Scales and Arpeggios

The novice does not practice scales unless he is forced to, while the professional trombonist practices scales because he wants to. Obviously the professional knows how he will benefit from scale practice.

Learning the scales is only the beginning, not the end. Once the scales have been learned, they can be **USED** to further develop all aspects of the technique. Not only can more technique and facility be learned, but better endurance, high register, low register, tone, attack, legato, staccato and vibrato can be achieved with scale and arpeggio practice. In order to receive the benefits from scale practice, the scales and arpeggios must be learned and practiced regularly with attention and purpose.

To benefit from scale practice, observe these points:

Memorization

Memorize them completely so that the pitches can be heard, the notes on the staff can be visualized, and the feel (kinesthetic sensations) of the slide and embouchure positioning are sure. Do not memorize the scales and arpeggios by learning the numbers of the slide positions only. When the scales and arpeggios have been completely memorized, you should be able to automatically play almost anything that you hear or see.

Patterns

Only playing the scale in one pattern, such as:

fails to develop the technique needed for the performance of the scalic passages as they are found in music. Patterns do not always begin on the tonic (key tone) on a strong pulse and end on the tonic on a strong pulse.

Diatonic

The scales should be practiced in a diatonic pattern or the "Arban's pattern," beginning on the next degree of the diatonic scale each time the scale is played.

Detached and slurred

uld also be practiced using the triplet
oupings recommended by Blazhevich.

In the triplet grouping, the beat only falls on the tonic
note in the last octave.

Many players think they know the scales and then find
they cannot play the scale from memory in a triplet
pattern. If the scale cannot be played in triplets, it
has not been mastered.

When learning the scale in triplet pattern, it is helpful
to remember on which scale step the beat is placed.

Then you can begin in the middle of the pattern without
having to play the first part. For instance, if the scale
can be played ascending and not descending, the scale
can be started on the sixth or seventh step and you
can practice completing the scale from this point.

6th Scale Step   7th Scale Step

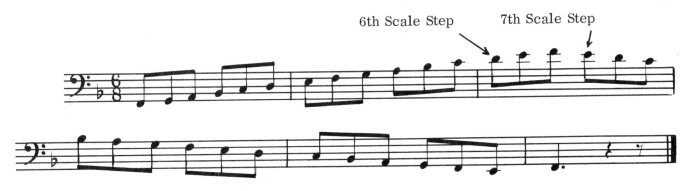

Quintuplets

The quintuplet pattern further develops the mastery
of the scale and when first learning the pattern you

should remember where the beat is placed so that you
can begin in the middle if you wish.

7th Scale Step

Thirds and Pedal Points

The two other scale patterns which must be practiced are scales in thirds and scales with a pedal point.

(Scales in thirds)

(Scales with pedal point—lower)

(Scales with pedal point—upper)

For additional practice, the scales can be played in fifths, sixths, *etc.*, but these are not recommended if memorization and practice takes too much time away from the patterns already mentioned.

Minor Scale Forms

Learning and working with only major scales will develop only part of your technique. Natural, melodic and harmonic forms of the minor scales must also be mastered. Since you played the natural minor scale when you played the major scale in the diatonic pattern beginning on the sixth scale step, this scale is already learned. The melodic minor scale ascending can be thought of as a major scale with a flat third and descending it is a natural minor scale, so this scale is nearly learned from the previous scale work. The harmonic minor scale is usually the most difficult to learn, *particularly when played in a diatonic pattern*. The intervals will almost fall into place naturally, if the augmented second between steps six and seven is remembered. After a few attempts with the diatonic pattern of the harmonic minor, (and a feeling that it can never be mastered) the scale falls into place and becomes as easy as a major scale in the diatonic pattern.

Diminished Scales

If you have a strong interest in jazz performance and improvisation, you should also memorize and practice diminished scales. Diminished scales are derived from the diminished seventh arpeggios and in one form have a half step above all arpeggio tones and in the other form have a half step below all arpeggio tones. Since there are only three diminished seventh chords, if enharmonic spellings are used, there are only six different sets of pitches to be learned.

Whole Tone Scales

The whole tone scales should be learned also. With enharmonic spellings there are only two different sets of pitches to be learned.

A music theorist would probably say that you **MUST** know the proper name for every note of a scale and arpeggio, and in time this ability will develop almost automatically. On the other hand, however, do not slow up the development of your ear and your feel of the slide with too much attention to the names of the notes.

Learn and use scales to gain a complete command of the instrument, and use the scales so as to have something to play while working on other aspects of your trombone technique. I do not object to the student playing scales and arpeggios automatically without thought of the individual note names, so long as he is thinking about and working on his trombone technique in some way. I do object to the student who tries to learn his scales by ear and hunts around for the proper notes instead of thinking the scale through. Only after the scale is learned can you think about the finer points of trombone playing and stop concentrating on the names of the notes.

Arpeggios

Although arpeggios are usually considered to be the individual notes of a triad or seventh chord, they can also be thought of as being selected notes from a scale. I suggest that if you have difficulty learning the arpeggios, that you temporarily return to the scale practice and accent the notes of the scale that form the arpeggio.

The major, minor, dominant seventh and diminished seventh chords must be learned and the augmented triads should be mastered also. The arpeggios must be played straight up and down, and in various broken forms.

Straight - Major

Broken - Major

Straight Major-Minor 7th

Broken Major-Minor 7th

Various other arrangements of the notes of the arpeggios should be practiced, but the memorization may take too much time and I recommend that when practicing these complex arrangements that you read the arpeggio exercises from a book. In order to avoid playing only certain patterns, you should own at least one book of arpeggios, such as Colin or Schlossberg, and you should read the other patterns from these books. The *66 Etudes* by Anton Slama are also excellent for broken arpeggio practice.

Rhythmic and Articulation Patterns

Except for some fanfare figures or the runs in a march, music is not written with uniform rhythmic patterns of scales and arpeggios. In many cases, a technical problem in a phrase is caused by the rhythmic articulation problems and not by the slide technique of the scale and arpeggio. To avoid these problems, practice the scales and arpeggios in several different rhythmic and articulation patterns.

Whether scales and arpeggios should be learned and practiced is not the principal point of this chapter. The main point is that scales and arpeggios should be **USED** to develop playing ability. When scales and arpeggios are thoroughly memorized, they are useful exercises for the development of all aspects of your playing. While reviewing the scale and arpeggio patterns, you can concentrate on many other qualities of playing without the distraction of reading an etude at the same time. Do some of this practice with your eyes closed or with the lights turned off, so that your complete concentration is focused on the **SOUND.**

Intonation

Of course, scales are to be used to develop precision tuning and all the righthand habits needed for good intonation, but while you are concentrating on intonation, you must play with the best possible tone quality. Pure intonation is impossible without a good and consistent tone quality.

Tone Quality

Developing consistent tone quality between the notes in the shorter positions as compared to the notes in the longer positions, and matching the tone quality between middle and high registers, and middle and low registers can be done with scale practice. Scales do not automatically develop the matching tone quality, and it is necessary for you to listen carefully to your playing. You must note the different settings of the embouchure, mouth, throat and breath control which are necessary to make two different pitches speak with the same quality.

Attacks

Attacks, and the consistency of the attacks between slide positions and between registers, are developed by the same techniques listed above. Note the different settings necessary to make the same sound on different pitches and then duplicate these differences on the next performance.

High Register

The high register can be developed by working the scales in chromatic order—proceeding upwards by half steps. The stress, when ascending, and the relaxation, when descending, develop the embouchure muscles in a scientific way. When building the high register, do not squeeze and pinch, but draw the relaxed middle register approach to tone production upward. Do not build barriers to your future development in the upper

register by always stopping the routi͏ note, such as high B flat, high C, h F. Always continue for one more half step, if possible, to B, C sharp, E flat, or G flat.

Low Register

The low register can be developed in the same way as the high register, only the order of the scales descends by half steps. Draw the natural embouchure for the middle register into the low register with each succeeding half step. Do not make any abnormal embouchure shifts. With this step by step approach, the low register is developed so that the flexibility between the middle and low registers is retained, and you do not get a special low register lip setting that cannot be used in any other register without resetting the lips.

Endurance

Endurance is developed by continuing to play one scale after another, while you concentrate on more relaxation, better breath control and less mouthpiece pressure.

Legato Control, Breath Control and Dynamics

Develop legato control by practicing the scales in long slurred groups. Develop breath control by placing the breath points further and further apart. Develop the consistency of attacks by reviewing all the scales with various dynamic levels and articulation styles.

Summary

All of the above benefits of scale practice can be accomplished only if you concentrate on these goals as the scales are being reviewed. Practicing scales and arpeggios with your mind wandering is a waste of time. When your mind wanders, not only are the benefits lost, but many bad habits are seated so well that it will take many more hours to break them.

Scales and arpeggios are not a cure-all and even with complete concentration, there is a limit to their benefits. They cannot be practiced to the exclusion of other exercises. I recommend that of a two-hour practice session, you do not devote more than 20 minutes to scales. Without too much repetition and without pauses of more than a second or two between scales, half of the scales and arpeggios can be reviewed each day. With this plan every scale and arpeggio is played in some form every other day—three times a week—over 150 times per year!!! With diligent practice the repetition accomplished over the year will have a noticeable and positive effect on your technique.

Chapter 14
Developing Facility

I suggest the following five procedures for the development of technique and facility.

Set Correct Habits

Many musicians fail to repeat the correct action often enough for it to become a habit. As you practice an etude, you make a mistake and stop to correct it. If you go on through the etude after playing the note or phrase correctly only once, the chances are only 50-50 that you will play that particular note or phrase correctly the next time. If you had repeated the phrase correctly *several* times before proceeding, you would have a better chance of playing it correctly the next time. If the phrase was repeated three times correctly after one mistake, your chances of playing it correctly the next time would be increased to 3 to 1. If you make a mistake at this point on the next time through, then work more diligently to set the correct habit. Repeat the correct action five or more times before proceeding.

Avoid Frustration—Develop Confidence

Many musicians attack a problem by starting a few notes ahead of the trouble spot to get a running start at getting past the problem. They try to force their way through the problem by running into it from a few notes away. Sometimes they repeat this several times in a row. They are neither solving the problem nor building a correct habit. They seem to be proving to themselves that they cannot get through the passage.

that it becomes a habit. This builds confidence. Repeating the same error in the same place builds frustration.

Practice Thoroughly and Completely

After stopping to correct an error, you should not start at the beginning again. You should proceed through the etude, or at least an entire section of the etude, before returning to the beginning. This way the etude is learned evenly without overlearning the beginning and underlearning the final sections.

Practice Slowly

To establish good habits, you should practice at a speed at which no errors will occur. At a slow practice speed, you must concentrate. If you do not keep your mind on the task, the errors will persist.

The tempo chosen for slow practice should be slow enough for you to play the phrase perfectly in nine of 10 trials. Positive reinforcement, which means being rewarded for a correct response, has the most effect when it occurs 80 to 90 percent of the time. Negative reinforcement, which means receiving a penalty for an incorrect response, *i.e.* playing the notes incorrectly, should be kept to a minimum of ten to 20 percent.

The tempo must be *increased gradually* until it is slightly faster than the desired speed. Many people practice slowly for a few minutes and then expect to play the phrase at tempo without difficulty. They are usually disappointed.

When attempting to learn the following phrase:

Do not try to force your way through a problem by repeating the wrong approach. Break your mental set and try some other approach.

You can learn from your errors, **BUT NOT BY REPEATING YOUR ERRORS.** You must attempt another approach and if that fails, try another and another until you find the correct one. When you discover the correct approach, repeat it several times in a row so

the phrase must be repeated slowly without error several times. When the phrase is comfortable at the first tempo, then you continue to repeat it while gradually increasing the speed. When you make a mistake, slow the tempo again for a few repetitions before you increase the speed again. You increase the speed until an error occurs one or two times out of ten and then you relax the speed for a few repetitions until the correct habit is established again. Continue this until you can perform the phrase *above* tempo.

To make the practice more interesting, change the rhythm so that the speed of some notes is increased. In a compound meter the rhythm has three variations.

After playing the phrase twice with each rhythm, **WITHOUT ERROR,** playing the exercise with the written rhythm will be noticeably easier. The rhythm change also exposes any difficult intervals that should get individual practice. Practice these repetitions intensely. Do not dawdle. Do not rest unless absolutely necessary. Make the break between each pass less than one second in length so that you make five to 15 passes every minute. If the phrase is extremely difficult and cannot be mastered in five to ten minutes, you will have to practice it at a later time in the practice period or leave it for the next day. The decision to stop is important. Do not continue to practice the phrase after the speed cannot be increased without errors. Once your learning has reached the saturation point, further practice must be delayed until later or you will develop a psychological block.

tempo, the phrase will never sound easy and relaxed at the correct tempo. Some cultures do not learn their music at practice speeds. They learn the music *a tempo*. The drummers of East Africa (Kenya, Tansania and Uganda) learn their extremely intricate xylophone technique *a tempo* and they break down when asked to slow the tempo so that a Western observer can analyze the patterns. The Suzuki Talent Education system (the teaching of music to very young children by teaching them to play the violin) also avoids practicing at a tempo which is slower than the concert tempo. To do this, they stop between notes or parts of the phrase and prepare themselves mentally for the next group of notes. They play that group and then stop to prepare for the next set. To learn the phrase above by using this method, the phrase is broken into groups of notes and each group is repeated several times at tempo.

Practice Rapidly

Practicing slowly sometimes develops a labored technique. Unless the speed is increased to *above* the desired

After this has been done, the groups are assembled
and repeated.

Larger groups are formed and repeated.

And finally, the largest groups are joined together for
the complete phrase.

Avoid errors. Repeat the correct habit several times
without error before proceeding to the larger groups.

Summary

One. Avoid making a mistake, and if a mistake is
made, avoid repeating the error. (Try something else
or make a different type of error rather then repeat
the same one.) Two. When the note or phrase is played
correctly, repeat it correctly a few times before continuing. Three. Learn a piece completely. Do not
overlearn the beginning and underlearn the last part.
Four. Practice slowly to set the correct habit and then
increase the tempo gradually until the correct tempo
is reached and exceeded. Five. Practice above tempo
so that in performance the phrase will be played below
maximum speed and will have a fluent relaxed flow.
(If the complete phrase cannot be played, break the
phrase into small note groups for rapid practice and
then assemble the small groups into larger groups.)

Chapter 15
Buzzing Practice for Embouchure Development

Buzzing the mouthpiece is often recommended for all players who want to develop better tone placement, tone quality and endurance. Because mouthpiece buzzing is very taxing to the lips it should be done only for a few minutes each day at first.

Buzzing with a Mouthpiece

First, learn to buzz a middle register note such as middle B flat. Use a normal attack and repeat this note in a half-note rhythm until the note is attacked, sustained and released *exactly* on pitch.

slightly detached

As your security develops, allow the center portion of your lips to relax and flap outwards so that the buzz develops a fuller and deeper tone. Adjust the throat and back of the tongue to enlarge the oral cavity to further deepen the tone quality of the buzz. Do not practice buzzing with tight lips, clenched teeth or a closed throat.

As your security develops further, begin to move away from the middle register note. For example, buzz:

or:

Again, buzz each note exactly in tune. Produce a loud and open tone.

In time, you should actually play etudes and solos by buzzing the mouthpiece. After buzzing, you will notice that the pitch placement on the trombone is more secure and that the tone is fuller and louder.

As with any exercise, too much work will be damaging. At first these buzzing exercises should be done for only a few minutes every day.

Buzzing without a Mouthpiece

Buzzing the lips without the mouthpiece is recommended for you who have a limited amount of time to develop your embouchure or have neglected some of your practice for that day. Without the support of the mouthpiece, the lips must form and hold an embouchure by themselves. This type of practice is very strenuous and should be limited to a minute or two even if you have a strong embouchure.

To buzz your lips without a mouthpiece, your embouchure must be formed naturally from a combination of a half-pucker and a half-smile. Your lips must be aligned normally and slightly rolled in. The buzzing is done with the center portion of the lips. Concentrate the pressure as if you were squeezing a pencil point with your lips. Do not stretch your lips sideways and do not blow through them as if they were stretched rubber bands. Make the tone color of the buzz as dark and open as possible by allowing the fleshy parts of the lips to relax and by opening your oral cavity.

An excellent daily routine consists of buzzing a folk tune or an arpeggio or scale for a minute. My personal routine each day consists of buzzing:

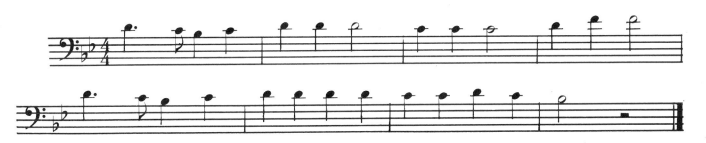

The tune is repeated in B major and sometimes in C major. Finally, a B flat arpeggio is buzzed and the routine is ended.

This method of building the embouchure has been criticized by those who only buzz using the mouthpiece. They contend that the work is unnatural and doesn't give the lips the feeling of the mouthpiece. Though their criticisms may be valid, I must repeat that the system works. In moderation, the practice will build a secure middle and upper register. The buzzing without a mouthpiece also makes it possible to practice while riding a bicycle or driving a car, when holding a mouthpiece to the lips would be both inconvenient and dangerous.

Regular Practice

The most difficult part of buzzing practice is to remember to do it regularly. I suggest that the buzzing be done at a certain time or place everyday. Either begin the first practice session of the day or do it at some time in the 24-hour period when you do not normally practice trombone. I prefer to do my buzzing at a time other than near when I will practice trombone. I begin buzzing when driving through a certain intersection on the way to work each day. Some memory crutch should be added to your daily routine to remind you to do your buzzing exercises.

I have found that buzzing either *with or without* a mouthpiece develops a firmness in the embouchure that can make trombone playing more sure. I recommend that buzzing in moderation be used to develop security, tone and endurance.

Chapter 16
Alternate Positions

The technical problems of the trombone will force you to use some alternate positions. Although alternate positions have intonation problems just as the alternate fingerings on other brass instruments, the trombone slide makes it possible to adjust this intonation. Thus, the slide is a mixed blessing. It forces you to use more alternates, but provides you with a way of correcting the intonation of the alternates.

General Rules

Two general rules govern the use of alternate positions:

1. Reduce the right arm's work load by using as many alternate positions as possible. Use alternate positions so that the slide can continue to move in the same direction as long as possible. After reversing directions continue to move the slide in the new direction as long as possible.

2. Do not use alternate positions if they cause bad intonation, produce poor tone quality or promote insecure playing. Use the positions which use the shortest amount of tubing when ever possible.

The listener usually does not care how creative you have been with the selection of alternate positions. The listener is concerned mainly with the correct notes with a good tone and with good intonation. Although you may be breaking your arm because you are not using alternates, you will get and hold your job as long as you produce the proper sounds at the proper time.

Therefore, I would caution you about using too many alternate positions. Intonation, tone and security must not be sacrificed for easier right arm work.

Look at the intonation chart in Chapter 17. Notice that as the slide is extended, many alternate position notes leave the position and must be played above or below the normal position. The extension of the slide makes the instrument as long as a French horn in F, and the tone becomes muffled and the tone placement becomes unsure with a tube of this length. Do **NOT** use alternate positions on high notes in extended slide positions unless absolutely necessary.

Common Alternate Positions

The most common alternate positions (in order of usage) are:

Middle F in Sixth Position

Play middle F in sixth position when the phrase drops to a C after extending the slide through a series of notes which includes the F.

Use it when the phrase jumps up to an F after you have already extended the slide.

When you do not have an F-attachment trombone, there are many patterns that demand the use of the sixth position for this F.

D in a Flatted Fourth Position

Most players play Ds in a flatted fourth position in scalic passages in B flat and E flat major.

Other players must play nearly all Ds in a flatted fourth position because their first position D is flat. If your instrument does not have springs in the receivers to allow the pitch to be adjusted upward, your Ds should be played in first position only in very rapid passages.

Middle B flat in a Sharpened Fifth Position

Playing B flat in a sharpened fifth position is used occasionally with shifts to or from other fifth and sixth position notes.

or

High F in a Very Sharp Fourth Position

High F in a sharp fourth position is used only rarely. The fourth position F has an inferior tone to the first position F and there is not much of a saving in slide movement distance. For security, many players do not consider the use of this alternate unless forced to. The alternate is used in combinations with E flats and G flats.

Middle E in Seventh Position

The middle E in seventh position is found mostly in slide combinations using a trombone *without* an F attachment. Combinations which would force the playing of middle E in seventh position rarely occur on an F attachment trombone.

These last three are occasional possibilities, but none of them have nearly the usage (**OR SECURITY**) of the first two listed.

Other Alternate Positions

There are many more possibilities for alternate positions when the passage is slurred. The Arthur Pryor solos use alternate positions so that many pairs of notes can be slurred naturally (*i.e.*, without the use of a legato tongue). In these cases, you play a natural lip slur and give your tongue a momentary rest from the otherwise constant 16th notes.

Alternate positions are particularly useful when playing legato passages in minor keys and sharp keys. An A sharp in sharpened fifth is more common in b minor than the B flat in the same position in phrases in B flat major.

E sharps in sixth position and in sharped fourth position in f sharp minor are more common than Fs in these same alternate positions in F major.

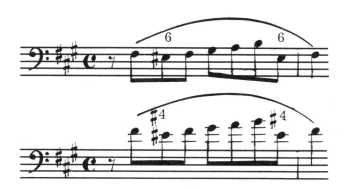

High Register Alternate Positions

When first building security in your high register, you should limit the use of alternate positions. Four notes, all within a whole step of each other, are available in first position.

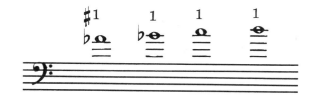

The same four notes are also available in third position.

I recommend that all B flats and Ds be played in first position and all A flats and Cs be played in third position. There is no acoustical reason for this, but simultaneously setting both your embouchure and your right hand in a certain position helps focus your mind and embouchure on the desired pitch. When the slide is in first position the embouchure is asked to play only two of the four notes available in that range. The lip sets for either a B flat or D when the slide is in first position. When the slide is in third position, the lip sets for A flat, C or E flat. Do not expect immediate security, but do expect the number of missed or cracked notes in this register to diminish. As your security develops you can then begin to use B flats in third, Ds in sharped third and Cs in first position. As before, consistent playing is more important than proper use of alternate positions.

Chapter 17
Intonation

The trombonist has two general intonation problems. One problem is caused by the construction of the instrument itself. The second problem is related to the different intonations of scales (equal temperament, just intonation or Pythagorean intonation) and even if the instrument were perfectly in tune with one of these scales, it would be out of tune with the others.

Intonation of the Overtone Series

No trombone is perfectly in tune with itself. This is not the fault of the manufacturer and the finest instruments generally have the same deficienceis at the same places in the various registers of the instrument.

All trombones usually have octave B flats in first position that are fairly close to being in tune although some adjustment may be necessary, particularly if an oversized or undersized mouthpiece is being used. For the purposes of this book, the B flats will be considered to be in tune, and if you are observed from the right side, it would appear that you play these B flats (first, second, fourth and eighth mode of vibration) in first position without lowering or raising the slide.

The third, sixth and 12th modes of vibration tend to be sharp and have to be lowered slightly. This lowering can be done by humoring the pitch down with the lips and throat or by moving the slide. Moving the slide is suggested. You achieve a truer tone with less chance of a missed attack if the slide is adjusted. In first position the third, sixth, and 12th modes are Fs and when observing you from the same location as above (the right side) it will be noticed that you play these notes slightly below first position. (The dotted line indicates the normal placement of first position.)

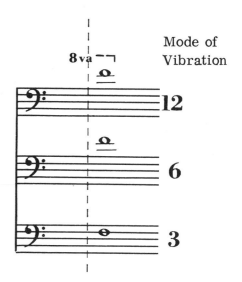

Mode of Vibration

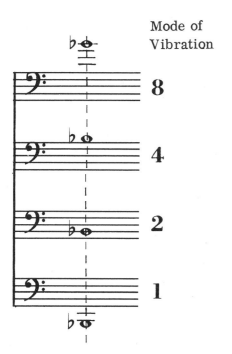

Mode of Vibration

Combining the notes discussed so far, a chart of the slide positions would appear as follows:

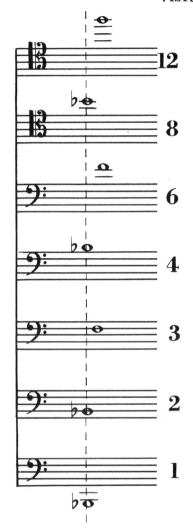

The fifth and 10th modes of vibration (both of these notes are Ds) tend to be flat and have to be raised.

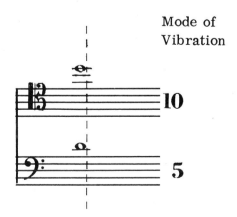

If the trombone has cork or felt bumpers in the receivers, you will have to lip up the notes in first position or else use an alternate position. If the trombone has spring bumpers, you can compress the springs about half of their extension and thus play the Ds slightly above first position.

The seventh mode of vibration (A flat) is very flat and is usually so flat that it is unusable in first position unless the springs are compressed completely and the lip raises the pitch of the note also.

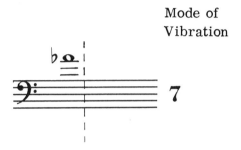

The ninth mode (C) may be slightly sharp. The tenth mode (D) is flat.

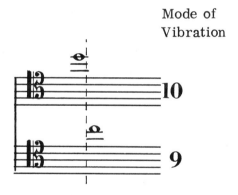

The 11th mode of vibration is so sharp or so flat that an in-tune note is found almost midway between the two slide positions. Thus a high E flat is played with the slide placed between first and second positions.

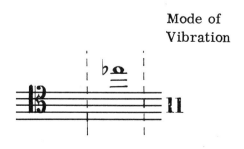

Thus the intonation of the first position would be:

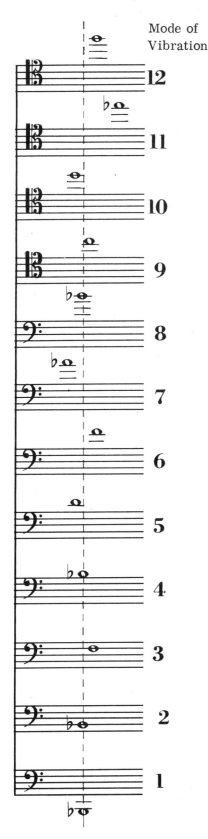

Intonation of the Slide Positions

Complicating this intonation problem is the fact that the intonation differences are magnified as the slide is extended. A larger percentage of the trombone becomes cylindrical when the slide is extended while the conical section (the bell joint) remains fixed in length. As a result, the adjustment for tuning is increased in the longer positions. The D above the staff is played only slightly higher than a regular first position, whereas the same partial in sixth position (the A on the top line of the bass staff), must be played nearly three-fourths of an inch higher. The flat partials get flatter and the sharp partials get sharper as the slide is extended.

The entire slide position chart would appear as: (See Fig. 46 Trombone Intonation Chart, Page 79.)

The dotted lines indicate the normal placement of the slide position and the notes are written either on, to the left of or to the right of the dotted lines to indicate the placement of the note on the slide. (You are at the left and the slide is being adjusted through the positions to the right. If the note is written to the left of the dotted line, it indicates that the note is played higher on the slide than the normal placement of that position). When testing these adjustments play with a straight and centered tone. Do not lip the note one direction while moving the slide in the other.

Learning the entire chart at one glance is impossible and I recommend that you study the chart in sections. For instance, note the relative positions of the notes of the B flat arpeggio above the bass staff:

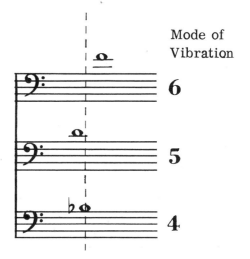

The B flat is in tune, the D must be pulled slightly sharp (above the dotted line) and the F must be flatted below the first position.

INTONATION CHART

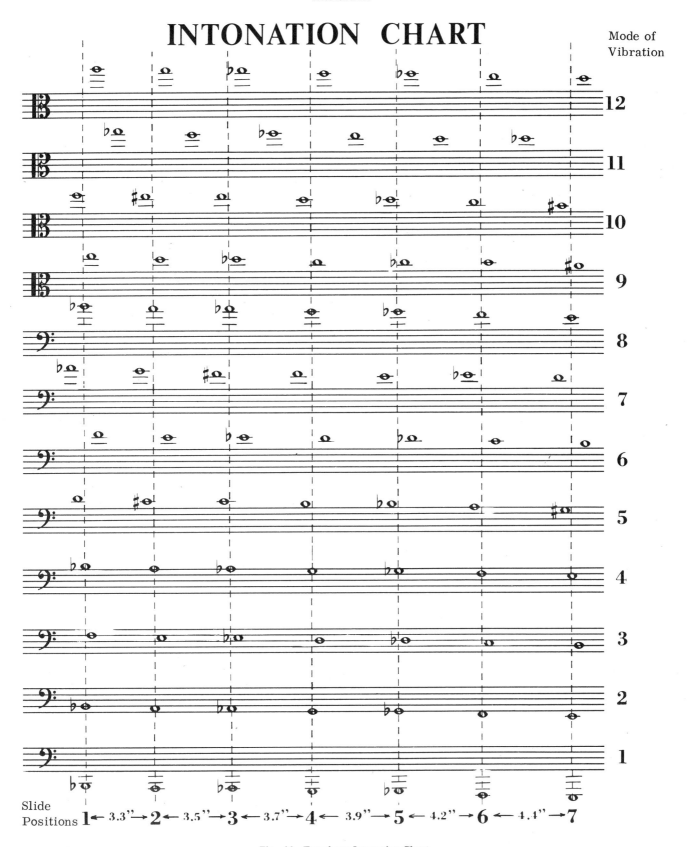

Fig. 46   Trombone Intonation Chart

Now study the same modes of vibration in the third position:

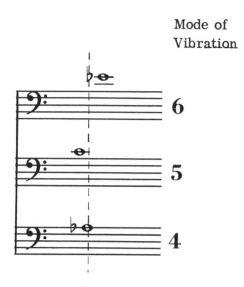

The A flat is in tune, the C must be raised and the E flat lowered from the normal third position.

Thirdly, study the same modes in the fourth position:

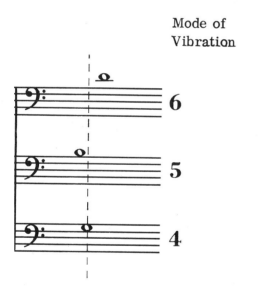

The G is in tune, whereas the B natural must be raised slightly and the D must be lowered a noticeable amount.

The most common intonation error of too many trombonists, is playing the seventh partial in the second, third and fourth positions too low. By not playing the high G, the high F sharp and the alternate position high F natural high enough, probably through carelessness, you begin to accept the flatter pitch as correct. It takes only a few months for the incorrect pitch to

be established in your ear. After this, the poor intonation sounds like good intonation. Take care that poor intonation does not become a habit.

Remember that this chart only shows the tendencies of most players on most trombones. The positioning of the notes will vary, but usually in the same general direction. **ALSO,** the ear is primarily responsible for and the final authority as to the proper intonation of a note. The chart is only a way of visualizing the pitch discrepancies so that you can improve your aim when trying to locate the proper pitch.

Intonation of the Scale Temperaments

In addition to the problems of playing the trombone in tune with itself, you must be concerned with the intonation of the various scales of music. There are at least three tunings of the major scale in common use today. These tunings are called temperaments or intonations and the three most common ones are: One, equal temperament, two, just (diatonic) intonation and three, Pythagorean intonation. Though some experts believe that everyone should play in equal temperament (as the piano is tuned for *one* octave) the richness of the overtones of a trombone makes playing in equal temperament almost impossible or at least undesirable.

Equal temperament equalizes all of the intervals of a scale by making all half steps the same size and making all whole steps equal to two half steps. Before the development of equal temperament, the half tones and whole tones in a scale were larger and smaller, depending on the color that the player wanted to add to his performance. To add brilliance to the melodic line, the performer could use Pythagorean tuning which enlarges the size of the whole steps and decreases the size of the half steps. If the player wanted to blend the intervals of a chord when playing with an ensemble, he decreased the size of many of the whole steps and increased the size of the half steps. As long as the members of the ensemble agree on the blend and color they wish to achieve, the pitches can be altered momentarily, but it is not possible to tune a harpsichord or a piano to more than one temperament or intonation at a time. Also, these other intonations change when the key changes and the attempts to build a piano that could modulate were never successful.

Note that when playing with ensembles without a piano, you will probably humor the intonation away from equal temperament in order to get a better sound. Below is a diagram of a major scale which is equally tempered. Each whole step contains 200 cents and each half step contains 100 cents. (A cent is a unit of measurement which has become a standard in the field of musical acoustics. The stroboscopes are graduated in cents, and it is not possible to determine the number of vibrations per second in a cent without doing some mathematical calculation or consulting a table. At A = 440 Hz, a cent is approximately equal to one-quarter of a vibration. One octave lower, a cent is equal to one-eighth of a vibration. For further explanation of the cent, consult a book on the acoustics of music.)

A diagram of an equally tempered major scale would appear as:

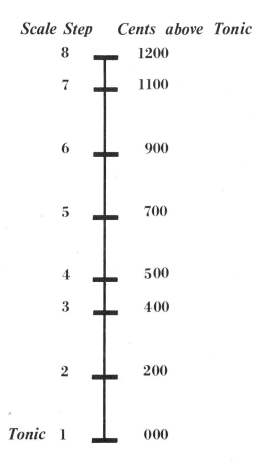

Scale Step   Cents above Tonic

Scale Step	Cents above Tonic
8	1200
7	1100
6	900
5	700
4	500
3	400
2	200
Tonic 1	000

Equal temperament when played as a scale by one trombone will sound fairly good, but when played in harmony it creates problems. If two trombonists play an equally tempered interval of a perfect fourth or a perfect fifth (500 cents or 700 cents), a slow *beat* will be heard. This beat sounds the same as when two players attempt to tune a unison and are very nearly, but not exactly, in tune. The harmony sounds better if the beat is removed and flatting the fourth by two cents or sharping the fifth by two cents will eliminate it. Professional trombonists have difficulty playing an equally tempered fifth. They will hear the beat, and one of them will move his pitch slightly so that the

interval will blend and the beat will disappear.

An equally tempered third is a compromise between the other two intonations. For the best possible blend, the equally tempered third should be lowered nearly 14 cents (just intonation). For brilliance, the equally tempered third should be raised nearly eight cents (Pythagorean intonation). Note on the chart below how the intonation of the just and Pythagorean scales differ. The small hack mark indicates the placement of that note in equal temperament. The large mark indicates the actual placement of that note. On that large mark is a number which indicates the number of cents in that interval. To the right of the mark is a positive or negative number which indicates the difference between that note and the same note in equal temperament. To locate these notes using a Stroboconn, the dial of the Stroboconn would be set sharp (+) or flat (−) as indicated on the chart which appears on page 82.

This chart need not be memorized nor even remembered when attempting to play in tune. The point to be made here is that what sounds best or blends best is the standard for how the intonation should be played. You should not be afraid to adjust the tuning of a note up or down ten or more cents, if it produces better intonation. Remember, no letter names were placed on the chart because when the music modulates the notes will change to fit the new intonation.

Intonation with a Piano

Though the piano is supposedly tuned in equal temperament, the acoustical construction of the piano makes this possible in one octave only. Because of the tension on the strings, the overtones are sharp and when the tuner adjusts the piano, he tunes the upper octaves sharper than A = 440 and the lower octaves flatter than A = 440. Therefore you cannot play at one pitch level when accompanied by a piano. You must adjust your tuning depending on the register in which the piano is playing and the note of the chord that you are playing.

Both the theory and practice of playing the various musical intonations are beyond the scope of this book, but in general you should be aware that:

1. Though the piano is tuned in equal temperament, the octaves are stretched, and the intonation of the trombone note will have to be adjusted either up or down from exact equal temperament.

2. When playing with other instruments than a piano there is a tendency to blend chords and brighten melodic

Comparison of SCALES
(measured in cents)

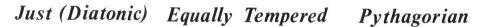

Just (Diatonic)   *Equally Tempered*   *Pythagorian*

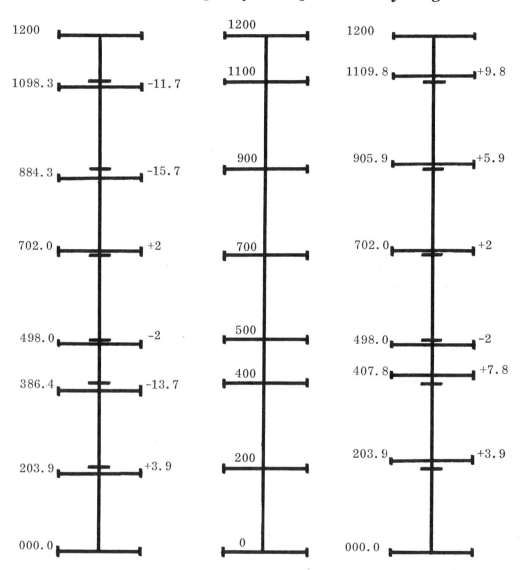

Numbers on the left of each column indicate distance in cents of
  each scale step above tonic.
Numbers on the right of each column indicate differences in cents
  from the equally tempered scale steps.
Small hack marks indicate the position of the equally tempered
  scale step.

Fig. 47   Comparison of Scales in Cents

lines and arpeggios. To achieve the correct intonation, you will have to leave equal temperament by as much as ten to 15 cents sharp or flat.

For further information about the nature of temperament, listen to:

W. J. Stegeman, *The Marvelous Building Blocks of Music* (Austin, Minnesota: The Author, 1962) and

Bell Telephone Laboratories, *The Science of Sound* (New York: Folkways Records # FX6007, 1959)

Developing Intonation with a Stroboscope

More precise intonation can be developed by using a stroboscope. Stroboscopes are available in different models, but the model which is most common is the one developed by the C. G. Conn Corporation which has the tradename, *Stroboconn*. All explanations in this book will be related to the Stroboconn, but with adaptation, the same methods can be used on other musical stroboscopes.

One of the rotating wheels of the Stroboconn will appear to be motionless when the note sounded is in tune. If the note is nearly correct, but not quite exactly in tune, the spokes of the wheel will appear to revolve in one direction or the other. The faster the wheel revolves, the further the pitch is from being correct.

Some criticize the use of the Stroboconn and claim that it teaches you to look, not to listen. This is a fault of the method, not the machine, and unless you consciously work to develop your ear, your study with the aid of the Stroboconn is wasted.

When first beginning work with the Stroboconn, take particular care with the adjustment of the volume control. The Stroboconn will not be damaged by playing too loudly, but the patterns on the wheels are blurry and difficult to read if the volume control is set too high. Adjust the volume so that the windows have just enough light appear in them to clearly outline the patterns on the wheels. Once this volume level is set, try to remain at about the same distance from the microphone and play with the same volume.

Begin work with the Stroboconn after completing your normal warm-up. If the instrument is tuned before it is completely warmed, the trombone will continue to change pitch as it warms, and you will become quite confused and frustrated because you will not play in tune to the satisfaction of the Stroboconn.

After a complete warm-up, tune a few of the middle register notes. Do not tune one note only. I suggest that you begin by tuning middle F (fourth line of the bass staff) then tune middle B flat and then tune low B flat. Test all three notes before moving the tuning slide. Notice the tendency of all three notes (they are all probably different), and move the tuning slide to accomodate as many of the three notes as possible. I have found that at first the middle B flat is not the best note to which to tune and that many players habitually lip this note sharper than the middle F or low B flat. Also, as discussed in Chapter 5—Tone Quality, it is unwise to pull the tuning slide too far. You should relax the pitch down to the proper level rather than pull the tuning slide more than one inch.

After tuning, begin to aurally memorize the *exact* pitch of the correct note. Once this is established, close your eyes while facing the Stroboconn, attack the note, and then open your eyes to check the accuracy of your aural memory. Then play several notes (a scale, an arpeggio or a short song) and end on the note to be checked. *After* attacking the final note, look at the proper wheel of the Stroboconn to see whether the pitch is correct.

Only look at the Stroboconn after the pitch has been started. Thus the machine is truly training your ear, not your eye.

Many players are confused at first by the Stroboconn model which has all of the notes of the chromatic scale displayed on it simultaneously. The arrangement of the windows corresponds to a piano keyboard, the five windows in the upper row are the black keys and the seven windows on the bottom row are the white keys. (See Fig. 48 Stroboconn on page 84.) Since you may not think of your notes in relation to a piano, I recommend that you learn the windows of the Stroboconn one at a time, beginning with the notes that are most important to you. F is found in the middle window of the bottom row and the B flat is found on the right hand end of the top row. Next, the D is found below and between the two upper windows at the left end of the display, or in other words, it is on the bottom row and is the next to the end on the left. After locating three notes, B flat, F and D, you can glance at the display from the corner of your eye as you play lip trainers, scales and etudes and correct the pitch of three fundamental notes of your technic. With these three notes established, the tuning of other notes will begin to improve as you compare them with these three notes.

Notice that as one note is played, the wheels in some of the other windows will tend to stop also. This is an illustration of the overtones that are present in the tone of a trombone. For example, when playing B flat, the wheel in the F window will nearly stand still. The wheel in the D window will slip slowly to the left

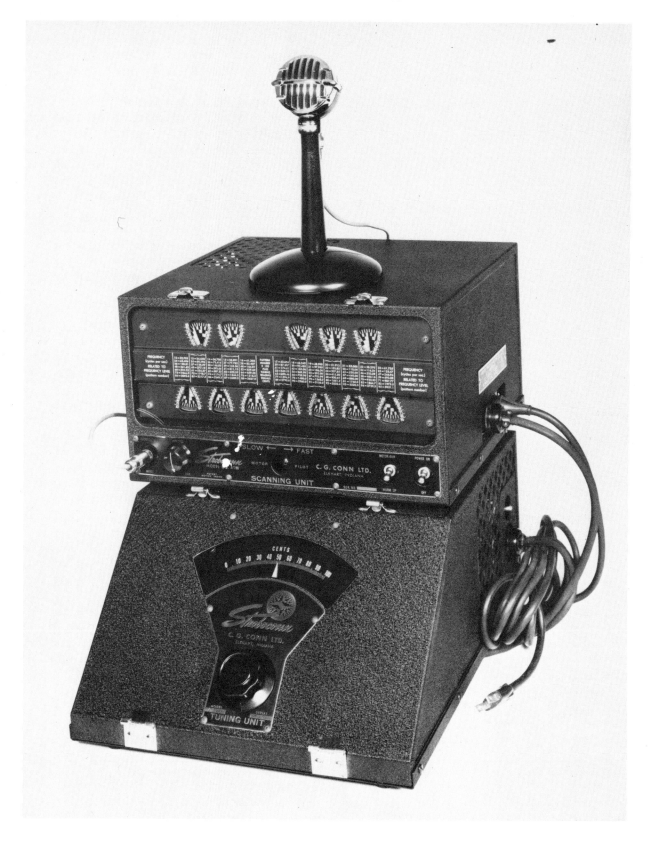

Fig. 48   Stroboconn (Photograph courtesy of C. G. Conn, Ltd.)

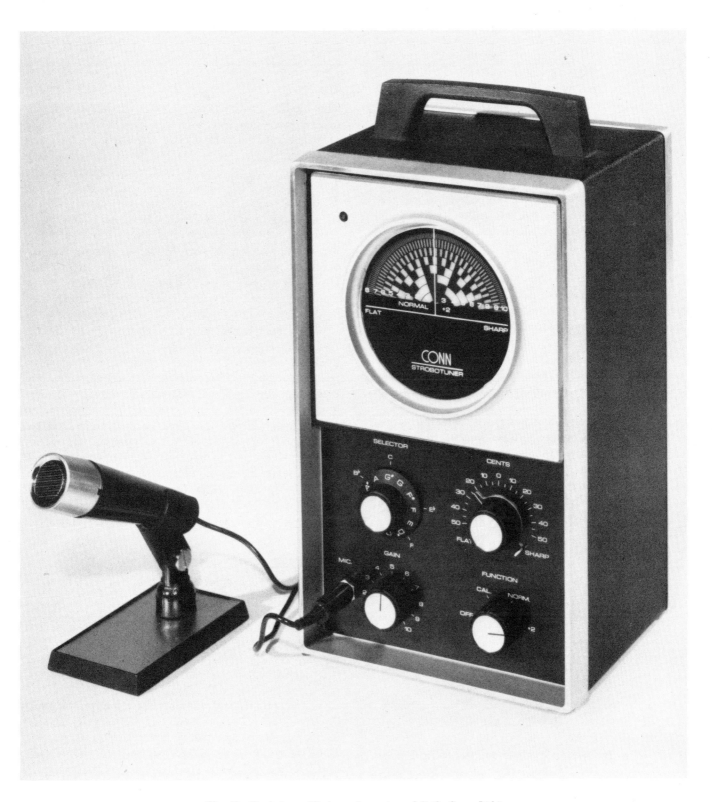

Fig. 49   Strobotuner (Photograph courtesy of C. G. Conn, Ltd.)

indicating that this overtone is slightly flat to equal temperament. (Do not try to stop the spin in the D window, when playing B flat, this overtone is supposed to be about 14 cents flat to equal temperament and is perfectly in tune with just intonation).

Notice also that with a good tone, the outline of the spokes of the wheels are sharp and clear (if the volume is adjusted properly) and that more than one set of spokes will stand still in that same window if the tone is very good. If the tone is poor, or the volume is adjusted improperly, the spokes will become blurred and only one set of spokes will be visible. Thus, if used properly, the Stroboconn can be used to improve the tone quality. For improving tone quality, relax and adjust the oral cavities while watching the display of the Stroboconn, and attempt to get as clear a pattern as possible. The Stroboconn faithfully picks up all sounds and attempts to show them on the display, and all pinched tones have overtones in them that are badly out of tune with the fundamental note. Tubby tones tend to not have enough overtones, and an airy sound will show as a haze on the display. Thus the best tone is the one which produces the clearest display both in the window of the note being tuned, and the other windows which are the overtones that are present in the sound.

If you only have a Strobotuner with which to work, you can take advantage of this overtone display to be able to check more than one note without resetting the dial. (The Strobotuner has only one display window and the note that is to be checked is dialed on the knob below the window.) (See Fig. 49 Strobotuner on page 85.) You are supposed to set the dial on the note to be checked. Only one particular note can be displayed and you must stop and reset the Strobotuner before checking another note. With a lip slur such as:

if the B flat is set on the dial of the Strobotuner, only B flats will stop the rotation of the wheel. Although it doesn't provide quite as clear a display, the Strobotuner can be set to F and then the wheel will tend to stop on both the F and the B flats (F is a nearly in tune overtone of the B flat). Thus with a B flat arpeggio, the F setting of the Strobotuner will make it possible to check all of the notes except the Ds.

This method of making one setting of the Strobotuner display more than one note is neither the best nor the most accurate for tuning. The display is a bit blurred and there is a difference in tuning between the overtone and the equally tempered fifth of two cents, so the spokes of the wheel will not give an exactly true reading. I would strongly recommend that you work with the Stroboconn rather than the Strobotuner, so that all pitches can be checked at an instant without stopping to reset the machine. If a Strobotuner is the only machine available to you, you may wish to set it to the fifth above the principal note, so that more notes during warming-up and arpeggio practice will be displayed without interrupting playing to reset the machine.

Remember: Being able to play every note on the trombone so that the wheels of the Stroboconn stop does *not* mean that you are in tune. The Stroboconn is calibrated in equal temperament and equal temperament may not be the best intonation to use. You must be prepared to move above or below equal temperament as much as 15 cents to improve the tuning. On the other hand, the use of the Stroboconn is necessary for all players since many of them have developed poor listening habits and believe that their poor intonation is fairly good. Equal temperament must be established *first*. Then the subtle pitch shading of just intonation or Pythagorean tuning can be developed.

Developing Intonation with a Trombone Ensemble

Playing trombone trios and quartets is an excellent method for the development of better intonation. The homogeneous sound of a trombone ensemble makes it easier to hear the overtones and the beats than the playing with a mixed ensemble.

As a general rule, all members of the ensemble must be willing and able to adjust the intonation and no member of the group can arbitrarily set a certain pitch and expect all of the other players to bend to meet him. In fact, tuning to the first player causes serious problems, because his part contains many Fs, Es and E flats above the staff all of which tend to be sharp. If the other members of the ensemble adjust to bring their notes into proper intonation, the entire group will raise the pitch above A = 440 Hz.

As another general rule, if there is a choice between two pitches at the unison, the lower one should be considered to be the correct one. Tune to the lower note, otherwise there is an ever rising spiral of pitch adjustments. When a layman hears an out of tune performance, he usually says, "Someone is flat." It could be, however, that someone is sharp. There are examples in music history in which the players continued to raise the pitch. After several years, they finally had to agree to lower the pitch a note or two to its original level.

Note that the brilliance of the Pythagorean major third demands that the person playing the tonic must remain on pitch. If the tonic is allowed to rise, the brilliance will disappear. Thus, an ensemble director who decides that raising the pitch to A = 444 will make the ensemble more brilliant is in error. If everyone plays a little sharper, the relative intervals within the harmony will remain the same and the brilliance that could be achieved by occasionally raising the thirds

set level of intonation or else an ever rising pitch spiral will begin.

To establish and to perfect intonation, the members of the trombone ensemble should play simple warm-up exercises together. The playing of the long-tone exercise of Emory B. Remington (*Warm-Up Exercises for Trombone*, Fairport, N.Y.: Rochester Music Publishers, n. d.) in which at first every other note is a middle B flat, then for awhile every other note is a middle F, and finally every other note is a low B flat, is an excellent exercise for a trombone ensemble to play in unison for the establishment of the primary tuning notes. Other lip slur exercises which use the overtone series are excellent for the tuning of octaves, fifths and fourths.

Exercises using harmony can be played after the ensemble becomes sensitive to the beats that they are working to avoid and sensitive to the blend for which they are striving. While the remaining members of the group play a lip slur through the overtone series, one member sustains a low note which is one of the principal notes of the overtone series.

and leading tones will be lost.

The members of a trombone ensemble should all be willing to adjust the pitch for the best blend and should as a group maintain a low pitch level. The low pitch level will allow the momentary raising of certain pitches for the added brilliance. After the rise, the player who was responsible for the rise must return to the previously

If the ensemble has more than four members, two players can play a perfect (just intonation) fifth as a basic drone for the exercises. The players with the drone must be able to play a perfectly in-tune beatless fifth before the exercise is attempted. They must also hold that tuning without being influenced by what is being played by the other members of the ensemble.

Simply playing the overtone series with the drone parts will not produce better intonation. The drone parts must be somewhat predominant and the other parts must be played easily so that the pitches can be matched with the overtones of the drone part. The players of the slur must adjust so that their notes blend into the sound. If your note almost disappears into the sound of the ensemble, you are probably very nearly in tune. If your note tends to carry or penetrate, you are playing too loudly and most probably playing out of tune. Consult the Intonation Chart for the overtone series and the diagram of just diatonic intonation earlier in this chapter so that you can adjust the various notes of the overtone series into proper intonation.

To further refine the intonation of the ensemble, the group should play chorales. The chorales should all be in the same key. From a collection of chorales such as *Early German Chorales* or *Bach Chorales* for trombone quartet as published by Robert King Music or *Bach Chorales* arranged for trombone trio as published by Ensemble Publications, Buffalo, N.Y., the group should play several chorales in B flat major. Before starting, you should set the pitch and intonation of at least the tonic and dominant chords. Then after playing one chorale, the players should switch parts for the next chorale. Rotate parts by having the first player move to the bottom part and have all other players move up one part. For the next chorale, still in the same key, the rotation should be done in the same manner (everyone move up one part with the top player moving to the bottom part). After three chorales with a trio, or after four chorales with a quartet, the ensemble can go to their usual literature or rotate parts while playing another set of chorales in another key.

Every member gets a deeper appreciation of the problems of an ensemble when rotating through the various parts. The first player and the bass trombonist are more able to appreciate the plight of the second trombonist after playing his part and trying to fit a note of harmony into an interval between the first and bass trombonist which are not quite in tune. The players learn that the bottom part must be established and have correct intervals, that the top part must not allow the upper register notes to rise in pitch and that the middle parts must blend to fit the intonation as established simultaneously by the top and bottom parts.

The team work of a trombone ensemble is the prime factor in the development of intonation which has the smoothness and blend of precisely adjusted pitches.

Chapter 18
Breath Control

This chapter is entitled Breath Control, *not* Breath Support. Breath support is only one specialized part of the total process of inhaling and exhaling the breath in trombone performance and we cannot talk about support without relating it to the other elements of breath control.

Breath control will be divided into three areas: One, the inhalation; two, the exhalation using a controlled relaxation of the breathing apparatus, and three, the exhalation using pressure developed by the contraction of the muscles of the rib cage and the lower abdomen.

Inhalation

Most breathing physiology lessons begin with a demonstration of the breathing apparatus which is constructed from a glass bell jar. This bell jar has two balloons fitted on a Y-shaped piece of glass tubing which represents the lungs and a rubber diaphragm across the bottom of the bell jar which represents the diaphragm. To demonstrate inhalation, the rubber diaphragm is pulled downward. The air pressure of the

jar is now below normal atmospheric pressure and air rushes in through the tubing to inflate the balloons. As the diaphragm is relaxed, the pressure within the bell jar exceeds atmospheric pressure and the air from the balloons is forced out through the Y-tube.

This demonstration only partially shows the breath action of a human being as he inhales and exhales. The use of a bell jar as a substitute for the rib cage is inappropriate, since an individual also expands and contracts his chest when changing from a full inhalation to a full exhalation and *vice versa*. To inhale, a vacuum within the chest cavity must be created. This is done by *contracting* the diaphragm and lowering it just as the rubber diaphragm was lowered in the bell jar demonstration. The vacuum can also be created by expanding the rib cage through contraction of the intercostal muscles which lace the rib cage. The chest cavity can further be expanded by making the upper chest expand.

False Concepts

There are many erroneous statements about breathing in brass pedagogy books. Two of the principal falsehoods are: One, the diaphragm contracts when it pushes the air out of the chest to support the tone; and two, clavical breathing (expanding the upper chest) is incorrect. The diaphragm, like all other muscles of the body, can only contract. It cannot push. To flex the arm the biceps muscles must be contracted. The biceps cannot push the arm from a flexed to a straight position. Some confusion about muscle contraction and relaxation occurs when the body is studied and the force of gravity is not considered. To lift a book from the table, the biceps must contract. To lower a book to the table, the already contracted biceps must relax so that gravity can straighten the arm. The diaphragm contracts to compress the organs of the lower abdomen and create a vacuum in the chest cavity. When the diaphragm is allowed to relax, the organs of the lower abdomen tend to return to their normal resting place, push the relaxing diaphragm up into the chest cavity, and create a pressure in the chest cavity. The belly muscles can also be contracted to further push the organs of the lower abdomen against the diaphragm and further increase the pressure on the chest cavity. Tensing the walls of the abdomen will squeeze the abdominal organs against the diaphragm. Tensing the diaphragm will squeeze the organs against the abdominal walls. Tensing *both* diaphragm and abdominal walls puts pressure on the organs of the abdomen and this may cause a hernia!

Clavical breathing is considered wrong by many texts, but it is impossible to take the deepest possible breath without allowing the upper chest to expand. This can be tested with a spirometer which will indicate that 15 to 20 percent less breath is inhaled and exhaled if the upper chest is held stationary. Clavical breathing should not be confused with the contraction of the muscles of the neck and hunching of the shoulders. True and efficient clavical breathing will allow the upper chest to fill without a constriction of the throat and upper thorax. Although many high brass texts disapprove of clavical breathing, the late William Bell, former tubaist of the New York Philharmonic, maintained that when he needed a breath, he needed all that he could get, and to do this he had to use clavical breathing. Many trombonists, particularly bass trombonists, find that they must take the deepest possible breath and that their upper chest must be allowed to or made to expand.

Deep Breathing

Most inexperienced trombone players have never learned to completely inhale to their fullest capacity. Although you may be physically fit and may be an active athlete, these physical activities do not usually teach you to breathe deeply. Many trained athletes do not have a concept of deep breathing and for many of them rapid shallow panting is sufficient to provide oxygen for their systems. You do not need a great deal of oxygen and you may become light headed when the hyperventilation of several deep breaths has supplied too much oxygen and removed too much carbon dioxide from your body. The athlete pants to get oxygen; the low brass player breathes deeply to get a quantity of air to use. Many performers believe that the basis for good breath control is to breathe as deeply as possible and to continually work to develop an even larger vital capacity.

Deep Breathing Exercises

Several exercises for the development of deep breathing have been advanced. The following are a few examples of these exercises:

1. While standing erectly, breathe fully and raise the arms outward from the sides to a position parallel with the floor. Hold the inhalation and return the arms to the sides. Notice the expanded lower rib cage.

2. While seated, bend over and grasp one ankle. Inhale and note the expansion of the lower ribs and the contraction of the muscles of the lower back.

3. Notice, while lying on your back on the floor, how during normal breathing the abdomen rises and falls. In the same position, inhale as deeply as possible and note the expansion of both the lower rib cage and the abdomen.

4. Without being concerned with the expansion, inhale while thinking of drawing the air along the bottom of the mouth. On successive inhalations where the air is drawn along the bottom of the mouth, note the expansion of the lower ribs and the abdomen. A similar idea is to breathe while thinking that a pleasant vapor, such as a cold medication, is being inhaled.

5. Kleinhammer recommends that the person always be aware of the additional breath that can be taken. To increase expansion and capacity, you should fully inhale and then take in even a bit more breath. Hardly anyone finds that the first inhalation is truly complete. There is always space for a little more air.

All of the procedures above are recommended because they all place your attention on the breath action first and then direct your attention to the position that parts of your body have taken. Attention to the muscles is always second and after the fact. You should be wary of any exercise which involves a conscious manipulation of the diaphragm muscle and the muscles of the lower abdomen. Some procedures that direct your attention primarily to the muscles of the lower thorax and suggest that they be contracted in a certain way may cause you to injure yourself. When inhaling, you must be as relaxed as possible. Only the muscles that must work should be active, and other muscles in the area must be relaxed so that your inhalation is not restricted. If the muscles of the abdomen are tensed, the diaphragm is then squeezing the organs of the lower abdomen against a wall of hardened muscle. Attempting a full inhalation while tensing the muscles of the abdomen can cause injury and strain.

The Spirometer

The fullness of the breath inhalation should be checked with a spirometer from time to time. A spirometer measures the vital capacity. Your vital capacity includes all of the air that you can inhale and exhale, and does not include the residual air that remains in your chest after full exhalation. Spirometers are usually available in departments of physiology, speech and physical education, or are used by physicians who specialize in respiratory illnesses and respiratory pathology.

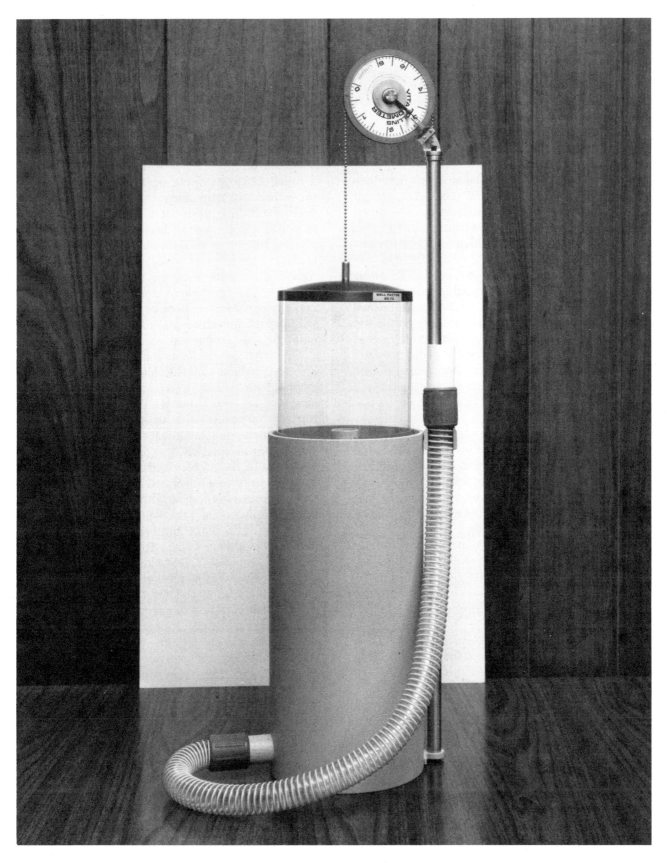

Fig. 50 Spirometer (Wet Type) (Photograph courtesy of Warren E. Collins, Inc.)

This instrument is an excellent learning device. If you are allowed several trials with a spirometer and told the results after each trial, you can learn which approach will give you the deepest breath. You should work with a spirometer to develop a way of thinking about breathing and a way of relaxing which helps increase your controllable breath supply.

Exhalation through Relaxation

Once a full breath has been taken, you must then control it. If you inhale fully and then relax, the air will rush from your mouth as the elastic ribs, lungs and lower thorax return to their normal unextended position. Your normal chest position is nearer to complete exhalation than to complete inhalation. The ribs and abdomen must be contracted to expel the remainder of the air. Therefore, to control your air when playing a low-resistance instrument, the air cannot be pushed from the beginning of a phrase to the end. At the top of the inhalation, the elastic parts of the thorax squeeze the air to a pressure that may exceed the pressure needed for middle and lower register notes. If you cannot feel this natural support at the top of the inhalation, you have not inhaled nearly deeply enough or are overly tense. If you do not partially hold the expansion, a large amount of air will rush through the embouchure during the first few seconds that you sustain the note. This rush of air can destroy the attack or ruin the shape of the note. (See Chapter 6—Attacks and Releases). This is not to imply that you will not feel any pressure or any resistance when playing at the top of an inhalation. There is a pressure in your mouth and lungs, but the thorax is not allowed to fully relax or the pressure would exceed the necessary pressure for the note.

Exhalation through Support

As a note is sustained, the elasticity of the body parts are not stretched as far as they were at first and they exert less pressure. At this point, you no longer have to hold back or hold a partial inhalation; the relaxation will sustain the note without help. An instant later, the elasticity will not supply the pressure needed for the note and then you must begin to actively push the breath to support the note.

How a note is supported without injury, is a topic that cannot be discussed easily. The textbooks on brass technique and singing technique have many contradictions among them. Some players advocate the pushing of the diaphragm in and up. As noted before, this is physically impossible. You cannot push the diaphragm

up, but you can relax it in a way which seems to be in and up as the abdominal organs press on it. Others argue strongly for the contraction of the lower thorax with the same action as one would use in the act of defication; instead of in and up, the pressure is down and out.

Some players insist that the abdomen must be held firmly when supporting the tone. As teachers, they demand extreme firmness and they push or strike the abdomen of the student with a hand or the end of a rolled magazine while he is playing to insure that the firmness is maintained. Other players and teachers believe that the firmness of the abdomen is detrimental to performance, or is at least not as important when playing trombone as with the playing of the higher brasses. Kleinhammer advocates using a relaxed abdomen and I concur with his approach. I believe that stiffening the solar plexis and the lower abdomen is not only unnecessary, but that it restricts the breathing, shallows the inhalation and promotes tension that will harm the tone production and the person himself.

The most natural approach is the safest and most effective method, and this natural approach places the emphasis on the air stream and not on any particular action of the lower thorax. Your attention should be focused on pushing the air stream through the lips. The breathing apparatus will then react with a natural and comfortable action.

Beware of the problems of oversupport. Low brass instruments have a lower resistance than trumpets. As your muscles strengthen with practice, you will not be able to feel them work—there is a natural anesthesism. Trying to make the breath control feel like it did a few months, or years ago, will demand muscular exertions that will far exceed the exertions you used originally. Damage and tension in the throat and embouchure will occur if you try to get the same feel of support that you used to get.

An excellent exercise for breath control for low brass players uses a glass half filled with water and a drinking straw. Submerge the end of the straw about a half of an inch. (See Fig. 51 on page 93.) Take a full breath and blow a long and steady stream of bubbles. At first it will be difficult to sustain the bubbles without a momentary break in their stream. Avoid using any more breath than necessary. As control is developed, the bubbles can be sustained for 40 seconds or more on a single breath.

The drinking straw exercise will help clarify the principles of this chapter. At the beginning of the note, the breath will have to be held back and at the end of the note, extreme tensions of the muscles of the thorax must be used. True breath control is not just

Fig. 51 **Breath Control Exercise Using a Drinking Straw and a Glass of Water**

one set of pressures, but a constantly changing set of adjustments as the air is expelled from the lungs.

Catch Breaths or the New Beginning

The greatest confidence and precision was developed by the horn students of the late Arkadia Yegudkin, affectionately known as "The General." The General's heavy Russian accent made the phrase "The New Beginning" sound like "Der Neu Beginick" and you may hear some of his former students refer to this procedure by the latter title.

The New Beginning simply involves treating every note as the first note—hence a new beginning is made on every note. After the mouthpiece is set on the embouchure, you relax and open the corners of your mouth and inhale. The second part of the new beginning follows immediately: the corners of your mouth close, the embouchure firms, the breath reverses direction and the attack is made. In other words the new beginning is much like the breath action of a small sneeze—an inhalation followed immediately by an exhalation.

The mouthpiece remains in contact with at least one lip and probably both lips during the inhalation. It is not removed from the lips and reset. Instead, the corners of the embouchure relax and open for the breath and then firm exactly (or almost exactly) as the attack is made.

The new beginning is practiced in two different ways: With the mouthpiece only or with the instrument. With

the mouthpiece exercise, the mouthpiece is set on the lips of a formed embouchure. Then in a steady rhythm of quarter notes at 60 to 80 per minute, a certain pitch is buzzed on the mouthpiece. Breathing and then quickly forming an embouchure and blowing just any pitch is wrong. You must aim at a definite pitch, and you restrike this note exactly on pitch several times. Sliding into the pitch from either above or below the note is not acceptable. Begin in the middle register. Repeat the note until you have full control of it.

Next buzz each note of an ascending scale eight times.

Next alternate between two different pitches.

Finally, practice buzzing three and four note arpeggios.

and

During all of this work, the setting of the embouchure and the attack follow the inhalation immediately. Also, the note must be exactly on pitch every time.

Applying the new beginning to the performance on the instrument is done with the etudes of Blume or Kopprasch. Using the same tempo as above (quarter note at 60 to 80 per minute) select an etude in even eighth or sixteenth notes and make all of the notes quarter notes. Thus, an exercise which is written:

would be performed:

Because so little breath is used for each note, you will soon become full of air and even if the exercise is begun with only a small breath, there will be a gradual filling up. Modify the exercise so that the action of relaxing and forming the embouchure is the same but little or no air is inhaled. In other words, there is a fake breath between every note.

The development of this technique makes it possible for you to begin any note without a lot of preparation. Many seem to confuse themselves before making the first attack. They wet the mouthpiece, dry the mouthpiece and then set the mouthpiece on the embouchure a half a dozen times before attempting the first attack. They are selfconscious before the attack is attempted. With the new beginning, you establish the security of beginning a note without all these needless preparations.

Some players are afraid to breathe between certain large intervals in a phrase. Instead they try to play the entire phrase on one breath, or they breathe at some less appropriate spot to avoid a breath before the leap. This causes poor phrasing or playing the phrase without enough breath. Once the new beginning is mastered, your fear of the leap is gone. You can breathe where you have to or where you want to without worrying about security. With the new beginning, a lengthy preparation is not used and you will not split

or chip the note after the breath because you did not have time to get ready or get set.

This new beginning is similar to the late Emory Remington's breathe and attack which develops the same security. Either of these techniques is used *only* after your embouchure and tone production are established. I cannot recommend them for you if you are having pitch placement problems. The new beginning develops further confidence after your security is established.

After learning the new beginning, learn to breathe fully and deeply with a catch breath. Most players do not like this exertion. The catch breath is difficult, uncomfortable and hard work, and most players shorten the note preceding the breath so as to allow more time for the inhalation. To develop this quick deep breath, you must drive yourself to sustain the last note of a phrase as long as possible, and then breathe quickly and deeply. Practice Blume and Kopprasch etudes that have constant eighth or 16th notes in them. First breathe on every bar line. Then breathe on every other bar line. Then every third bar line. Develop your ability to inhale fully without breaking the tempo of the constant rhythm of the notes. Playing ensembles with players who can inhale faster than you can is also excellent catch-breathing practice.

Chapter 19
Low Register

The low register of the trombone depends primarily on the sensitive adjustment of the oral cavities. As discussed in Chapter 5—Tone Quality, you must develop a controlled relaxation of the red portions of the lip. I assume for this chapter that you have already developed this lip relaxation.

General Development

The development of the low register depends on your learning to feel the focus of the tone in your throat. Use the muscles in the back of your mouth and around the walls of your throat to open these cavities as if you are yawning. Use a breath control that supports the note with an easy unforced flow of warm breath. To develop the proper image of the low register, you must think: Open the jaw, depress the back of the tongue, lower the larynx, and feel the back pressure

of the tone in the lower trachea. You may not really make some of these movements and some may be physically impossible, but you can think of these movements and thinking of these images in your mind will help open your low register.

Special Exercises

If your range stops on a certain note or your tone quality changes as you pass a certain note in the low register, I suggest that you practice the following exercises:

1. Lip the tone down, one half step at a time. You play a sound like a *glissando*, but do NOT move the slide. For example, if the last good note in your register is G, bottom line of the bass staff, you would play the following:

Glissando WITHOUT Moving the Slide

continue to descend using valve register notes

2. Pull the tone into the low register with descending *glissandos*. The slide actually moves as you sound your best (and lowest) note and *slowly* pull this tone down by half steps.

By either method, you will get little benefit once you have gone further than one whole step past the note where your tone began to deteriorate. Once the tone quality has been lost, you should return to the good note and begin pulling the tone down again from this point.

Never allow a fake embouchure to be used in the low register. The embouchure must be the same one that is used in the middle register. If you use a special low register embouchure, you will develop a definite break between your middle and lower registers.

To develop the low register on a natural embouchure, begin exercises in the middle register and proceed into the low register without resetting your lips on the mouthpiece. One excellent exercise for this embouchure work is Exercise No. 4 in R. H. Fink, *36 Studies for Trombone with F Attachment* (Carl Fischer). At first, play the fourth beat of each measure as a quarter note, omitting the second and third notes of the triplet.

Also, practice scales that descend into the low register. Begin on Middle B flat.

detached and slurred

continue pattern descending by half steps

Tonguing and Breath Control

Do not make the mistake of blowing and tonguing with two much force as you attempt to make the low register respond. Until you can focus the tone, until you have a feel for the note, it is a waste of time to attempt to make the low register respond by increasing physical effort. Though the low register requires slightly more air, it does not require a great deal more and it usually requires far less breath than many beginners try to push through the instrument. You may have to change your attack from a *T* to a *D* stroke for the low register, particularly on loud attacks. This does not mean that you use a slow or lazy stroke of the tongue. A *D* stroke is pulled from the teeth just as rapidly as a *T* stroke, but it does not have the explosive chiff at its beginning that the *T* attack has. The *T* attack, though it puts an edge on an upper register note, may blow the lips apart and keep a low register note from sounding for a fraction of a second.

Summary

In summary, the low register is developed through the learning to control the size and shape of the oral cavities. This control can be developed by experimenting with the focus of your tone by lipping down and glissandoing the chromatic scale. This focus must be developed without using an overpowering air stream nor crude percussive tonguing.

Chapter 20
High Register

High register development must take place over a period of time. It is useless for you to try a lot of different methods or experiment by looking for the trick or the secret that will give you a high register with only a few days of work. Many players experience an improvement in high register after having some lessons dealing with breath support, and they continue to attempt to improve their high register by using more and more support. Trying to force the upper register with excessive breath pressure develops many tensions which finally defeat the development of the high register.

Air Pressure

A high register which has an excellent tone must be developed through a relaxed system of tone production. Many methods erroneously state that the higher notes must be played with a faster moving and thinner air stream. Some of these methods even use the analogy of a nozzle on a garden hose and state that to give the water more pressure so that it will spray further, the nozzle is tightened to reduce the size of the hole. Unbelievable as it may seem to a person who is unfamiliar with physics or the application of Bernoulli's principle, this garden hose analogy is not appropriate to the playing of the high register on the trombone.

In truth, a faster moving stream of air has *less* pressure than a slower moving stream of air. An airplane wing does not get its lift primarily because it moves through the air at an angle. Instead, it gets the majority of its lift by the application of Bernoulli's principle. As the air moves over the wing, it moves at a higher speed as it bends around the wing at point A than it does at point B. The higher the speed, the lower the pressure, and it is this difference in pressure over an airplane wing that gives the wing its lift.

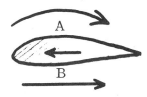

Another demonstration of the low pressure of a fast moving stream of air uses a spool and a cardboard disc. The cardboard disc is cut to the same size as the end of the spool. A straight pin is placed through the center of the disc so that the disc will remain centered over the small hole through the spool. To begin, lightly hold the disc against the spool and blow air through the spool at point A. As soon as the air stream is started, release the finger holding the disc and attempt to blow the disc away from the spool. The air enters the spool from a narrow channel at point A and passes under the cardboard disc at points C and D, but the pressure of the atmosphere at point B will hold the cardboard disc in place. Even when inverting the spool, the cardboard disc will not fall off until the high speed air stream (which has an air pressure which is less than the atmospheric pressure) is stopped.

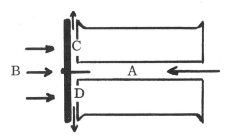

To further demonstrate how weak a high-speed stream of air is, take a piece of paper and blow across the top of it. Pucker your lips as when whistling so that the air stream flows rapidly over the paper. As the air speed is increased, the pressure falls and the atmospheric pressure will raise the paper to almost a horizontal position.

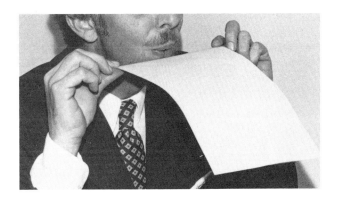

IF high pressure is needed in order to play the high register, the demonstrations above prove that using a narrow fast-moving stream of air is not the way to develop high pressure. Instead, the reverse is true. To achieve a high pressure stream of air, the air should move slowly through a large column. Kleinhammer states that when playing in the upper register, the player should hold the mouth open as if just having taken a bite of a hot potato. This technic will use Bernoulli's principle to produce a high pressure air stream.

Relaxation

You must develop a relaxed approch to tone production in the upper register. Relaxation is developed most easily by playing in the middle and low register. The fundamental lip slur exercises which are quite easy for you should be reviewed while you concentrate on more efficiency (more tone with less effort) and even more relaxation. This relaxation is further promoted by playing exercises in the valve register such as *36 Studies for Trombone with F Attachment*.

Exercises

You cannot expect your high register to just develop by itself while you play middle and low register exercises. On occasion, you must go to the high register and become familiar with these notes. One way of combining relaxation with the high register is to practice lip slurs which slur from the low register to the high register. These slurs should draw the relaxation and open oral cavity settings from the low register to the high register. Secondly, you must place demands on your embouchure and breath control by playing in the high register. The body will compensate for and adjust to the demands placed on it and to teach it what is needed for the high register, you must work in the upper register. This does not mean that you should force the tone production or smash the embouchure. It only means that to learn to play in the upper register, you must continue to work in this register.

Once you can get the sound of the high note you desire, even if this sound is only a squeak, you have made the first important step in the development of this note. If you work for less strain and more tone with every attempt at this note, this note will surely become more familiar and more secure. "Familiarity breeds contempt" is an appropriate quotation for the high register. The more you play these upper notes, the less fear you will have of them, and as your familiarity develops you become contemptuous of the fear that these notes used to give you. Once the fear is conquered, security in the upper register can be developed in a short amount of time.

When someone asks me which is the highest note I can play, I wonder whether they mean the highest note that I ever played, the highest note I played at the beginning of a practice session with my lip in the best possible shape, the highest note ever demanded on a formal concert or the highest note that can be played, loud or soft, slurred or tongued, even when my lip is beginning to tire. A professional trombonist does not get paid for lucky squeaks. He is paid to consistently produce the note, even if it is to be played at the end of a two hour concert after five or six hours of rehearsal that day. Therefore, your high register must extend well above the highest note needed on the concert, so that you are always secure.

You should think of your high register as being those notes that you can play at all dynamic levels, slurred or tongued, even when tired. You should then work on your register so that in a practice situation you can play notes a fourth or fifth higher. You then have a reasonable margin of safety at the concert.

To develop this margin of safety, your register should be developed in a logical and methodical manner. Everyday your practice routine should include some lip slurs into the upper register and some scales and arpeggios should be played in chromatic ascending order.

For example, begin lip slurs in the seventh position and progress up the slide by half steps.

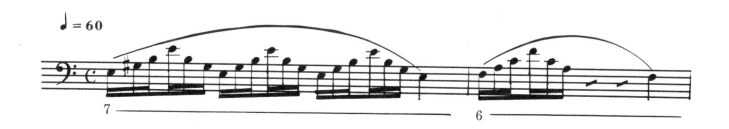

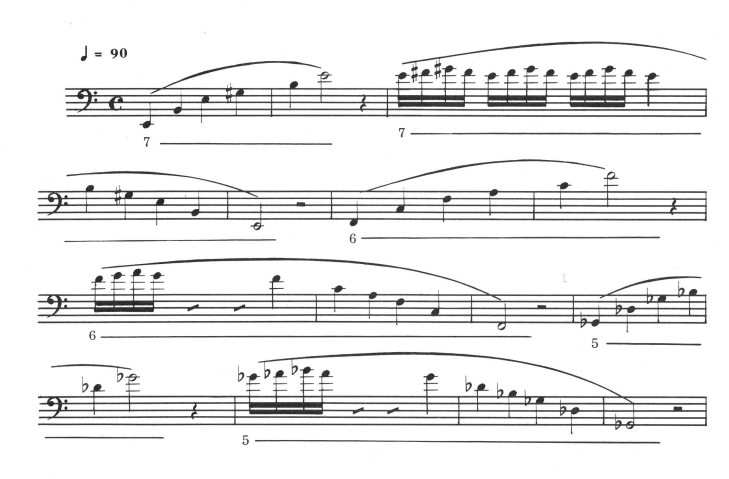

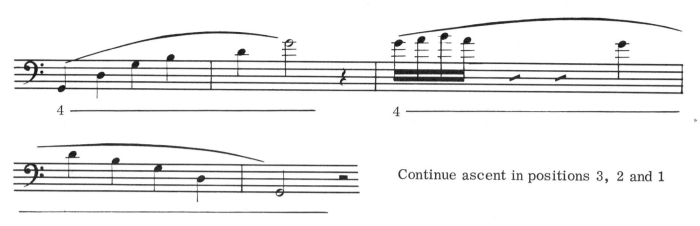

Continue ascent in positions 3, 2 and 1

Also play arpeggios both broken and straight in ascending chromatic order.

Continue ascent chromatically

Play two octave scales or play one octave scales in the *diatonic pattern*. (See Chapter 13).

IMPORTANT: Never allow a certain note to become the upper limit or boundary. Some players habitually stop their practice on high B flat, high D or high F. They then develop a block to further progress and have difficulty playing a high B natural, high E flat or high F sharp. **ALWAYS PUSH ON DURING PRACTICE ON THOSE GOOD DAYS** and play the *next highest* slur, arpeggio or scale.

Additional Exercises

To further develop the high register, spend at least half of the practice period playing R. H. Fink's *Studies in Legato*, or Bordogni-Rochut's *Melodious Etudes*.

After Volume 3 of the *Melodious Etudes* is nearly completed, more intense work can be undertaken to further build the high register. Charles Colin's *Progressive Technique*, currently out of print, if available, should be practiced for five or ten minutes a day. Proceed through the exercises so that these five or ten minutes are spent at the limits of your upper register. The same exercises in a different order are printed in Colin's *Daily Warm-Ups*. When using the *Daily Warm-Ups* book, play only exercises in the same key. First master F major, then F sharp major, then G. After completing the book, continue the work in the book by practicing the exercises *one octave higher*.

Once the register has reached a high E or high F, you should return to *Studies in Legato*, this time one octave higher than written. (Only if at least one complete phrase can be played an octave higher without strain, should you attempt this procedure.) Caution: You will only hurt yourself and your lip if you play with strain and force. In the back of *Studies in Legato*, the procedures for building the upper register are outlined. In brief, you begin one octave higher and when you tire you continue to play but return to playing in the octave in which the study is written. When the lip is rested and relaxed, the exercise is played one octave higher again.

Many high register building systems use the same training system that is used by athletes, particularly weight lifters. These systems are to be practiced every other day, or only three times a week. In the intervening days, the normal practice routine proceeds as usual and your lip is given a chance to recover from the taxing work of the previous day. I would recommend that the extreme upper register be practiced only three times a week and if unusual stiffness or tension develops, that it be reduced to twice or once a week until the stiffness disappears.

Summary

In summary, the upper register is developed by using a relaxed (open mouth) approach so that the tone production is not choked. The relaxation is further developed by practicing middle and low register etudes and then drawing this openness into the upper register with lip slurs and scales. The high register notes are developed by playing them and not by avoiding them. A logical sequence of exercises should be practiced every other day so that you lose your fear of these high notes and your body learns to develop the necessary strength. The necessary strength for the high register must be developed over a period of time while proceeding through several study books, each one of which is a bit more difficult than the last. There is only one secret to playing in the high register, you must work on it steadily for a period of time. There are *no* secret short cuts.

Chapter 21
Multiple Tonguing

Trombonists do not use multiple tonguing (double tonguing, triple tonguing and flutter tonguing) as much as trumpeters do, but in time all trombonists must learn to execute these multiple tonguings with moderate dexterity. When double tonguing, every other note is articulated with a *ku* syllable. For example, *Tu, Ku, Tu, Ku, Tu, Ku.* When triple tonguing, every third note is articulated with a *ku* syllable. For example, *Tu, Tu, Ku; Tu, Tu, Ku.* Sometimes the *Ku* is placed after the first *Tu*, and then occurs every third note thereafter, so that the syllables are, *Tu, Ku, Tu; Tu, Ku, Tu.* The flutter tongue is made with the tongue rolling an Italian *R* and begins with a *T*: *TRRRRRRRRRRRRRR.*

Uses of Multiple Tonguing

Multiple tonguing is usually needed in a fanfare rhythm figure which has three or four notes in rapid succession.

The speed of this figure exceeds the speed of the single tongue. The single tongue may be able to repeat fast enough for some figures at soft dynamics, but when playing louder, the tongue tends to get heavy and slow. Multiple tonguing is used so that you can play rapid figures loudly enough to suit the music.

Double tonguing is needed in *alla breve* (cut time) marches that have eighth-note runs. These figures are found in the marches of Sousa, Fillmore, Alexander and others. If the speed of the march is about 120 beats per minute, a single tongue is usually possible, but should the speed be increased to 132 beats per minute or more, a double tongue will be needed.

Unfortunately, many players do not learn to double tongue a scale passage (even though they can double tongue on repeated notes) and find out too late (at the concert or audition) that the tempo is slightly faster than they are able to single tongue. Double and triple tonguing should be developed so that they can be played at any speed from slightly slower than the fastest single tongue up to very rapid figures. Double and triple tonguing should be developed on scale and arpeggio figures as well as on repeated notes.

Typical of the demands of multiple tonguing is the triplet figure in some editions of *La Gazza Ladra:*

103

etc.

A particularly difficult double tonguing passage is located in the bass trombone part of *Finlandia*. Not only is the figure rapid, but loud and low:

Another excerpt which is not considered easy is the passage in the fourth movement of *Scherezade*.

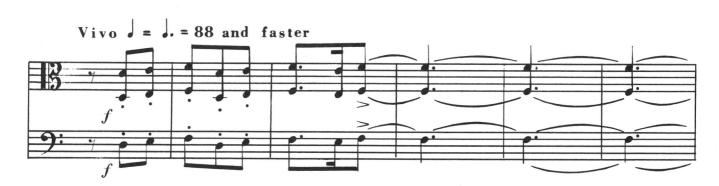

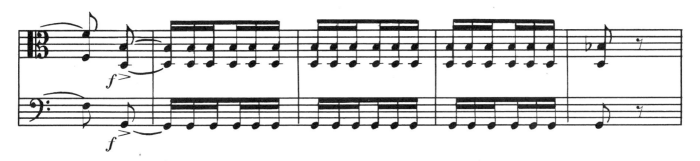

Though the rhythm is grouped in triplets, some players use a double tongue and begin on the *Ku* syllable. They misplace the accent of the double tongue so that the figure retains a triplet pulse.

Others begin with a *T* syllable, play one group of double tonguing and follow with groups of triple tonguing.

Whether the *K* is placed in the middle or the end of the triplet group is also an arguable point. For evenness, many prefer to play slow-speed triple tonguing with the *K* syllable in the middle of the group.

Developing Double Tonguing

Double tonguing requires that every other note is articulated with a *T* consonant and the alternate notes are articulated with a *K* consonant. A comfortable vowel is added to these consonants and the figure becomes: *Tu, Ku, Tu, Ku*; or *Tah, Kah, Tah, Kah*; or *Toe, Koe, Toe, Koe*; etc.

These same method books suggest that the tonguing be developed from a slow and controlled speed with a definite space between the notes and an overemphasized accent on the *K* syllable. Thus an exercise such as:

Would be practiced:

When the articulation is clean and controlled, the speed is increased gradually. As you continue to practice over a period of weeks, you increase the speed while you retain control and a balanced sound. If you want a study method with progressive exercises, I recommend the double tonguing exercises in the Arban's Book.

Developing Triple Tonguing

The same procedure is suggested for the development of triple tonguing. The consonants for triple tonguing are a *T*, another *T* and a *K*. With addition of a vowel, the figure becomes *Tu, Tu, Ku; Tah, Tah, Kah; Toe, Toe, Koe; etc.*

Again, the tonguing is developed from a slow and a controlled speed. Space between the notes and overemphasize the accent on the *K* syllable. An exercise such as:

would be practiced:

Over a period of weeks, with regular daily practice, the speed is gradually increased. Evenness and control must be retained at all times. Some players mistakenly believe that they can double or triple tongue if they can play the exercises at the fastest tempo marked, even though they can neither play it slower nor faster than the suggested tempo. The trombonist must be able

to control his multiple tonguing at all speeds.

In an emergency, when multiple tonguing is needed and there is not enough time to proceed through the normal series of exercises, the consonants *D* and *G* can be substituted for the *T* and *K*. Thus in the fanfare figures:

The syllables used would be:

Many teachers recently have developed a method of teaching multiple tonguing that does not require you to interrupt the air flow between notes. Thus the standard Arban's exercises would be played on one steady stream of air.

The teachers using this system claim that multiple tonguing when finally developed uses an articulation of the tongue and throat that uses one steady stream of air. They also claim that the arduous chore of practicing double and triple tonguing can be shortened with this approach. I developed my own multiple tonguing using the traditional method, but believe the claims of these teachers for this new system are valid and would suggest that you use this new system if you are developing multiple tonguing without instruction.

Begin by practicing the syllables without the instrument. Sing the syllables in a monotone voice. Use a very open vowel and keep the throat open as much as possible. Learn to relax the front part of the tongue so that it can articulate the T without tension. Hold the back of the tongue and the jaw motionless. Consciously make the throat cavity as large as possible with the vowels ä as in *call*, *oo* as in *too*, or ō as in *toe*.

After you can pronounce the syllables automatically at many different speeds, play the multiple tonguings on the instrument. Begin slowly as with the traditional method, but do not separate the notes.

Double

Triple

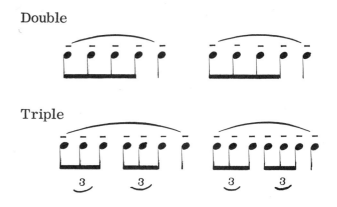

Gradually increase the speed while retaining control. Be sure that the throat remains open and that the K syllables are played strongly and evenly so that the rhythm does not limp.

Flutter Tonguing

Flutter tonguing is indicated in the music with either the word flutter or the phrase flutter tongue written over the note. Occasionally there are extra beams placed on the note stem indicating that the note is to be played as a tremolo (repeated as many times as possible during the duration of the note).

The tongue pronounces an Italian rolled *R* af note is begun with a *T.* Pronounce *TRRRRRRRR* If you are having difficulty rolling an *R,* practice th tonguing without the instrument. Elevate the base of the tongue and hold it still while relaxing the tip of the tongue so that the tip will flutter as the air is blown through the mouth. Blow rather forcefully at first while you try to relax the tip of the tongue. Do not become discouraged if the roll will not develop immediately. Some persistent practice will solve the problem.

Chapter 22
Volume

Breath Control

Developing volume is more than just blowing more, pushing more air through the horn, or using more breath support. These three suggestions are all very good rules to follow, but there is a limit to how much additional breath support and additional air can be used.

Oral Cavities

Blowing more, pushing more air, or using more support will not produce more volume unless the body makes several other adjustments. Many players unconsciously tense their throats and lips when they increase their support and as a result, no more air moves and they simply get red in the face. To move more air, the throat and mouth must be relaxed so that the air can move from the lungs into the instrument. When working on the development of volume, always be conscious of the openness of ALL of the oral cavities.

Though it is possible to develop more volume by blowing harder and moving more air *at a higher speed*, the more efficient way of using the breath is to learn to enlarge the air stream so that your air stream seems to move in a large slow column. Move the air stream through a large open mouth as when fogging a cold window.

Resonance

The most important skill to develop is a FEEL for the resonance of the trombone. I will probably have difficulty using the proper amount of breath with the correct breath pressure when first playing a new model trombone. The instrument either has a tone which does not center well or has a resistance that seems to prevent playing a full *fortissimo* tone. Within a few minutes of experimentation though, the trombone seems to improve. The trombone doesn't really improve, but I discovered the proper resonance of the instrument by adjusting my head cavities and my breath flow. You will have to work for many months to be able to discover the full resonance of your instrument, but once the proper FEEL has been obtained, the volume will increase without an increase in physical exertion. In fact, many players overpower the natural resonance of their instruments and they could achieve a better and more powerful tone by *pushing less*. This is not

to say that the beginner can play louder by relaxing. At first, you must develop all the support that you can and even more. After several years of playing (and forcing) there are many players who are supporting the air too much and not allowing the instrument to develop the resonance of its own. Developing a sensation of the resonance of the instrument is achieved by being very sensitive to the sensations of the lips, mouth, throat and upper chest. When your body is adjusted to the proper resonance, you can almost feel the tone of the instrument coming back up the mouthpiece pipe and resonating in your oral cavities. The late Louis Armstrong said, "I know my horn and my horn knows me." This applies to the development of volume.

Tone

In addition, more volume can be developed if the tone is fully developed. The tone of any musical instrument is not one note, but a combination of several notes. A tone is determined by the relative strengths of all of these overtones. If the lower partials are very strong and the upper partials are not present or are very weak, the tone will be tubby and dark. If a lot of strong high partials are present, the tone will have a thin whiny sound. In either case, the tone will not have volume. The dark tone will be covered easily and the bright tone will cut through an ensemble with a whining buzz, but will not be full bodied. The tone will be muffled and turgid if the overtones are not in tune with each other. You cannot directly tune the overtones of your sound, but if you develop a relaxed, singing sound, the overtones will be in tune. Thus you must develop a tone which is full and relaxed if you are to develop your volume to a powerful level.

Summary

In summary, the development of the volume of the tone depends on your ability to: Support, but not force; play with open oral cavities, but not strain; work with the resonance of the trombone, but not try to overpower it, and develop a free open relaxed singing full tone, but not try to force a deficient tone into an acceptable sound.

Chapter 23
Endurance

Endurance depends on both strong and efficiently working muscles. Some players develop strong embouchures and strong breathing muscles yet have no endurance because they have developed habits that tax these muscles. They use too much mouthpiece pressure, do not warm-up properly, tense the throat or force the breathing. Although they are strong, their bad habits weaken and damage the muscles so that they can only retain their strength for an hour or so. More rare is the player who has a natural approach to playing the trombone, uses his muscles efficiently, but because playing has always been easy for him, has never disciplined himself to the regular routine of strength development. Unless these natural players work regularly at a muscle building program over a long period of time, they will never develop endurance.

Strength Development

To develop strength, you must regularly *play* lip training exercises and lip slurs. You should also *play* etudes and studies in legato which are more than a few minutes in length. Notice that the word used was *play* and this means working at less than maximum effort. A trombonist must do a great deal of *playing* to build up long term endurance. In addition, the muscles of the embouchure and breathing apparatus should be pushed to their maximum exertion so that these muscles become used to increased demands. As the body adjusts to these demands it grows stronger and then you can *play* at higher levels of exertion without fatigue.

Relaxation

Most important to endurance development is the efficient use of the embouchure and breathing muscles. In many cases my students have strength, but appear to waste more energy than I use to produce a tone. Rather than simply run through the standard warm-up, you must constantly think of relaxation and always try to relax even more while playing these exercises which are so familiar to you. The tendency for most is to day-dream while playing the old exercises. Day dreaming sets the bad habits even more firmly. When playing melodious etudes and studies in legato, the least forceful approach must be used, even when playing *forte*. Particularly when the melodic line descends, you must use less force and coast so that your strength returns for the more difficult phrases. You must take *every* opportunity to rest while playing.

Special Exercise

Alternately sprinting and jogging has become a standard training method for long distance runners. An instrumentalist can use this same technic to develop endurance. After warming-up, you sprint by playing at extreme dynamic levels in extreme parts of your range. As soon as fatigue begins to develop, you jog by resting while continuing to play in the middle register with dynamics which are neither loud nor soft. You remain in the middle and low registers until the fatigue disappears and then you return to the difficult exertion again. You alternate between this maximum exertion and the easy middle and low register playing until no amount of easy playing will rest your muscles. You must then stop and rest or you will damage your embouchure.

Whether you are working for more endurance, or simply trying to accomplish more in the allotted time in a practice period, you should have several exercises and etudes to be played as the sandwich between regular portions of your practice routine. Exercises and etudes which should be inserted into the practice routine for resting the lip are easy lip slurs, softly sustained pedal tones, scales in the low register, easy studies in legato and F attachment studies.

After several weeks of a regular lip-building routine, and if the work is done in the most relaxed manner possible, you will "break through" and find that your endurance limit is no longer just one or two hours. Instead you will find that you can continue playing for hours without end.

It is important that you do not punish your lip when working to build endurance. There are moments when the exertion is at a maximum, but this does not mean that you are to force or use mouthpiece pressure. On the other hand, you must push yourself. The building of endurance involves placing demands on your lip while playing with the easiest most relaxed approach. To develop endurance, you must use a standard and scientific training routine which neither beats nor babies your lip.

Chapter 24
Interpretation and Style

Playing the correct notes with the proper dynamics and the correct articulation will not produce a musical performance. In order to play musically, you must add some interpretation and style to the performance. This interpretation and style will include the addition of small tempo changes (rubato), small dynamic changes (nuances), variations in the speed and width of the vibrato, variations in the actual rhythmic length of the notes and the silences between these notes, and the variations of the volume, tone color and vibrato within the individual notes. When music psychologists attempt to analyze the various parts of musical style, they usually can only analyze one factor at a time and usually develop findings that cannot be directly applied to performance of other music. There seems to be a point at which the more the musician thinks about his performance, the less musical the performance becomes. Therefore, you must develop your ear so that when you interpret or play with a style, the music will have a musical flow and an emotional feeling rather than a thoughtful sound.

Proper Style and Creativity

Don't make the mistake of believing that playing with style, or using interpretation is a matter of personal freedom or creativity. Some believe that when a teacher corrects their style that the teacher is engaging in a battle of wills or is trying to restrict them. Nothing could be further from the truth. A musician does not develop a style by just sitting down and imagining a new or different way of playing a certain phrase. Only with a composition of his own can the trombonist decide how to perform the piece without considering other factors.

When a teacher corrects your phrasing, he is not trying to suppress your individuality. The teacher is only pointing out that you have exceeded the limits of good and proper taste. You are free to interpret, but this interpretation must be within the limits of proper style and this is learned from others who have an ear for such style. When observing an excellent conductor for the first time, you may get the impression that all of the suggestions or demands about musical style are only whims of his. You may also wonder how he

can remember all of these fine points from one rehearsal to the next. But after a few rehearsals, the careful observer will note that the corrections are always the same at these points and the conductor will continue to work for that interpretation until he achieves it.

Learning Proper Style

To learn musical style, you must actively participate in the making of music with the best possible musicians, teachers and conductors. Only after years of study and listening will you have enough background in interpretation to be able to correctly interpret a composition by yourself. In the meantime, you should perform with many musical groups, and not only learn style from the corrections which the conductor gives directly to you but also by listening to the corrections that the conductor gives to the other sections of the group. You should listen to many different artists and absorb as much of their style as possible. On occasion, you may be excused from rehearsals when the accompaniment for a visiting soloist does not include a trombone part. In such cases, you should not go home, nor join the other members of the excused group in conversation in the tacet room.* Instead you should remain in the rehearsal room and listen to the rehearsal of the visiting artist. Musical taste and style can be absorbed by listening to vocalists, string players, pianists, *etc.*, and elements of their taste can be applied to your style.

To develop a musical style and learn how to interpret music, you must first imitate the styles of established musicians. You must become sensitive to the fine points of nuances, vibrato, rubato, note shape and note length. You must compare the styles of these musicians and synthesize these styles into your own way of playing. Finally, when you have truly studied the best styles of the best players, you will be ready to create your own style with proper taste and balance. To the truly dedicated musician, this learning and development of style never stops. It continues for his entire musical life.

Tacet room—back stage or a room near the rehearsal area where players who are tacet congregate to pass the time.

112

Chapter 25
Vibrato
(vē-brä ´tō)

There are three basic types of vibrato which can be used on trombone.

Slide Vibrato

The most obvious type is the slide vibrato. This can be done by rapidly vibrating the slide to and fro when performing commercial, dance or show music. Many jazz players prefer to stylize their playing with a slide vibrato by waiting until the end of a long sustained note and then wiggling the slide a few times in a broad almost jerky motion. Slide vibrato is primarily a pitch variation. Its use is prefered *only* in jazz and commercial music. Even the sight of slide vibrato offends most classical conductors and besides, it tends to be wide, slow and difficult to control. Only in special circumstances with particular orchestral solos with certain conductors is a slide vibrato ever used in classical music.

Diaphragm Vibrato

A diaphragm vibrato is executed by pulsating the breath flow. After the note is begun, you vary the flow of your breath by relaxing and tensing your diaphragm, *e.g. TUuUuUuUuUuUuUu.* Unlike the slide vibrato, the diaphragm vibrato is a variation of loudness not a variation of pitch. If it is produced at the proper speed, it warms the sound without being offensive to the listener. Again, this type of vibrato is difficult to control. In addition, I find it to be very taxing and it tends to tighten my throat and breathing muscles, although there are some players who use such a vibrato without encountering either of these ill effects.

Lip Vibrato

The lip vibrato is the type of vibrato which I prefer and use for most styles of music. Some people can produce a lip vibrato almost naturally because they are innately dissatisfied with a straight tone and instinctively *warm* the sound by alternately tightening and relaxing the lips. The lip vibrato is also known as the jaw vibrato since the jaw usually moves in and out or up and down as the lip tenses and relaxes. The lip vibrato varies not only the pitch, but also varies the loudness and tone color of the sound in much the same manner as a vocal vibrato.

If you think about using a *jaw* vibrato, the emphasis will be placed on the wrong part of your embouchure. You will alternately slide or smash your lips against the mouthpiece as you make the jaw vibrato. The unnecessary bruising of the embouchure muscles would not be good, even if it produced a nice tone with vibrato.

Learning Vibrato

To learn the lip vibrato, use as little mouthpiece pressure as possible on both lips. Start by using a rather low note—middle F. Now relax your lips almost to the point of dropping off the note to the low B flat of the overtone series.

When the tension is at a minimum, stop playing and imagine that you are holding a pencil point in the center of your mouth without holding it with your teeth. Now alternately squeeze and release the pencil point with your lips. Compress the imaginary pencil point from all sides. Do not simply smile or press the point from only the top and bottom.

Now play the middle F on your trombone. Be sure that you are using only a slight amount of mouthpiece pressure and a minimum of lip tension. Slowly pinch the pitch of the note sharper by using the same compressing action as described above. Continue to sustain the note and relax, then compress the lips and raise the pitch again, *etc.* Somewhere in the middle of this pitch variation is the true pitch of the instrument. As the note is sharpened, it passes through this true pitch center and then becomes somewhat thin in quality as it gets sharper. At the lowest point of the pitch, the tone quality is somewhat foggy and flatter than the centered tone.

If the sound somewhat resembles a car engine being started on a nearly dead battery (on a cold morning), the action is correct. If you have difficulty raising and lowering the pitch with this tensing and relaxing action, the lips are too tight. You will have difficulty with the lip vibrato if you are in the habit of playing too near the top of the pitch rather than in the center of the pitch. Check the tuning of your trombone. If at 72° F., the tuning slide has to be pulled out quite far to be in tune with the Stroboconn or a tuning bar, lower the center of the tone as described in Chapter 5—Developing the Tone.

If the trombone is in tune and you still have difficulty changing the pitch, you have a weak embouchure. The vibrato cannot be developed until your embouchure is strengthened. Lip slurs, studies in legato and buzzing tunes with your lips are good exercises for increasing lip strength.

Once you can control the raising and lowering of the pitch, the speed of the vibrato must be increased and the width (the variation of pitch) must be diminished. Increase the speed gradually. Do not allow the vibrato to become an uncontrolled quiver.

Some players, especially those who are singers also, have difficulty developing a vibrato that is controlled by the lip action. They have a natural relaxed undulation of the throat that they use when singing. This throat vibrato is easier for them to use than a lip vibrato and the results seem to be nearly the same. If you have a natural throat vibrato you should cultivate it rather than attempt to develop a lip vibrato.

Whether you think you use a diaphragm, throat, jaw or lip vibrato, you have to vary the tension of your lips throughout the cycle of the vibrato. The musical results are more important than the type of vibrato you think that you are using. No matter which type is used, if the sound is modulated in pitch, volume and tone color, the vibrato is acceptable.

Vibrato Speed

How fast should a vibrato vary? Many people state that it must be in good musical taste and they stop there. This is the best answer, but not very practical. Most American musicians vary their tone with a vibrato at the rate of five to seven times per second. A French vibrato varies at the rate of from eight to 12 times per second. Very few performers in this country use a vibrato which approaches the speed of a French vibrato.

Vibrato Variations

The vibrato must never become too precise nor too mechanical. Its speed and width change with a change in dynamics, range and style of the music. A musician usually varies both the speed and width of the vibrato while sustaining a single note. A consistent vibrato is as boring to the ear as a straight cold tone.

Above all you must remember that a vibrato will not make a poor tone beautiful. The poor tone will still only sound like a poor tone with a vibrato. A good tone with a musical vibrato can be developed with industrious practice and careful attention as to how established musicians use it.

Chapter 26
Clefs and Transposition

All serious trombonists must learn to read the tenor clef, the alto clef and a few of the most common transpositions. The reading of a clef is not a transposition. You are transposing when you change the letter name of a note, *i.e.* you read the third space (treble clef) of a trumpet part and play a B flat. The name of the note has been changed from C to B flat. Although some trombonists begin reading clefs as a transposition, the clef only repositions the notes on the new staff and the letter names of the notes do not really change.

Tenor Clef

The first clef you will need to be able to read in addition to bass clef is the tenor clef. It is found in advanced solo literature, advanced etudes, modern American band literature, moderately advanced ensemble music and is very common in symphony orchestral parts. The C clef sign indicates the location of middle C and takes several forms. The most common form of the C clef found in printed music is:

In some manuscript music it looks like a "K" in which the lines join on the line which is to be designated as middle C.

Occasionally, the clef uses cross bars to indicate the location of C. This form of the clef is common with a few French engravers.

When the C clef designates the fourth line of the staff as middle C, the music is then in the tenor clef. The lines and spaces of the tenor clef have the following names:

Some players learn to read this clef by simply learning the new names for the lines and spaces. Others read the tenor clef by transposing every note up a fifth (placing every note either two lines or two spaces higher):

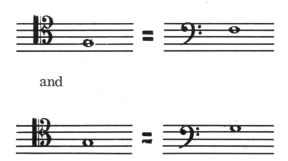

Still others who can read the treble clef prefer to lower the note one step and read the note in the treble clef.

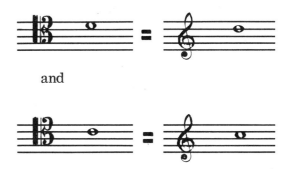

Of course, by this transposition method, the note is one octave too high and must be lowered one octave. No matter which method is used, in time all trombonists learn the names of the lines and spaces of the tenor clef without any mental crutches.

Alto Clef

The alto clef is not nearly as common as the tenor clef, but it is used regularly in certain types of music. The alto clef is found in the scores of the Baroque period (G. Gabrieli and Pezel to name two), the orchestral parts of Mozart, Haydn, Beethoven, Brahms, Berlioz, Schubert, Schumann, Rimsky-Korsakov and early Wagner; and is a commonly used clef in modern Russian orchestral works. In the works of the Baroque, Classical

115

and Romantic periods, the alto clef is used in the highest trombone part. The alto clef is used in all three of the trombone parts in the modern Russian works and at times the Russian composers prefer to write the parts (including the bass trombone part) on ledger lines *below* the alto clef rather than use the bass clef.

The lines and spaces of the alto clef are as follows:

Remembering the location of the Cs and Fs in the alto clef is a helpful base for learning the other notes.

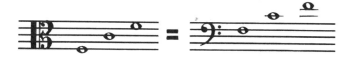

Some players learn to read this clef as a new clef, while others read it as a transposition from treble clef:

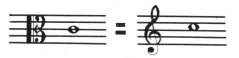

As with reading the tenor clef by transposing from treble clef, the above method sounds one octave too high and must be lowered accordingly.

Treble Clef in C

Reading the treble clef for non-transposing instruments is used mostly by jazz musicians who must read from lead sheets or "fake" books. There is no simple interval transposition crutch for reading this clef. Learning to read treble clef music in C is best done by simply learning the names of the lines and spaces of the clef.

Imagining the music to be bass clef and then transposing the music up a sixth tends to be a rather cumbersome process.

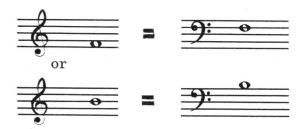

Treble Clef in B Flat

The B flat treble clef can be read by using the tenor clef and altering the key signature. The transposition of B flat treble clef music allows you to read music that was written for B flat trumpet, treble clef baritone, B flat tenor saxophone, B flat bass clarinet, *etc.* To read a B flat treble clef part, you imagine that the clef has been changed to tenor clef and that the key signature has two more flats or two fewer sharps than are printed.

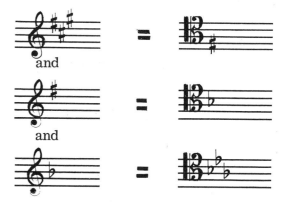

When using this method of tranposition, the added accidentals are read as indicated, except for those accidentals on the notes that would be read as Bs or Es. These accidentals must be played one half step lower than written, *i.e.*

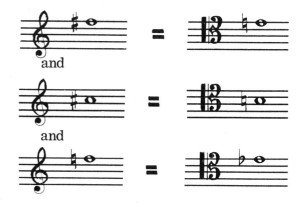

Treble Clef in E Flat

The transposition of E flat treble clef music, which is used for reading parts for E flat alto clarinets, E flat alto saxophones, E flat baritone saxophones, E flat contra-alto clarinets, *etc.* is not as difficult as the B flat treble clef transposition. To transpose a part written in E flat treble clef, the clef sign is changed from treble clef to bass clef, and three flats are added or three sharps are subtracted from the key signature.

The notes may have to be raised or lowered one octave depending on the instrument for which the part is written.

E flat Alto Saxophone

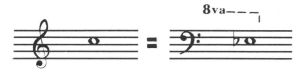

E flat Baritone Saxophone

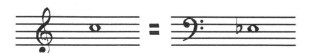

E flat Contra-Alto Clarinet

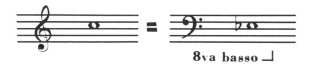

As with the transposition of accidentals in the B flat treble clef, the added accidentals are read as indicated, except those notes which are read as Bs or Es. On notes which are transposed as Bs and Es, the accidentals are lowered one half tone—sharps become naturals, naturals become flats, flats become double flats.

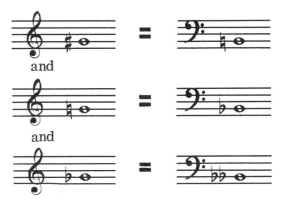

Treble Clef in F

The most difficult transposition for you may be the F treble clef transposition. The trombonist who is a brass instrument teacher needs this when playing in unison with a French horn student. The symphony trombonist may have to use this tranposition when covering the tuben in F parts in Bruckner and Richard Strauss, or the Wagner tuba parts in the *Ring*. These Wagner tuba and tuben parts are to be played by French hornists, so the symphony trombonist can always refuse to attempt to play the parts.

The brass teacher will probably learn to read the F treble clef French horn parts, by reading the treble clef and transposing the part down a perfect fifth. After a little practice, you will be able to see the notes down a fifth from where they are written.

All symphony orchestra trombonists must be able to read both tenor and alto clef. The bass trombonist will have fewer parts in the tenor and alto clefs, but must be able to read both clefs and should be prepared to read alto clef with notes written on the ledger lines below the staff.

Other trombonists will encounter parts and etudes written in the tenor and alto clefs as they study more advanced literature, and should develop the ability to read the B flat treble clef and the E flat treble clef transposition, particularly if they plan to teach brass instruments.

Chapter 27
Lip Problems

Chapped Lips

Many minor physical problems plague brass players. Chapped lips can be soothed by applying one of the commercial balms, but these preparations should be used only when they are absolutely necessary. If they are used habitually, you will become completely dependent on them. The wind, sun and cold will chap your lips, but the chapping is intensified if you habitually moisten your lips. Therefore, to avoid part of the necessity of chap cream, consciously avoid wetting your lips with the tongue except when playing trombone. Chap creams tend to protect the skin on the lips too well and keep the skin cells from shedding. As a result, your lips become thicker and less sensitive when treated continuously with chap cream. For best response and sensitivity, your lips should have only a normal layer of epidermus on them. Sparingly used, lip cream will prevent chapping, yet keep the lips sensitive and responsive.

Fever Blisters

Fever blisters are both a curse and a blessing. They tend to appear on your lip somewhere near where the rim of the mouthpiece is placed, a short time before you are due to make an important appearance as a trombonist. The appearance of a lip pimple before a public performance is almost too common to be a matter of chance. If might be that you are psychosomatically providing yourself with an excuse for a poor performance. In other words, you get a fever blister, so that *if* you do not play well, you have an excuse for doing poorly. This is not always the case, and there may be some changes in body chemistry that cause the blister.

A herpes virus can also cause the lips to swell and break out. Intense exposure to ultraviolet light is thought to encourage the virus. Once the lip begins to break out, most people treat it with patent medicines containing alcohol and camphor which dry the weeping blisters. As with other viruses, the infection is never completely removed. The infection recurs at regular intervals with some people and they should avoid long and intense exposure to sunlight (ultraviolet light) and protect their lips when exposed to the sun with appropriate salves. They should also keep the medicine available so that the drying process may be started immediately.

Care should be taken to avoid infecting pimples and fever blisters that are on your lip when the skin is broken. Keep your mouthpiece clean and do not touch your lips with your fingers or your hand. If you stop playing and practicing when you have a small pimple, you risk losing your audition, losing your position in an ensemble to someone else, losing irreplaceable practice time, and you may begin to develop a psychosomatic escape. You may develop other pimples the next time you come under stress.

When playing on a lip blemish which has not broken the skin, you should place the mouthpiece on your embouchure in its normal position even though it is uncomfortable. Do not move or disturb your embouchure and do not move the mouthpiece to a more comfortable spot and begin to develop a new embouchure. Ease the discomfort of the mouthpiece resting on or near the blemish by consciously using less mouthpiece pressure than you normally use. Playing on a minor embouchure blemish is a great aid to learning to play with less pressure.

Braces

Braces do not have to cause the problems that they usually do. Braces will teach you to use less pressure. Also, to avoid the cutting and scarring of the lips, use *Kerr's Boxing Wax* instead of the usual soft wax which most dentists recommend to cover the braces. *Kerr's Boxing Wax* is available from your dentist and is usually used when making dental models. It is packaged in strips which are about three inches wide and a foot long and is both the color and consistency of red licorice. Cut a strip of wax which is about three-eighths of an inch wide and three inches long. Press this strip onto the teeth on top of the braces. If the strip is too thick, peel the strip off of the braces, stretch it slightly and reapply it. With a little practice, you will be able to work the wax to the proper thickness so that your lip will be backed by a smooth surface. Not only does the wax cover the wires and loops of the braces, but it fills in the depressions between the teeth and in some cases provides a supporting surface that is more uniform than the player had before he acquired his braces.

Colds and Sore Throats

Head colds and sore throats can be a serious impediment, and some trombonists risk serious ear damage by blowing the infection through the Eustachian tubes into the middle ear. Any trombonist with a weakness in the throat and ears for such infection must not play when the infection is present.

On the other hand, minor discomforts from a cold must not stop you from playing. The late Emory Remington's answer to a student who complained of a cold was, "you need to play and practice so that a lot of fresh air is pumped into your lungs." Birgit Nilsson, the famous soprano, comments, "One day . . . I had a bad cold, and I discovered how I could produce a tone without hurting my throat. It was so simple . . ." Thus, she learned how to be more relaxed and efficient with her tone production, by working when she had an impediment from a cold. I have found that continuing to practice with a chest cold is an aid to learning. Trying to inhale deeply, so as not to trigger a cough, opens and relaxes the throat and breathing apparatus.

When the sinuses are stuffy, and the hearing dulled by a simple cold, it is difficult to hear the type of tone that is being produced. Avoid forcing to make the tone brilliant. Instead, feel the tone and if the tone feels easy and open, your normal sound is being projected from the bell.

In summary, the broken skin or an embouchure infection or the serious infection of the throat and ears is cause to suspend playing, **BUT** practicing and performing when only mildly disabled can be a great help to the development of correct habits. Using less mouthpiece pressure, feeling the tone in the throat, relaxing the throat and breathing mechanism in order to compensate for the presence of a lip pimple or common cold can help you learn things about playing trombone that you would have otherwise not experienced. In addition, if you can continue to meet your obligations with your ensembles, you both develop confidence for your playing under less than ideal circumstances, and also you avoid the risk of being permanently replaced by another player.

Other Lip Problems

Temporary Stiffness

There are times in every trombonist's life when the lip just does not work right. This could be caused by changes in body chemistry because the individual has either altered his living habits (eating, sleeping, exercise or the lack of it) or is caused by some type of bacteria or virus (cold or flu). The lip changes may be caused by external sources such as sunburn, windburn and excessive pressure from the mouthpiece. Problems connected with any of the above upsets will disappear as you resume normal living habits and allow your body to recover from the physical damage.

If your lips are swollen and unresponsive because you have a fever or a sunburn, you must try to continue playing in as normal a manner as possible. I assume that you are dedicated to the art and that you do not use these problems as an excuse to cease playing and practicing for a time. Most players and all professionals do not or cannot let these problems bother them. They have won their positions in the musical world by being dependable and consistent.

Do not place stress or unusual pressure on your lip during this period of recovery. As you work to make your lip respond, you cannot use extra pressure from the mouthpiece, or change your embouchure in a way that could set back or ruin your recovery. Therefore, **DO NOT PRESS AND DO NOT MAKE EMBOUCHURE ADJUSTMENTS** when playing on lips that are momentarily not right because of sunburn, fever, lack of sleep, *etc.*

If the lips should be functioning normally and there is no apparent reason for their lack of response, then you must work in a logical way to recover the lost response. First, I recommend that you change none of your procedures. There are days when everything should be all right, but as you begin playing you find that the response is not as it should be. In many cases, the response will return with a few more minutes of warm-up or by extending the easy portion of the warm-up a little longer. In other words, remain calm, slow down and do not force the warm-up to proceed at the standard pace. Many lip problems disappear in these extra few minutes.

On the other hand, it is unwise and a waste of time if the extending of the warm-up period becomes an everyday necessity. Do not fall into the habit of long warm-ups; it will become a time-wasting crutch.

Extended Stiffness

Those lip response problems that are not a one day stiffness, must be solved with careful analysis. The stiffness is caused by one of two things: a change in the warm-up or practice procedures; or the loss of confidence in playing caused by self-doubts or a traumatic experience in performance, rehearsal or audition.

Locating that one exercise in the practice routine that is causing the stiffness of the lip is difficult. All of the lip trainers and exercises that you are doing are very important features in someone's routine. But remember that what is a benefit for one person may be a problem for someone else. Realize that the difference between the success and failure is not caused by the exercise itself. The problem is probably being caused by playing the exercise incorrectly or with the wrong goal in mind, *i.e.* lip flexibility exercises must be relaxed before they are increased in speed—pushing for speed first tenses the lip and produces stiffness. Also, an easy warm-up exercise for one player is an intense lip training exercise for the less advanced performer.

If you are lucky enough to be able to remember which exercise was added to the practice routine a few days before the lip response problem began, the solution of the problem is easy. Eliminate that particular exercise! Being able to trace the trouble to one exercise or one procedure is probably too much for which to hope.

Tension in your entire production system is most probably the cause of your trouble and relaxing this hidden tension is a difficult problem. Relax as much as possible and return to an old routine. The late Emory B. Remington, "The Chief," helped eliminate these problems in his students by returning to his standard warm-up routine and following this with relaxed work in the Bach *Unaccompanied 'Cello Suites*, which were part of the student's past. The problems dissolved as the student was reestablished in the original routine.

There are a few other procedures (but don't let them become fetishes) that can be used to restore confidence and flexibility.

1. Warm the mouthpiece to above body temperature before beginning. Do this by running warm water through it for a few seconds. Then when this warmed mouthpiece first touches your lips, it helps to relax your orbicularis oris (your embouchure muscle). Some players set the mouthpiece on a steam radiator if the trip to the hot water spigot is too far away.

2. Warm your trombone completely before beginning by blowing your breath into the lead pipe (not the mouthpiece). If the instrument has the mouthpiece inserted, not only do your lips touch the cold mouthpiece, but the expanding air as it passes the throat of the mouthpiece is colder than the breath and slows the warm-up of the instrument.

3. Raise the relative humidity of the air within the instrument by blowing warm air into the instrument or by actually pouring water into the instrument.

All three of the above procedures do not directly affect the lip, but do prepare the instrument for normal performance and thus do not demand that the lip compensate for a cold, dry instrument.

In summary, to eliminate the stiffness or unresponsiveness of the lip: one, Temporarily eliminate any new exercises; two, Extend the time given to warming-up, particularly the easy portions of the routine; three, Return to set procedures of the past which always produced excellent results, and four, Take more care with the warming-up of the instrument so that the lip is not required to compensate for a cold instrument.

Chapter 28
The Contest and the Performance

A successful performance, audition or contest usually depends on several weeks of careful preparation. Contest and recital solos must be chosen several weeks before the performance, and the repertoire for an orchestral audition must be learned in detail long before the audition.

Physical Preparation

An excellent procedure for preparing for a contest or solo audition is outlined in Volume III of the Leduc edition of the Arban book for trumpet. Study this outline in detail for a complete understanding. In brief, the system begins three weeks before the performance with a daily practice schedule which consists of 75 minutes of practice with the instrument, several minutes of study without playing the instrument and several rest periods that range in length from five minutes to several hours. Fifteen days before the performance the practice time is reduced to 50 minutes; ten days before it is further reduced; and during the final week before the performance, the practice time is reduced a little more every day. Finally, the preparation consists of a short warm-up and one play through of the piece the day before and no playing, except for a brief warm-up, on the day of the contest.

In summary, the system uses intensive work at the beginning of the period and gradually discontinues practice as the day of the contest approaches. Too many players use exactly the opposite procedure. They panic and gradually intensify their work, until the lips and mind are so tired that on the final day they can hardly complete the piece.

Avoid last minute practice sessions that attempt to assure success and sometimes only prove that nothing is fully prepared. Prepare in advance so that there is no doubt about your ability to play the selection.

If the conductor of your ensemble becomes panicked and demands last minute rehearsals, do everything possible to avoid being weakened by his actions. Players cannot explain to the audience that the reason that they missed so many notes was because they had been goaded into extra rehearsals that day. The audience has no way of knowing that the poor playing was caused by the forced extra rehearsals. All things being equal, the conductor will look good and the tired performers look bad. Rest as much as possible during the panic rehearsal, use as little pressure as possible, play the loud dynamics softer than they could be played, and do not spend energy trying to play the soft passages too softly. In other words, TAKE IT EASY until performance time.

Mental Preparation

Along with the musical preparation for the performance, you must prepare yourself mentally for the job. Whether it is a contest, solo audition or orchestral audition, you should attempt to learn what the actual procedures will be. If possible, you should rehearse before hand in the room to be used. If you cannot rehearse in the room, you should try to see the room, note the possible positions of the audience, the music stand, the piano and make a quick check of the acoustics of the room. To check the acoustics you should play a few notes if possible and if not, talk, shout or clap your hands in order to get a feel for the liveness of the room. If you have a feel for the room you will not be surprised or disarmed by deadness or excessive liveness of the room when you attempt to play. How you sound in the room cannot be changed, and helpful advice from someone who suggests that you change your tone should be ignored. Do not attempt to adjust the brilliance of your tone on the spur of the moment.

Nervousness

A little nervousness may stimulate you to a better than average performance. When nervousness becomes excessive, however, the performance deteriorates rapidly, and excessive nervousness must be fought and controlled. This panic nervousness can either build up before the performance or strike after you have gone on stage. Therefore, it is wise to be prepared for the onset of nervousness at anytime and have positive steps planned to control it.

Dry Mouth

Dry mouth, caused by a lack of saliva flow, does not necessarily mean that a drink of water is needed. For some people, a drink of water is an aid, and they can keep a glass of water nearby so that they may have a sip when the dry mouth strikes. For other people, the water washes the remaining saliva away and in a few moments their mouths are drier than before the drink. You can induce a flow of saliva by chewing the sides of the base of your tongue, or by rubbing your tongue on the floor of the mouth with a sucking action. The flow of saliva can also be started by touching the tip of the tongue to a slice of lemon or a few drops of a commercial breath sweetener.

Drinking a moderate amount of water over a period of time *before* the performance aids players with chronic dry mouth and helps all performers from becoming dehydrated during the performance. On the other hand, avoid drinking from water fountains, particularly those with refrigerated water. If you drink water from a cold water fountain, you are bathing your lips in the cold water. This is particularly damaging when done after the lips have been warmed-up. You should carry a plastic or collapsable metal cup in your trombone case, so that if there are only cold water fountains available at the performance, you can get a drink by first filling the cup. You can then drink the cold water with open lips, or warm the water with your hands before drinking it and thus avoid chilling the warm lip muscle.

Shaking

Uncontrolled shaking of the body can sometimes be controlled by inhaling deeply several times. The nervous player tends to roll his shoulders forward and crouch, much like a boxer, and this may inhibit normal breathing. If you are shaking before you go on, lean against a wall, straighten your back and neck against the wall and take several deep breaths. The shaking will usually subside. If the shaking returns or begins while on stage, breathe deeply during rests, stand (or sit) erectly but not stiffly, and try to relax the muscles of the back and neck. Avoid trying to grip the floor with your feet.

Uncontrolled shaking in the breath control is caused by tensions in the lips, throat, chest, lower abdomen or many other muscles of the body. Some people encourage tenseness in their breathing, by tensing an arm, a leg, a foot or a hand. If you try to grip the floor with your feet, the muscles of your legs will tense and then this tension will creep from muscle to muscle along the route of your blood veins. As the tension reaches the lower abdomen, the breathing begins to shake. This flow of tension can be demonstrated by clenching your fist—notice how your upper arm, your shoulder and your neck begin to ache in a few minutes.

Some recommend relaxation; others suggest deep breathing to ease the trembling breath. Some believe that deep breathing makes them tremble more and they must direct their thoughts elsewhere. One colleague imagines his breath returning back through the lead pipe of the instrument to counteract the tremble of nervous breathing.

Breaking-In a Solo

In general, a positive mental attitude assures a successful solo performance and is the best control of nervousness. This positive attitude is developed by learning the composition thoroughly, proceeding through logical and well planned preparatory routines, developing correct playing habits and constantly reviewing this set of habits. Never play a new solo under formal concert conditions, but always break it in at informal gatherings and studio recitals as preparation. In addition, it is quite helpful to prepare mentally for the performance by imagining everything about the event (lights, the sight of the audience, the darkened house, the heat of the stage, the odors of the concert hall) while rehearsing the work in the hall of the performance. This type of preparation is further explained in Maltz, *Psychocybernetics.*

In particular, you should remind yourself of your capabilities, and realize that the audience favors you and wants to hear the best possible performance. There is no good reason why you should not expect to do nearly as well as you can.

Performance After a Wait

It is always best to warm-up as near to the performance time as possible, but there are times when you must sit quietly for several minutes before playing. At auditions or contests, you should anticipate the time for your performance and begin silent (or nearly silent) preparations a few minutes before hand. First, warm your instrument completely by exhaling warm breath into it for a few minutes. Warm the mouthpiece by holding it in your hand or by placing it in a pocket next to your body. Do not warm the mouthpiece with the lips, because a cold mouthpiece will chill your warm lip muscle. Within a minute or so before the performance, buzz your lips in the mouthpiece while holding a wadded handkerchief around its stem to muffle the sound. Finally, just before playing, sound a few warm-up notes while tuning to the piano. Playing one note, the tuning note, is usually not enough and you should test a few notes related to the tuning note.

When playing fanfares, church anthems, church recessionals and symphonic compositions where the wait may last 30 minutes, your preparation will be the same as above, except that you cannot play any tuning notes. You should prepare for these situations when practicing by warming-up normally, waiting for several minutes, silently re-warming the instrument and the mouthpiece, buzzing the lips in the muffled mouthpiece and then playing without tuning or sounding any preliminary notes.

Stage Deportment as Soloist

Stage deportment must be rehearsed, otherwise you will be distracted by the last minute concerns about how to enter and leave the stage.

Entrance

Many players are so shaken by their entrance that it takes them several minutes to recover their composure completely and the solo may be finished by that time. Many novices enter the stage area too slowly, look at the audience with a silly grin and then proceed to wander in the general direction of their position for the performance. If the entrance is slow enough, they arrive at their place and prepare to take a bow (as they had planned to do) and find that the applause has stopped. They are surprised by the situation and it continues to bother them as they begin to play.

The entrance should be made with all possible speed. It should not be hurried, but your stride should be lengthened so that you get to your place as soon as possible. Walk with a style that is both business-like and relaxed. Do not saunter or allow your body to jangle. Do not look at the audience directly until you have reached your position on stage and do not smile unless you are inclined to do so naturally. A fake smile very easily appears to a strange audience as a somewhat stupid grin, and the question occurs to some, "What is he laughing about?"

First Bows

Once in place on stage, and *after* your accompanist has arrived at the piano, acknowledge the applause with a bow which is a relaxed bend at the waist. Allow your head to drop naturally, and do not attempt to duck your head as a substitute for a genuine bow. Do two things during the applause and the silence that follows. First, thank the audience for their attendance and their applause with a bow or two. Allow the sound of the applause and the presence of the audience to lift both your mental spirits and the adrenalin flow of your body, so that the performance will benefit from this added lift. Secondly, do not rush into the beginning of the performance. Collect your thoughts, tune with care but without delay, and then focus your concentration on the opening mood of the composition to be performed. Allow enough time for the audience to settle and then begin the performance. If there is an introduc-

tion to the solo, signal the accompanist that you are ready with a slight nod.

The Performance

During the introduction and the interludes which follow, you should listen to the accompaniment and remain as motionless as possible. Do not upstage the accompaniment with distracting activity. Delay all facial grimaces of checking your embouchure or moistening your lip until the last possible moment before beginning to play. Release the condensation from the trombone silently with the slide held to the side and slightly behind where you are standing. Audiences do not like to see the release of condensation and besides you may slip on it when leaving the stage if you place it in front of your feet. Avoid spraying the slide while the accompaniment is being played. Do not wipe your face or your mouthpiece with a cloth! Waving a white cloth is quite distracting to a sophisticated audience. If spraying the slide or wiping your face must be done, partially turn away from the audience and perform the necessary acts with slow, gentle and discreet movements so that the effect of the accompaniment is not lost. Wipe your face or spray your slide *only* during breaks between movements or between compositions. The flourishing of a towel is completely unnecessary *at any time;* use a folded handkerchief.

The ending of the piece is as important to the mood of the composition as the beginning. For those compositions which end with a flourish, the instrument can be removed from your lips and lowered to rest position with a motion which is more rapid and more emphatic than normal. This is a visual signal to the audience that the piece has been completed, and it acts as a trigger for the beginning of the applause. For pieces that end slowly and softly, you should remain still for a few seconds and sustain the mood into the silence before relaxing. When the accompaniment completes the composition, you should remain attentive to the end. The trombone should be held in playing position if the accompaniment is not too long, or slowly lowered to rest position if the accompaniment will last several seconds. In no case should you make any rapid motion until the piece has been completed. Do not upstage the accompaniment. Finally, let go or relax by lowering your shoulders or by moving your feet to signal the end of the composition.

Final Bows

Finally, you acknowledge the applause and leave. One or two bows should be sufficient, before sharing the applause with a nod or gesture toward the accompanist or the conductor of the ensemble. At this point, they may take a bow alone, or your bow can be syncronized to coincide with theirs.

Exit

After two or three bows, leave the stage area with a swift yet unhurried walk. As when you entered, the length of the applause is somehow predetermined by the audience as a group. Most audiences will lengthen their applause slightly so that you will be allowed to disappear behind the side curtain before they stop. Other audiences will stop when they intended to, and leave you to finish your walk in embarrassed silence.

Additional Bows

Once you are out of sight, you should take two steps and **STOP**. Do *not* begin a conversation with friends backstage. Do *not* express your relief that it is over. Do *not* criticize the accompanist or yourself for errors or problems which occurred during the performance. After you take those two steps and stop, you must listen to the applause for not more than two seconds. If the volume is diminishing during those two seconds, it will probably stop very soon and the performance has truly come to a close. If the volume of the applause is not diminishing in those two seconds, you should return immediately to the stage area and thank the audience with an additional bow or two. If after arriving back on stage, you believe that the applause will not continue for much longer, you should take your bows within a few feet of the exit rather than waste time returning to the center of the stage. After thanking the audience with two or three bows, depart quickly and take your place two steps outside the exit. A third bow may be in order, and the decision for this bow is made in the same amount of time as it took to decide the second bow, two seconds. The mutual respect, appreciation and warmth between the soloist and the audience cannot be shared with the soloist standing outside while the audience applauds an empty stage.

Many soloists delay their second and third bows for fear that they will arrive on stage just as the applause stops. They have seen this happen to at least one person, and they do not want it to happen to them. True, it is a mutually embarrassing situation, but usually it was caused by the soloist staying off stage too long. Either the performer was not paying attention to the audience, or took too long to decide whether the applause was really going to be continued. If the soloist takes too long to return for a bow, the audience will tire of applauding an empty stage, loose their concentration, begin to think about other things and decide with the same single mind which determines the length of their applause that the soloist is not going to return. The inexperienced may choose to wait three seconds (instead of two) before deciding to return to the stage, and in those three seconds anyone will know whether the audience would like to applaud any longer. For further insurance against the possibility of arriving on stage to silence, some soloists touch the side curtain as they begin to move toward the stage. This movement of the curtain signals the audience that the soloist is returning for a bow and will reappear in a moment. This helps everyone and prevents mutual embarrassment.

Etiquette

If the soloist and accompanist are both male or both female, there are no problems with stage etiquette. The soloist enters first and, depending on the position of the piano, the soloist can either lead or follow the accompanist on departure. On second bows, which are close to the exit, the soloist can lead the entrance and the accompanist can lead the exit thus avoiding the problems of who leaves first and whether one person crosses in front of the other. More commonly, the soloist always leads on the first exit, and crosses in front of the accompanist to exit after a second bow.

When the soloist is female and the accompanist is male, the pianist will always follow, and on second bows he must stand so that the soloist can cross in front of him when she departs. He should take care not to stand in her way as she attempts to exit.

When the soloist is male and the pianist is female, the rules are changed (not withstanding the women's liberation movement). The pianist enters and departs first. On second bows, the soloist can lead the pianist on by the hand, but this would be the only circumstance where the soloist would precede the pianist. Otherwise, the accompanist enters ahead of the soloist, and crosses in front of him to lead the departure. The soloist should rehearse all stage action before hand with someone in the audience to criticize the action and offer advice. The action should be rehearsed for speed and *in concert dress*, particularly with a male soloist and a female pianist. High heels and a narrow formal dress could greatly slow the speed that was rehearsed with a street dress and moderate heels. The female pianist should move with her greatest speed and grace so that the applause will not be wasted on labored entrances and departures.

The page turner is invisible by present day concert manners. He or she enters last, departs last and moves as inconspicuously as possible.

Stage Deportment with a Large Ensemble

The stage deportment of the players in a large ensemble is just as important as that of a soloist. Although often ignored by most of the audience, there have been times when poor deportment has led to the firing of a player. Particularly in highly competitive positions, no deviation from proper deportment is tolerated. Notice how still both television and symphony orchestra players remain while resting during or between pieces. Their posture is not rigid in a military way, but they remain motionless with their heads and eyes facing forward. Just as you do not flourish a towel or handkerchief in a solo recital, you do not withdraw and replace music in the folder in a way that distracts the audience and breaks the mood. Many amateur groups forget the conductor and the audience when one number is completed, and they begin preparing for the next composition. They return one piece and remove the next piece from the folder while the conductor attempts to acknowledge the applause. This music change looks like a flock of white winged birds about to take off. The mood of the concert is further ruined when the conductor attempts to have the group stand to accept some of the applause. Since they are not paying attention, the group is not aware of the request to stand and they get to their feet one by one rather than as a group.

A professional group is attentive to the conductor and the audience during applause. If the music for the next part of the program must be prepared, it is removed from the folder by curling it so that it is not seen by the audience. The movement of the arms, head and torso are restricted so that there is no illusion of movement, and the conductor is watched so that should they be asked to rise they can do so as a group. This standing and sitting is usually controlled by the concertmeister (or a solo woodwind player in a wind ensemble), and the group stands when he stands and sits when he sits. Should the conductor enter from the wings and gesture for the group to rise without going to the podium, another person should indicate to the concertmeister that the signal to stand has been given. The group should not sit again until the conductor has left the stage, and since the concertmeister cannot see this either, the principal 'cellist usually gives him a cue.

The trombonist may have the feeling that since he is seated in or near the back row that he is not seen and therefore the rules of deportment do not apply to him. The deportment is the same whether it is a solo recital or a large symphony orchestra. Members of the audience have good eye sight and some have expensive binoculars. One of these persons may be the manager or the conductor's wife. The trombonists must remain attentive even during tacit movements of a long symphony. Their eyes and heads must face forward, and if they must exchange information such as what the count of a long rest is, it must be whispered through still lips while looking straight ahead or signalled with the hands or fingers which are resting on the thighs well below the line of sight of even the highest seat in the balcony.

The basis of deportment is a respect for music, a respect for the conductor and a respect for the audience. Everyone benefits when nothing is done to distract from the performance. Most decisions regarding deportment which have not been discussed in this chapter, can be solved logically if the respect for and mutual appreciation of music are considered first and foremost by all concerned.

Chapter 29
Performance in Large Ensembles

A trombonist in a large ensemble has problems similar to those of any other instrumentalist who sits five or more rows away from the conductor. In addition, he has problems that are particular to his own instrument.

Successful performance with either a symphony orchestra, large concert band or medium-sized wind ensemble depends on the following rules:

Anticipate the Beat

The trombonist must play slightly ahead of the beat, particularly in rapid staccato passages. If the note does not precede the beat, the trombonist is criticized for being late. The lateness of the sound is sometimes attributed to the distance between the trombonist and the conductor, but since sound travels over 700 miles an hour, the difference in time between a tone produced five feet from the conductor and one produced 50 feet from him is very slight (approximately 4/100 of a second). Occasionally the conductor will explain that to fill that long pipe of the instrument requires an anticipation of the beat, but again, filling the pipe at the speed of sound takes only about 1/100 of a second. There are good physical and psychological reasons, though, for hearing the trombones (and other distant and low pitched instruments) as being late. For a full explanation consult: Fritz Winckel, *Music, Sound and Sensation: A Modern Exposition* (New York: Dover Publications, Inc., 1960, 1967) p. 173. In brief, the tone of the trombone does not reach full intensity until a fraction of a second after it is begun; the ear does not perceive low tones as well and as rapidly as higher tones; and the resonance of the room increases the volume of the note after the note has been started. As a result, although the note was begun on time, the perception of the attack is delayed and the conductor (and the audience) will hear the attack as **LATE**. The Winckel formula for the calculation of this sense of lateness is stated as follows:

$$\tau_{res} = \sqrt{\tau_1{}^2 + \tau_2{}^2 + \tau_3{}^2 + \ldots}$$

The formula is of no value to you except to remind you that if you do not anticipate the beat, you will be late. When standing back stage near a good trombone section, notice how on any moving and rhythmic passage they drive or push the beat constantly. Of course, the trombone section must learn to feel this drive as a group or the ensemble will be poor. How much to anticipate the beat is not something that each player does on his own. The amount of push is determined by the principal of the section and the other members of the section place their notes precisely with his.

Develop an Internal Sense of Ensemble

In a soft or legato phrase, it is difficult to see the exact point of some conductors' beats, and it is necessary for the section to develop an internal sense of ensemble. If each trombonist calculates the point of the beat by himself, poor ensemble will result. On the other hand, if the section learns to feel the attack and breathe together, the ensemble of the section will likely be better. (The attack may not be exactly where the conductor desired, but at least members of the section are spared the individual disapproval of the conductor). For the best ensemble, the principal player should breathe in a way that tells the other members of the section when the attack will be made. With experience, the ensemble of the trombone section will improve without a distinct beat from the conductor.

Never Play too Loudly

Remember that at the concert the conductor's gesture may indicate more tone, even though your volume was more than adequate during all of the rehearsals. Do not assume that the volume levels of the concert have changed from rehearsal. Once you have passed a safe level of volume, you will probably crack or split notes and the most unsophisticated listener knows when a note was missed. Therefore, remain within safe levels of volume and, if necessary, raise the bell of your trombone an extra inch or so, if the conductor *truly* wants more volume. Try to provide the *true* volume desired, but **DO NOT CRACK!**

Develop a Breath Attack

Although seldom discussed and seldom taught, it is possible to begin a note without a stroke of the tongue. Conductors like to have strings and clarinets enter at a very soft dynamic level and occasionally attempt to make the trombones enter in the same manner. An attack without using the tongue is particularly useful when the passage is very soft and the point of the beat is indefinite. To develop this attack, the lips, throat and mouth cavity must be set as if you are already playing the note. Slightly before the attack is desired, the air stream is started and momentarily the note appears.

Always Have a Breath Reserve

In rehearsal, do not play a phrase which demands all of one breath. Maintain a reserve, learn to breathe deeper or sneak a slight extra breath into the middle of the phrase. At the concert, the phrase may be slightly louder, the phrase may be slightly slower, a *fermata* may be held slightly longer or your nervousness may use a little extra breath. If you do not have a reserve of breath, the phrase will not be completed successfully. Always play phrases with a reserve supply of breath. This rule is somewhat related to the third rule, and demands that you never pass a point at which you have a safe margin of control.

Be Prepared for Different Beat Patterns

Under the pressure of the performance, the conductor may place an extra curl on a certain beat, over cue solo entrances, or conduct in a style that pleases the audience, but is far more flamboyant than he used in rehearsal. Although these different conducting patterns are disturbing, you must be prepared for them and not let them destroy the ensemble of the section or distract you so that you miss notes. Your performance should imitate the rehearsal. Do not make any on the spot changes to accomodate the more vivacious conducting patterns.

Assist Your Colleagues

Develop a spirit of cooperation among the other players of the section so that the performance in public sounds as professional as possible. Occasionally when a phrase ends *diminuendo*, the section may sense that a colleague is tiring and cannot play any softer without loosing control of his note. In such cases, the trombone section will not continue the *diminuendo* as rehearsed, but continue to sustain the note to help support him instead. In cases where the conductor is insistent that the passage be played softer, it seems better for all to assume a pained expression on your faces and **HOLD A SAFE DYNAMIC,** rather than continue the *diminuendo* and let a colleague of the section fail. The same cooperation applies to a momentary intonation problem which is caused by fatigue or nervousness. As the pitch begins to change slightly, the other members of the section should give in the direction of the change, if they can do so without jeopardizing themselves and without causing intonation problems with other sections of the ensemble.

Many of the individual's problems with large ensemble playing can be solved by a cooperative spirit among the members of the trombone section. The development of sensitivity among the various members of the section can be improved by playing trombone ensembles and by occasionally warming-up in unison. The difference between a trombone section that is never a concern to the conductor and the section that is constantly displeasing him is that the good section has an ensemble sense and a cooperative professionalism that solves or eliminates their problems before the conductor hears them.

Chapter 30
The Euphonium and Baritone

Sooner or later it is to your advantage to learn to play baritone and to develop a competent control of the instrument. Throughout this chapter, the euphonium and baritone will be referred to as the euphonium, even though there are differences between the instruments, or at least there is a difference between tone concepts when playing them.

Mouthpieces

When playing euphonium, you should choose a mouthpiece that has the same rim as the one you use on trombone. This will prevent the development of embouchure problems. Vincent Bach notes that a brass mouthpiece tends to break down the fat particles in the lip muscle as it "rides in place" on the embouchure and in time, even though you are not using excessive pressure, a "groove" is worn into the lip muscle. He believes that this "groove" is good because it enables you to "find the spot" when placing the mouthpiece on your embouchure. He believes that you can become proficient on more than one brass instrument if the mouthpieces of the instruments are exactly the same or are quite different in size. With all mouthpieces the same size, you develop only one groove in your lip. With mouthpieces which are quite different, you develop several individual grooves in your lip.

DO NOT use a euphonium mouthpiece that is only close to the same size as your trombone mouthpiece. Two similar mouthpieces will develop their own grooves, but these grooves will be so close together that the two grooves will become one: then neither mouthpiece can find its spot. Therefore, you must use a euphonium mouthpiece which has a diameter exactly like or quite different from your trombone mouthpiece, so that only one lip groove or two separate and distinct lip grooves will be developed for the placement of the mouthpiece.

Note: This concern about the size of the mouthpiece is limited to the diameter of the mouthpiece and the width and contour of the cushion. The mouthpiece you use on the euphonium may have cup, throat and orifice dimensions which are quite different from the trombone mouthpiece and not cause any embouchure damage.

Holding the Instrument

Any one of several grips can be used to hold the euphonium so that the mouthpiece meets your lips at the proper spot with the correct angle. Avoid resting the instrument on your lap, **UNLESS** this is the best position. In most cases, resting the instrument on your lap puts the vertical placement of the mouthpiece too high or too low and has the mouthpiece meeting your embouchure at the wrong angle. If you rest the instrument on your lap and play on a different embouchure, or contract your neck and jut out your jaw in order to reach the proper spot, you will ruin your trombone embouchure.

Usually the instrument must be held with your left hand or cradled with your left arm so that the mouthpiece meets your face properly. The exact method is determined by the shape of the instrument and the playing technique of the euphoniumist. If the instrument has only three valves and no triggers, the left hand and arm posture can be any one of several possibilities. The most comfortable one can be chosen after experimentation. If the instrument has a trigger that extends the third valve slide, then the instrument must be held so that a finger or the thumb of the left hand can reach the trigger. If the instrument has a trigger that extends the main tuning slide, it will probably be necessary to cradle the instrument with your arm so that the entire left hand is free to move the trigger. If the instrument has a side mounted fourth valve, the left arm must support the instrument so that a finger of the left hand can operate the valve with dexterity. Some players who first learned to play a euphonium with a side mounted fourth valve, like to continue to use the left hand (rather than the fourth finger of the right hand) to operate the fourth valve after changing to a euphonium with four valves mounted in a row. They find that one of the first fingers of the left hand has more strength and agility than the fourth finger of the right hand.

No matter which grip is chosen, it is important that the euphonium be held so that the mouthpiece rests on the embouchure at the proper spot and meets the jaw at the correct angle. At first, the grip needed may be uncomfortable and quite tiring, but the muscles of your left arm will adapt to the demands placed on them, and with a little work the discomfort will vanish.

Choosing the Instrument

Euphoniums have several distinct shapes and sizes. The trombonist usually has no choice; the instrument that is available is the one he plays, but should a choice be possible, there are several items for you to consider.

Small Bore Versus Large Bore

The small bore euphonium is similar in bore to the dimensions of a .500″ bore trombone and a mouthpiece from one usually fits the other. Larger bore euphoniums are becoming more popular in the United States and their mouthpieces are larger than that of the .500″ bore trombone yet smaller than the mouthpieces used in the symphony bore (.547″) trombones. As a result, neither a small nor a large shanked trombone mouthpiece will fit this larger euphonium. A sleeve or adapter shank is usually provided, or can be purchased separately, so that a small bore trombone mouthpiece can be fitted into the larger bore euphonium. The sleeve is placed in the lead pipe of the euphonium and the mouthpiece is inserted into this sleeve. There are acoustical objections to this procedure, because the air stream now has to make two steps into the main pipe (from the mouthpiece to the sleeve, and from the sleeve into the lead pipe). Although the acoustical argument is valid in theory, in practice it does not cause problems for most players.

Bell Front Versus Upright Bell

The bell front euphonium projects its tone better than an upright euphonium when played in a marching band or an ensemble that is not using an acoustical shell. The player is not as bothered by showers of confetti, rain or snow when playing outdoors. The projection of tone, which is desired in outdoor work, is objectionable to some conductors for indoor concerts, particularly when a stage shell is used. The upright bell diffuses the sound upward and projects the tone outward by reflection off of the roof of the stage shell.

It is possible to rotate the bell of some instruments so that it is pointed forward during outdoor work and pointed upward during indoor concerts. An alternative is to purchase two bells, one bell front and one upright, and attach the proper one as needed.

More and more solo and ensemble compositions are scored for muted euphonium, and if mutes are to be used, the upright bell is more desirable. Although it is possible to construct a bent cone mute for a bell front euphonium, it is easier to buy or construct a straight coned mute for a euphonium with an upright bell.

Tuning Triggers

Baritones and euphoniums have intonation problems just as any other brass or woodwind instrument. Without some device to adjust the intonation, you must lip the untrue notes or simply play out of tune. All brass instruments have overtones that are sharp and flat, and valved brass instruments have certain valve combinations that are out of tune (usually sharp). Some intonation problems can be solved by using alternate fingerings, but other tuning problems (particularly on three-valved instruments) must be solved with triggers or slide rings which can be used to momentarily extend the length of the valve slide.

All brass instruments need a way of lengthening the tubing when valve combinations one and two, one and three, and one, two and three are used. In order to lengthen the pipe for these combinations, some manufacturers have installed a trigger or finger loop that will extend either the first or the third valve slide. A third valve slide will flatten one and three, or one, two and three valve combinations, but if all three combinations are to be lowered, the trigger must be on the first slide. The third valve slide may be set a few notes ahead of time in preparation for the combination and it is not necessary to retract the slide immediately unless the combination of two and three is the next note. On the other hand, one and two tends to be sharp, and if the trigger is placed on the first slide it can work to flatten all three combinations (one and two, one and three, and one, two and three). Since many of the notes preceding the sharp combinations are first valve alone, the first valve slide must be extended at the last moment and retracted immediately or it will flatten the first valve notes also.

A main tuning slide trigger has an advantage in that it will adjust any note no matter what valve combination is being used. Some triggers only extend (flatten the notes), others have a spring barrel arrangement which holds the slide at a middle point and then the slide can be contracted to sharpen a note and extended to flatten a note. With the triggers that only extend, the euphonium could be tuned sharp and then you could keep constant pressure on the trigger to keep it extended until you reached a note that had to be raised. You could then relax the pressure and allow the slide to contract.

The disadvantage of main slide tuning triggers is that it cannot be preset for a certain note, like a first or third valve slide can be. Since it influences all notes, it must be set at the instant the adjustment is needed and released immediately afterward.

Many trombonists prefer the main tuning slide trigger

to the others, apparently because they have become used to humoring all the notes with the main slide, and they adapt to the idea of a left hand slide more readily than the individual valve triggers. Also, since trombonists do not lip notes into tune on trombone, they find that lipping notes on a euphonium is very tiring and prefer a slide so that they can fix the intonation without lipping.

Fourth Valve

The fourth valve on a euphonium is used to solve some intonation problems and also to extend the range of the instrument downward. It also adds weight and expense to the euphonium, but the weight and expense are negligible as compared to the advantages.

The fourth valve is either placed beside the other three valves and is to be operated with the fourth finger of the right hand, or it is placed at the side of the instrument and is to be operated with one of the fingers of the left hand. When the fourth valve is depressed alone, it lowers the fundamental overtone series a perfect fourth, just as the valve combination one and three does. Since one and three is usually sharp, the fourth valve is tuned either in tune or slightly flat. The one, two and three combination is very sharp and by using two and four instead, these notes are more nearly in tune. The fourth valve on some instruments can be extended an additional half tone, making other notes in tune and extending the range a half tone lower. (See the section later in this chapter for a complete discussion of intonation problems).

The fourth valve extends the lower range of the instrument an additional *major third*, **NOT A PERFECT FOURTH!** The tubing will lower the open concert B flat a perfect fourth, but when used with other combinations, its effectiveness is diminished. If it is tuned so that it lowers concert B flat an augmented fourth, it will extend the range of the instrument nearly a perfect fourth. The fingering for the lower register when the fourth valve is tuned to a perfect fourth below B flat is:

Notice that only a few of the notes are in tune. The other notes must be lipped or compensated for with a tuning trigger.

Automatic Intonation Systems

It is possible to build a euphonium which will automatically add the extra tubing length needed for certain valve combinations, and subtract it again when it is not needed. One manufacturer has a patented system in which the air column is diverted through additional tubing when certain combinations of valves are depressed. The advantages of the system are offset in part by the increased cost and weight of the instrument, and the inflexibility of the combinations. On certain notes which are played sharp by most performers, the compensation system does not operate, and without any triggers to lower the note, you *must* lip the note flatter or use cumbersome alternate fingerings. Another maker has a compensating system which also has a main slide trigger. The player then has the advantage of the intonation of an automatic compensating system while retaining fine control of the intonation with the main slide trigger.

Tone Production

The trombonist usually finds that the euphonium is quite responsive and free blowing as compared to the pressures used for tone production on the trombone. At the same time, this free response usually inhibits the trombonist's development of an excellent euphonium tone.

Trombonists tend to continue to blow the euphonium much like the trombone, rather than developing a more yawning, low pressure approach to the instrument. They tend to overcontrol the air stream, almost spitting at the throat of the mouthpiece, and as a result, they play with a bright and dry sound.

To develop your euphonium sound, use the warm-up and lip training routines used on trombone, yet constantly work to use less breath pressure with a warm airflow. Work to find that combination of control and relaxation which encourages the euphonium to respond to its own resonance. The breath is focused into the instrument, or through the instrument. Particularly when playing notes using two or more valves, the tone may be dull and lack luster. The lower notes must almost be coaxed to respond with a tone quality that is similar to notes that are fingered open or with just one valve.

Care and Maintenance

Oiling the Valves

The valves should be oiled regularly and this should be done every few days, before a regular practice period. Occasionally, the new oil will dislodge dirt that will soon foul the action of the valves; therefore, you should not oil the valves immediately before a concert unless absolutely necessary.

Oiling euphonium valves is the same as oiling trumpet valves, but because the instrument is larger and more difficult to hold, you have a better chance of dropping oil on your clothing, scratching the valves and their casings, stripping the threads on the caps and dropping the valve springs on the floor. Carefully follow these steps:

1. Hold the euphonium so that the valves are upright (perpendicular to the floor). Unscrew the retaining ring and remove the valve from the casing. (If the euphonium is not held so that the valve casing is upright, the valve spring will fall out onto the floor and will soon be stepped on.)

2. After removing the valve, wipe the valve and the inside of the casing with a lint free cloth (not facial tissues) and then apply several drops of valve oil to the valve.

3. Carefully return the valve to the casing, and note that near the top of the valve there is a key (a little bump) which is supposed to fit into a key way (a groove) inside the valve casing. Since the key can be easily smashed, broken or bent, slide the valve into the casing carefully.

4. Carefully tighten the retaining ring. The threads on the valve casing and the retaining ring are made of brass, a rather soft metal, so carefully align the threads before screwing on the cap or the threads will be stripped.

Spinning the valve in the casing to find the key way will add scratches to the plating of the valve and the side of the casing. Removing the valve from the casing in a rough manner will also scratch both the valve and the casing. Notice the placement of the valve spring. A few euphoniums have the spring attached to the valve, but most simply have the spring resting unattached at the bottom of the valve casing. If the casing is to be wiped out, reach down into the casing with a finger and remove the spring. (Remember to replace it before inserting the valve again.)

Each valve is different. Each has the ports placed at a different point, and even though any valve can be returned to any casing, the instrument cannot be played if the valves are mixed. Therefore, it is wise to oil and replace each valve individually. Most manufacturers have placed numbers on the valves somewhere to aid in the indentification of them.

If the valves become mixed and the numbers cannot be found, follow this procedure: Begin by locating the second valve. Pull out the second valve slide and put a valve into the casing. When the second valve is depressed, both valve ports can be seen through the open valve slide. Once the second valve has been found, replace the valve slide and install the other two valves. There is now a 50–50 chance of having installed them correctly. Play a chromatic scale; if the valves are in the correct casings there is no problem. If some notes of the scale do not sound, reverse the first and third valves.

Cleaning

If the euphonium has just been removed from storage, it is best to assume that its care has been neglected and that a complete cleaning is in order.

For a complete cleaning, remove the valves, the valve springs, the lower valve caps and all of the slides. NOTE: there are many crooks in a euphonium which are supposed to be soldered permanently, so do not mistake them for slides and attempt to remove them. On the other hand, some valves have several removable crooks, so check all of them. Before removing a slide which appears to be stuck look to see whether it is a permanent crook or a removable slide. Look at the construction of the slides that have already been removed and compare them with the slide in question and with the other joints that you know are permanent. Slides usually have ferrules (small metal collars) and permanent joints usually do not. The stuck slide can be removed by using a rope or twisted handkerchief and a few drops of penetrating oil. If penetrating oil must be applied, be sure to allow sufficient time for it to work. (See Erich Brand, p. 144, or Clayton H. Thiede, p. 8).

Wash all of the euphonium using water which is no hotter than lukewarm. A little mild soap can be used if desired. Scrub the inside of the mouthpiece with a mouthpiece brush. Use a plastic coated metal snake brush to remove dirt and fungus from the inside of the valve slides and the main tubing of the instrument.

A euphonium does not need a complete washing very often. Once or twice a year is usually sufficient. Between major cleanings, the mouthpiece and the lead pipe should be cleaned with water and a brush. The lead pipe must be kept clean because an accumulation of dirt and fungus will narrow the bore and distort the tone. Also, the dirt will ooze down the pipe and foul the valve action. Cleaning and oiling the valves only helps temporarily in these cases, because as soon as the euphonium is played again, the ooze begins to foul the valves. The valves will not be dependable until the ooze is washed from the lead pipe.

Lubricate and reassemble the euphonium after it has been washed and dried. Replace weak valve springs or stretch each one a little before returning them to the valve casings. Some players switch the stronger springs from the third and fourth valves to the first and second valves and *vice versa*.

Valve Slides

Valve slides and the tuning slide should be lubricated with petroleum jelly (Vaseline), tallow or clarinet cork grease. Remember to depress the valve before removing or inserting the valve slides. If the valve is not depressed, the compression or vacuum of the moving slide tends to make the valves leak and places a strain on the walls of the valve slide.

Condensation

Almost every baritone and euphonium has one point in its tubing where condensation will tend to collect. The first time this collection of water occurs with your new euphonium, it may take quite a while to discover its location. First, empty the water from the main tuning slide. Second, remove the water from each of the valve slides. If the valve slide has a water key, depress the valve, open the key and blow air into the instrument. If the slide does not have a water key, remove the slide, **AFTER** depressing the valve. Remember gravity! The instrument must be in a normal upright position if you expect to find water in the "bottom" of a valve slide. Many people tilt the instrument and pour the condensation back into the instrument as they try to pull the valve slide.

Finally, there is usually one spot on every euphonium that is not near a slide or water key. After a week or two of practice, the condensation finds this specific spot and the gurgle of condensation begins. To find this water, blow air **GENTLY** into the instrument and determine whether the water is in the main tubing. Gently blow air and press each valve down individually if the water is not in the main slide. Remember to blow **GENTLY**. With force, the water is blown up the pipe and the gurgling stops temporarily, but in a few moments the water returns and the gurgling begins again. If the condensation is in the main pipe, study the instrument and guess in which low point on the pipe the water has likely to have collected. Select the smaller bore tubes first. Then study how the instrument can be rotated (clockwise or counter-clockwise) so that the water will run into a section of tubing where there is a valve slide or a water key.

If the condensation is in a certain valve, first check the tubing of the valve slide. Follow a tube that leaves the valve. If that tube **BOTH** begins and ends in a valve casing, it is a valve slide. (If the tube leaves the valve and goes on to another part of the instrument, it is part of the main tubing). Study the tubing and select a low point where the moisture could collect. Then rotate the instrument so that the water will run to a relief point.

Some tubas must be rotated twice to get this moisture to a relief point, but most euphoniums need to be rotated only once. If the moisture is in the main tubing, it probably is in a small bend in the tubing as it enters or leaves the valve section. If the moisture is trapped in a valve slide, it is probably in the third or fourth valve. On some euphoniums the tubing for the third and fourth valves have two slides instead of one, yet many still do not have enough slides to take care of the condensation without rotating the instrument.

Valve Oil

Some euphonium valves do not operate well with regular trumpet valve oil. Some players prefer to use straight kerosene. Others use kerosene with some tincture of wintergreen added to kill the kerosene smell. Others add a few drops of olive oil, so that the oil adheres to the valves longer. On euphoniums on which the lead pipe enters the valve casing without making any bends, the moisture of the breath washes the oil off the valves very rapidly. With these instruments, some players have increased the amount of olive oil that is mixed with the kerosene. Others add a few drops of olive oil or regular household oil to a regular brand of commercial valve oil, to make it adhere to the valves for a longer period of time.

Building Technique on Euphonium

The trombonist who is learning to play the euphonium does not have to work through all the method books that a beginning euphonium player would have to study. The trombonist needs to learn the fingering technique of the euphonium as rapidly as possible, and does not need all of the fundamental work of learning rhythms and the names of the lines and spaces. Thus, after you have learned the fingerings, you should begin work in advanced technical exercises. The scale and arpeggio exercises by Pares are excellent for the development of the automatic patterns that every euphoniumist must learn.

All technical exercises must be performed with precision and a steady tempo. Technique must be built over a period of time, and you should not expect to be able to cram and get any long term results.

In addition to Pares, H. Clarke's *Technical Studies* should be mastered, and some time should be spent with Anton Slama's *66 Etudes in All Keys.* As your technique advances, study the trumpet etudes such as A. Laurent's *Etudes Pratiques* and the *36 Etudes* by T. Charlier. One of the best books for the development of both technique and the characteristic tone of the euphonium is *all three* volumes of Bordogni's *Melodious Etudes* as edited by J. Rochut.

Trill Fingerings

Euphonium trill fingerings are the same as trumpet trill fingerings. The most common is the substitution of third valve for the first and second combination. This substitution is not only used for trills but in rapid passages, examples of which are found in Clarke's *Technical Studies.* For the most part, the third valve has a noticeably poorer tone quality than one and two, and is quite flat. In the long run you should develop the correct fingerings, rather than take many of the suggestions as they are found in technical studies such as Clarke.

Intonation—Euphonium

The euphonium player has three types of intonation problems. One. The overtone series of all brass instruments is only approximately correct, even on the best instruments; two, the valves used to increase the length of the fundamental pipe do not always add the correct amount of tubing; and three, the intonation of the various scales, other than equal-temperament, cannot be built into the instrument.

The Overtone Series

Although it is theoretically possible to construct a piece of tubing which will produce an in-tune overtone series, thus far it has not been done. As soon as the pipe is bent, the overtone series is changed, and with the several bends necessary for the construction of a euphonium, the problems are overwhelming. Over the years, through experimentation, various instrument designs have been improved, though not perfected. The modern euphonium has an overtone series which is more nearly in tune than many older models, but it is not perfect.

Most euphoniums have a fifth mode of vibration which is somewhat flat, a sixth mode which is usually sharp, and sometimes they have an eighth and a third mode which are sharp. You must humor notes which are on these modes either by lipping the note, by using some sort of slide device or by substituting an alternate

fingering. Work with a Stroboconn when learning the intonation of a new euphonium so that you will not allow your imagination to influence your ear and so that you will not learn to tolerate poor intonation.

The Valves

If the euphonium is to be completely chromatic, it must be possible to lower a note on the open horn through six half steps. To do this at least three valves are needed. When an open pipe is lowered one half tone, the total length of the tubing is increased by about seven percent. If the open tone is in tune, the second valve can be made long enough to lower that note exactly one half tone. As the pitch is lowered it takes a little more pipe with each step (notice the gradual stretching of the slide positions on the chart in Chapter 17). Thus to lower an open pipe one whole step, the pipe is lengthened seven percent of the open pipe, **PLUS** seven percent of the sum of the open pipe and the first seven percent. The first valve will have to be more than twice as long as the second valve in order to lower the open pipe one whole tone. It is possible to build a valve of this length, and so far the instrument is still in tune through two half steps.

From here on there is difficulty. The usual fingering to lower an open note a minor third (three half tones) is first valve plus second valve. But second valve only has enough pipe to lower an *open* note one half step. It will not be long enough to lower a pipe that includes the first valve, a full half step further. Therefore, the first and second valves combined do not have enough length in the slides to lower the open pipe three half steps and the first and second valve combination is sharp. The third valve could be tuned correctly for this interval, since it has not been used yet, and many European instruments are tuned this way and the players taught to use third valve instead of first and second (See *Methodo per Flicorno* published by Ricordi), but this causes the second and third valve combination to be very sharp. For the moment the fingering for lowering an open tone three half steps will be first and second valves and the third valve will be tuned flatter than the minor third interval. The third valve, combined with second valve, will be tuned so that the interval of a major third (four half steps) will be in tune. Now all of the valves have been used to make at least one interval correct, but there are two more combinations remaining. First and third valve, for lowering by a perfect fourth (five half steps) will be sharp and first, second and third valves for a diminished fifth (six half steps) will be very sharp. Note also that with the above tuning, second and third are in tune, and had the third valve been tuned as a substitute for first and second, the second and third combination would be more sharp than with the American tuning.

Ideally, to have the valve slides at the proper lengths of tubing in each of the six half steps, the instrument should have six valves. As early instrument makers worked to solve this problem they even added extra bells to the instrument and for the best design, the euphonium should have six valves and seven bells. For other considerations though, the present day arrangement of one bell and three or four valves with various compensating devices is the most efficient manner of playing in tune.

Just Intonation, Pythagorean Intonation and Equal Temperament

Even if it were possible to have the proper overtone series, and have the valve slides of the proper length, an instrument that was perfectly tuned to equal temperament would still be playing out of tune. Although equal temperament is the standard, ensemble players have instinctively humored certain notes to blend or add brilliance to their playing. For a fuller explanation of these other temperaments listen to the Bell Telephone Laboratory recording, *The Science of Sound*, the William Stegeman tape, *The Marvelous Building Blocks of Music* and refer to the section on temperament in Chapter 17.

Chapter 31

Selected Literature and Annotated Bibliography

Graded List of Literature and Technic

Level 1

Fundamentals of tone production, embouchure development, breath support and attack.

Typical Material:

Studies: W. Beeler, *Method*, Book 1 (Remick); Cimera-Hovey, *Method* (Belwin); J. Kinyon, *Breeze-Easy Method*, Vol. 1 and 2 (Witmark).

Solos: J. Kinyon, *Breeze-Easy Recital Pieces* (Witmark); J. Arnold (ed.), *Easy Trombone Solos* (AMSCO); Warren Benson, *Aubade* (Marks).

Technic: Major scales in G, C, F, B flat, E flat, A flat, and D flat, one octave, in quarter notes, M.M. quarter note = 72.

Level 2

Work in elementary legato style. Continued development of fundamentals.

Typical Material:

Studies: W. Beeler, *Method*, Book 2 (Remick); J. E. Skornicka and E. G. Boltz, *Intermediate Method* (Rubank); R. Clarke, *Method* (C. Fischer).

Solos: G. Mullins (ed.), *Twelve Easy Classics* (Summy); J. Arnold (ed.), *Elementary Trombone Solos* (AMSCO).

Technic: All major scales and arpeggios, one octave in eighth notes, M.M. quarter note = 72.

Level 3

Studies in tone control, breathing, flexibility and articulation.

Typical Material:

Studies: R. Fink, *Studies in Legato* (C. Fischer); A. Slama, *66 Etudes in All Keys* (International); H. Voxman, *Advanced Method*, Vol. 1 and 2 (Rubank).

Solos: B. Beach, *Suite for Trombone* (Associated); G. Cords, *Romanza* (Cundy-Bettoney); E. Paudert,

Fantasie Marziale (Cundy-Bettoney); H. C. Smith III (arr.), *Solos for the Trombone Player* (G. Schirmer).

Technic: All major scales and straight arpeggios, one or two octaves, in simple and compound rhythmic patterns, M.M. quarter note = 72.

Level 4

Further development of range, tone control, breathing, flexibility and articulation. Work on double and triple tonguing. Introduction of tenor clef.

Typical Material:

Studies: R. Fink, *Introducing the Tenor Clef* (Accura); M. Bordogni-J. Rochut, *Melodious Etudes*, Vol. 1 (C. Fischer); continuation of A. Slama, *66 Etudes.*

Solos: F. J. Haydn, *Adagio* (Witmark); J. Galliard, *6 Sonatas for Bassoon* (McGinnis & Marx); A. Guilmant, *Morceau Symphonique* (Remick); H. Berlioz, *Recitative and Prayer* (Remick); Croce-Spinelli, *Solo de Concours* (Belwin); H. C. Smith III (arr.), *Solos for the Trombone Player* (G. Schirmer).

Technic: All major and minor scales and straight arpeggios, one or two octaves, in simple and compound rhythmic patterns, M.M. quarter note = 72.

Level 5

A review of all the fundamentals of trombone playing. Advanced flexibility exercises. Introduction of B flat treble clef transposition.

Typical Material:

Studies: O. Blume, *36 Studies*, Vol. 1 (C. Fischer); continuation of Bordogni-Rochut, *Melodious Etudes*, Vol. 1 (C. Fischer); H. Voxman (ed.), *Selected Studies* (Rubank); B. Gregoriev, *78 Studies* (International); L. Gillis, *70 Progressive Studies for Bass Trombone* (Southern); A. Ostrander, *The F Attachment and Bass Trombone* (C. Colin).

Solos: J. E. Barat, *Andante and Allegro* (Belwin); V. Blazhevich, *Concert Piece No. 5* (Belwin); A. Vival-

di, *Sonatas for 'cello* (Editions Salabert); G. P. Telemann, *Sonata in f minor* (International).

Technic: All major and minor scales, same as Level
4, plus diatonic pattern, all at M.M. quarter note =
84. Major and minor arpeggios in straight and broken
form at M.M. quarter note = 72.

Level 6

Work with improvisation. Introduction of the alto
clef. Further development of range and flexibility.

Typical Material:

Studies: R. Fink, *Introducing the Alto Clef* (Accura);
C. Kopprasch, *60 Studies* (C. Fischer); Bordogni-
Rochut, *Melodious Etudes*, Vol. 2 (C. Fischer); V.
Blazhevich, *Clef Studies* (International); C. Colin, *Pro-
gressive Technique* (C. Colin); O. Blume, *36 Studies*,
Vol. 2 (C. Fischer).

Solos: G. F. Handel, *Concerto* (Leduc); F. David,
Concertino (C. Fischer); A. Corelli, *Sonatas for 'cello*
(International); Otto Luening, *Sonata* (Galaxy).

Technic: Scales as in Level 5 with increased speeds,
plus quintuplet grouping. Arpeggios as in Level 5, plus
augmented, dominant seventh and diminished seventh.

Level 7

A study of the more advanced material with emphasis
on recital literature.

Typical Material:

Studies: O. Blume-R. Fink, *36 Studies for Trombone
with F Attachment* (C. Fischer); K. Kahila, *Advanced
Studies* (R. King); continuation of V. Blazhevich, *Clef
Studies* (Int.); continuation of Bordogni-Rochut, *Melodious Etudes*, Vol. 2 (C. Fischer); R. Fink, *Studies
in Legato for Bass Trombone* (C. Fischer).

Solos: P. Vidal, *Second Concert Piece* (Leduc); P.
McCarty, *Sonatina for Bass Trombone* (Ensemble Pub-
lications); R. Sanders, *Sonata in E Flat* (Remick); L.
Bernstein, *Elegy for Mippy II* (G. Schirmer); R. Monaco,
Sonata (Autograph Editions).

Technic: Same as in Level 6 with increased speeds.

Level 8

Further emphasis on clef reading and solos. Begin
study of the standard orchestral repertoire.

Typical Material:

Studies: V. Blazhevich, *26 Sequences* (C. Fischer);
continuation of Blazhevich, *Clef Studies*; J. S. Bach,
Six Suites for Unaccompanied Violoncello.

Solos: S. Stojowski, *Fantasie* (Leduc); J. Takács,
Sonata (Mills); J. Davison, *Sonata* (Shawnee); C.
Salzedo, *Pièce Concertante* (Leduc).

Technic: Same as Level 7 with increased speeds.

Level 9

Comprehensive study of Bach's *Six Suites for Unaccompanied Violoncello.* Further emphasis on orchestral
excerpts and recital pieces.

Typical Material:

Studies: J. S. Bach, *Six Suites for Unaccompanied
Violoncello.* Orchestral excerpts.

Solos: J. Castérède, *Sonatine* (Leduc); P. Hindemith,
Sonata (Schott); G. Jacobs, *Concerto* (Mills); G. F.
McKay, *Sonata* (Remick); T. R. George, *Concerto for
Bass Trombone* (Rochester Music), George Green, *Suite
for Solo Trombone* (Autograph Editions); P. McCarty,
Aria and Rondo (Rochester Music), D. H. White,
Sonata (Southern).

Technic: Same as in Level 8 with increased speeds.

Level 10

A coverage of all types of styles and techniques used
for solo, orchestral and ensemble playing. Memorization
of standard orchestral excerpts and selected recital
pieces.

Typical Material:

Studies: Continuation of J. S. Bach, *Six Suites for
Unaccompanied Violoncello*; orchestral excerpts; V.
Blazhevich, *Concert Duets* (MCA); R. Borden, *15 Dia-
logues for Trumpet and Trombone* (Ensemble Pub.);
G. Maxted, *20 Studies for Tenor Trombone* (Boosey
& Hawkes).

Solos: W. Hartley, *Sonata Concertante* (Fema); B.
Childs, *Sonata* for unaccompanied trombone (Tritone);
D. Milhaud, *Concertino d'Hiver* (Associated); P. Cres-
ton, *Fantasy* (G. Schirmer); J. Castérède, *Fantaisie
Concertante* for bass trombone (Leduc); R. Croley,
Divertissement (Ensemble).

Technic: Same as in Level 9 with increased speeds.

Annotated Bibliography

Texts

Arban, J. J. B. L. *Célèbre Méthode Complète de Trompette, Cornet à Pistons et Saxhorn.* Paris: Alphonse Leduc, 1956.

A modern version of the Arban's book, with a great deal of text to guide the musical study. Of interest to the trombonist is the "Preparation for the Contest" in Volume III.

Bahnert, Heinz, Th. Herzberg, and Herbert Schramm. *Metallblasinstrumente.* Leipzig: Fachbuchverlag, 1958.

An East German publication which includes a brief history of brass instruments with many drawings of ancient instruments and a complete description of the development of brass instrument valves. Includes many scale drawings of mid-20th century European instruments.

Bate, Philip. *The Trumpet and Trombone: An Outline of Their History, Development and Construction.* New York: W. W. Norton & Co., Inc., 1966.

One of the most scholarly books available in English. Traces the development of trumpets and trombones with many illustrations. Devotes a complete chapter to the development of valves and includes cut-away diagrams of several. Has several appendices and an excellent selected bibliography. Recommended as a standard reference book.

Brand, Erick D. *Band Instrument Repairing Manual.* 6th Edition. Elkhart, Indiana: The Author, 1946.

The most complete repair handbook available. Also includes a list of necessary tools and equipment for a commercial repair shop.

Colin, Charles. *Daily Warm-Ups with Vital Brass Notes.* New York: The Author, 1959.

A 32-page book which combines two works which were previously published separately. The *Vital Brass Notes* are a set of decisive easily read articles on brass playing. The *Daily Warm-Ups* is a reordered publication of his *Progressive Technique.* (See Chapter 20—High Register.)

Everett, Thomas G. *Annotated Guide to Bass Trombone Literature.* Nashville, Tenn.: The Brass Press, 1973.

A complete listing with scholarly annotations of all known works for unaccompanied and accompanied solos, chamber music, duets, methods and orchestral excerpts for bass trombone. It also includes a selected list of articles and texts related to bass trombone performance and a selected list of recordings with bass trombone.

Farkas, Philip. *The Art of Brass Playing.* Bloomington, Ind: Brass Publications, Inc., 1962.

A treatise which focuses principally on the embouchure used with brass instruments. It examines the specific idiosyncracies in the formation of the embouchure on each instrument. It contains numerous valuable illustrations and photographs.

Fennell, Frederick. *Time and The Winds: A Short History of the Use of Wind Instruments in the Orchestra, Band and the Wind Ensemble.* Kenosha, Wisconsin: G. Leblanc Co., 1954.

A brief history of the development of wind instruments. Discusses the orchestral use of wind instruments. Lists the instrumentation of various concert bands during the past 100 years.

Hall, Jody C. *The Proper Selection of Cup Mouthpieces.* Elkhart, Indiana: C. G. Conn, Ltd., 1963.

A report by Dr. Hall on experiments done in the C. G. Conn research department. Though the research was confined to trumpet mouthpieces, some implications can be drawn for trombone mouthpieces. The effects of enlarging certain dimensions of the mouthpiece on the intonation and tone quality were tested and diagramed.

Kent, Earle L. *The Inside Story of Brass Instruments.* Elkhart, Indiana: C. G. Conn, Ltd., 1956.

A small pamphlet describing the acoustics and the design problems of brass instruments.

Kleinhammer, Edward. *The Art of Trombone Playing.* Evanston, Illinois: Summy-Birchard Company, 1963.

One of the books in the Summy "The Art of . . ." series. Has a strong emphasis on breathing and embouchure, and advocates mouthpiece buzzing for the correction of many problems. The information about instruments and equipment is too general to be of help to an instrumental teacher and the selected literature is neither selected nor accurate.

Knaub, Donald. *Trombone Teaching Techniques.* Fairport, N.Y.: Rochester Music Publishers, 1964.

Although brief and inexpensive, it contains a wealth of information. Gives specific recommendations about trombones, mouthpieces and equipment. Contains a brief, but selected list of solos and an annotated bibliography of suggested methods. Also has a concise description of trombone playing problems. The second half of the book is devoted to music for the instruction of a college-level class of trombone minors.

Kunitz, Hans. *Die Instrumentation, Teil VIII: Posaune.* Leipzig: VEB Breitkopf & Härtel, 1959.

An exhaustive examination of the development of the trombone and its use in orchestral writing. Though in German, the orchestration examples can be studied without a reading knowledge of German. Also discusses the tenor-bass, the contra-bass, the alto and the soprano trombone in detail.

Leno, H. Lloyd. *Lip Vibration Characteristics of Selected Trombone Performers.* College Park, Washington: The Author, 1970.

A printing of the author's doctoral dissertation. Also available as microfilm or Xerox copies from University Microfilms, but the definition in the pictures is better in the printed version. An excellent high-speed-camera study of the lip vibrations of three symphony trombonists. This study proves that both lips vibrate (not just one), that they vibrate at the frequency of the pitch being sounded and that the lips do close during the vibrating cycle.

Maxted, George. *Talking about the Trombone.* London: J. Baker, 1970.

An informative booklet written in an entertaining conversational style. Briefly touches several aspects of performance including anecdotes about and suggestions for orchestral playing.

Porter, Maurice M. *Dental Problems in Wind Instrument Playing.* London: British Dental Association, 1967-1968.

The only complete book available at this time for teachers and students with dental problems. Gives specific instructions for the making of dental appliances. Also provides details for making partial and full dentures that will retain the embouchure of the player. Suggests that study models or life size photographs be made before any teeth are removed.

Porter, Maurice M. *The Embouchure.* London: Boosey and Hawkes, 1967.

An excellent discourse on the physiology of the embouchure. The discussion includes the teeth, the tongue, the oral cavities and the physiology of breathing. Includes a short medical glossary and a list of references. Contains 56 detailed illustrations. Should

be one of the fundamental reference books in any wind player's library.

Rasmussen, Mary. *A Teacher's Guide to the Literature of Brass Instruments.* Durham, New Hampshire: Brass Quarterly, 1964. 2nd Edition published by Appleyard Publications, Box 111, Durham, New Hampshire, 1968.

The best annotated bibliography of brass literature. Includes solos, methods, ensembles for like instruments and mixed brass ensembles. Should be one of the principal books of a brass player's library of reference books.

Reinhardt, Donald S. *Pivot System for Trombone: A Complete Manual of Studies.* Philadelphia: Elkan-Vogel Co., Inc., 1942.

Contains both an explanation of the pivot system and exercises for the implementation of the pivot system ideas.

Tiede, Clayton H. *The Practical Band Instrument Repair Manual.* Dubuque, Iowa: Wm. C. Brown Co., 1962.

A well-illustrated easily ready text on fundamental repairs of instruments.

Weast, Robert. *Brass Performance: An Analytical Text.* New York: McGinnis and Marx, 1961.

A report on a collection of experiments carried out by the author. Though some may have questionable validity, one experiment is a particularly useful way of thinking about lip vibrations and breath support. (See the description in Chapter 5—Developing the Tone.)

Wick, Dennis. *Trombone Technique.* London: Oxford University Press, 1971.

A recent addition to the Oxford series ". . . Technique." Well-written and covers many important aspects of trombone playing. Mr. Wick makes many firm statements which will help the reader. He does not hide behind generalizations which leave the reader without a concrete opinion. An excellent book.

Wiesner, Glenn R., Daniel R. Balbach, and Merrill A. Wilson. *Orthodontics and Wind Instrument Performance.* Washington, D.C.: Music Educators National Conference, 1973.

Written more to the American adolescents' orthodontia problems than Porter's *Dental Problems . . .*, this book concentrates on the problems encountered by a brasswind player when a dental appliance is used to correct a malocclusion. It describes various dental appliances and suggests ways to ease the player through the embouchure problems caused by them. This book should be a part of every wind instrument teacher's library.

Wright, Frank (ed.). *Brass Today.* London: Besson & Co., Ltd., 1957.

A collection of articles dealing with the various aspects of brass playing in the British brass band tradition. Includes articles on playing technique, intonation, balance, contests, microphone placement, festivals and schools.

Methods

Beeler, Walter. *Method for Trombone, Book 1.* Remick, 1944.

An excellent book with many pieces from the classics along with well-chosen technical exercises. Noticeably more difficult than the Kinyon or Cimera-Hovey methods. Best used with beginning junior high students as a beginning method, or with elementary students after they have learned some fundamental material in either the Kinyon or the Cimera-Hovey methods. Level 1.

Beeler, Walter. *Method for Trombone, Book 2.* Remick, 1962.

A continuation of the material in Book 1 with emphasis on technical studies and pieces from the classics. Some of the material is excellent for baritone or trombone with F attachment, but is very difficult for a trombone without an F attachment. Level 2.

Blazhevich, Vladislav. *Clef Studies for Trombone.* International, n.d.

Difficult studies which switch among bass, tenor and alto clefs. Excellent for the development of orchestral style. Should probably be prefaced with clef reading work in other methods before attempted. Uses unusual meters for some etudes. Level 6, 7, and 8.

Blazhevich, Vladislav. *26 Sequences for Trombone.* C. Fischer, n.d.

Excellent studies for the development of range, endurance and orchestral style. Each sequence has two parts. The A section ascends repeating each pattern eight times and each B section descends in a style similar to the A section in eight repetitions. Only recommended for the serious student. Level 8.

Blume, O. *36 Studies for Trombone, Vol. 1.* C. Fischer, 1899.

Volume 1 contains the first 12 studies of the 36. Study No. 1 repeats a four-line sequence of scales and arpeggios in all 12 keys and is especially useful for the establishment of precise intonation. The remaining studies are less difficult than Kopprasch, but more difficult than Slama. They are always tonal and do not use any unusual rhythmic figures. Level 5.

Blume, O. *36 Studies for Trombone, Vol. 2.* C. Fischer, 1899.

The second volume includes studies Nos. 13 through 24 and are noticeably more difficult than Vol. 1. The studies remain tonal and use common rhythmic figures. Level 6.

Blume, O. *36 Studies for Trombone, Vol. 3.* C. Fischer, 1899.

Only slightly more difficult than Vol. 2. The studies have a higher range and utilize more difficult keys. Continue to be tonal and use rhythmic figures which are in the same style as the first two volumes. Level 6 and 7.

Blume, O., Reginald H. Fink (ed.). *36 Studies for Trombone with F Attachment.* C. Fischer, 1962.

Transposed a fourth or fifth lower than the original studies. Editings suggest the use of the F attachment and other editings suggest methods of practicing the studies. The tonal quality of the studies aids the development of valve intonation. Moderately to extremely difficult if played at the marked *tempi* and dynamics. Level 7.

Bordogni, Marco. Johannes Rochut (ed.). *Melodious Etudes for Trombone, Vol. I.* C. Fischer, 1928.

A must in every trombonist's development of tone, breath control, endurance and legato control. The etudes frequently use high Gs and As, and occasionally include a high B natural. Should not be studied until preliminary legato control has been developed. Level 4 and 5.

Bordogni, Marco. Johannes Rochut (ed.). *Melodious Etudes for Trombone, Vol. II.* C. Fischer, 1928.

An often-neglected volume. Technically demanding and utilizing difficult keys, the studies develop advanced technique and control. Level 6 and 7.

Bordogni, Marco. Johannes Rochut (ed.). *Melodious Etudes for Trombone, Vol. III.* C. Fischer, 1928.

An excellent volume for the development of high register and endurance. Technically not always as difficult as Volume II, the etudes are much longer and use a higher *tessitura* than Volume II. Level 7, 8 and 9.

Cimera, Jaroslav and Nilo Hovey. *Cimera-Hovey Method for Trombone, Book 1.* Belwin, 1940.

A standard method for many years. Does not progress as slowly as the *Breeze-Easy Methods* and covers in 40 pages what is covered in both books of the *Breeze-Easy* series (over 60 pages). Useful as a method for students brighter or more mature than the average fourth grader. Contains a balanced selection of pieces and technical exercises.

Clarke, Robert. *Method for Trombone.* C. Fischer, 1913.

Originally a complete method. One that began with basic fundamentals and progressed through advanced technical exercises. Now used as an upper-level intermediate method for serious students. Exercises range in length from a half page to a full page and more, and are excellent for the development of stamina and concentration. All exercises are in a detached style although a teacher can easily pencil in slurs if he wishes to work on legato technique. Level 2, 3 and 4.

Colin, Charles. *Progressive Technique for Trombone.* C. Colin, 1958.

See Colin, *Daily Warm-Ups with Vital Brass Notes* in text bibliography. Level 6.

Fink, Reginald H. *From Treble Clef to Bass Clef Baritone.* Accura, 1972.

Though designed as a bass clef reading method for treble clef baritone players, it is an interesting method for trombonists who are learning euphonium fingerings. Moves rapidly from elementary pieces to more technically demanding arias, folk songs and etudes, while retaining a progressive approach to the introduction of new notes and their fingerings.

Fink, Reginald H. *Introducing the Alto Clef.* Accura, 1969.

A primer for reading the alto clef. A preparatory book for Kopprasch, Blazhevich and the orchestral repertoire. Progressively reviews rhythm and keys, while slowly introducing new notes of the alto clef a few at a time. Incorporates folk melodies, classics and arias. Includes some etudes in alto clef and in bass, tenor and alto clef. A few pages of orchestral excerpts. Level 6.

Fink, Reginald H. *Introducing the Tenor Clef.* Accura, 1968.

A primer for reading the tenor clef. Begins with five pitches in half notes and very slowly adds notes and introduces more complicated rhythms. Incorporates many folk melodies, classics and arias. The final few pages contain etudes in tenor clef, etudes which change between bass and tenor clef and a few orchestral excerpts. A preparatory book for Kopprasch, Blazhevich, *etc.*, and an excellent review of rhythm, keys and legato for the student who has advanced too rapidly. Level 4.

Fink, Reginald H. *Studies in Legato for Bass Trombone and Tuba.* C. Fischer, 1969.

Selected from the vocalises of Panofka, Concone and Marchesi, studies are progressively arranged in the same order as *Studies in Legato for Trombone*. An octave below the trombone book, these studies are moderately difficult for a bass trombonist, but are an intermediate book for tubists. Edited to show the use of the bass trombone valve. Also contains some written suggestions for the performance of the studies. Level 7.

Fink, Reginald H. *Studies in Legato for Trombone.* C. Fischer, 1969.

Designed to provide legato material that is more advanced than primary methods, yet easier than the *Melodious Etudes* by Bordogni-Rochut. Selected from the vocalises of Panofka, Concone and Marchesi and progressively arranged, studies purposefully limit upper register work so that a smooth legato can be developed without straining for high notes. Each study has a brief sentence or two of suggestions for the performance of the studies. Level 3.

Gillis, Lew. *70 Progressive Studies for the Modern Bass Trombonist.* Southern, 1966.

Progressively arranged etudes which creatively build tuneful exercises from the rudimentary tonal patterns that every F attachment trombonist must master. Level 5.

Gillis, Lew. *20 Etudes for Bass Trombone with "F" Attachment.* Southern, 1965.

Suggested as a sequel to Gillis' *70 Progressive Studies*. Tonal and creative etudes which will build advanced bass trombone technique. Level 6.

Gregoriev, B. *78 Studies for Trombone.* GMI, 1961.

Advanced intermediate studies with some musicality. Not as musical as Blazhevich, but not as patterned as Kopprasch or Blume. Makes use of some unusual meters and some use of tenor clef. Level 5.

Kahila, Kauko. *Advanced Studies in Tenor and Alto Clef.* R. King, 1948.

Difficult studies in a more contemporary style than the Blazhevich clef studies. Level 7.

Kinyon, John. *Breeze-Easy Method, Book 1 and Book 2.* Witmark, 1958, 1959.

A well-organized and progressively arranged method which is used successfully with young elementary school students. The printing is well done and the visual appeal of the book is excellent. The emphasis of the book is placed on thorough mastery of the fundamentals and the range and technique are limited to make this possible. Level 1.

Kopprasch, C. *60 Studies for Trombone.* C. Fischer, 1905.

Published in two volumes. The studies progress from intermediate technical pattern exercises to studies that are quite difficult. Some of the studies are in tenor clef and a few are in alto clef. A few others change through all three clefs. Level 6.

Maxted, George. *Twenty Studies for Tenor Trombone.* Boosey and Hawkes, 1954.

Extremely difficult high register studies. Uses alto clef for the most part. Almost every etude ascends to high Es, Fs and occasionally G flats. Not as tonally or rhythmically complicated as some other studies, they are difficult because of the extremely high *tessitura.* Mr. Maxted composed these studies for the development of high register. Recommended only for the advanced and serious student. Level 10.

Ostrander, Allen. *The F Attachment and Bass Trombone.* New Sounds in Modern Music (C. Colin), 1956.

A method which begins with elementary valve exercises and ends with orchestral bass trombone exercises. Should probably be supplemented with other material. Level 5 and 6.

Remington, Emory. *Warm-Up Exercises.* Rochester Music, n. d.

A booklet of the most popular warm-up exercises of the late Emory Remington. The selections range from the first exercises to the most advanced. Level 1 through 10.

Schlossberg, Max. *Daily Drills and Technical Studies.* Baron, 1947.

A transposition of the trumpet exercises of the late Max Schlossberg. Contains a wealth of material both for lip building and for technique development. Level 1 through 10.

Skornicka, J. E., and E. G. Boltz. *Intermediate Method for Trombone.* Rubank, 1938.

Best used to follow either Kinyon, Book 2 or the Cimera-Hovey Method. Originally designed to follow Newell H. Long, *Elementary Method for Trombone* (Rubank, 1934), but many find the Long book too demanding for beginning students. Level 2.

Slama, Anton. *66 Etudes in All Keys for Trombone.* C. Fischer. 1922, International, 1957.

A series of exercises which concentrate on scales and arpeggio patterns in all the major and minor keys. With a few exceptions, all etudes have a melodic character that can be stylized in an orchestral manner with a little imagination. The exercises do not tax the embouchure of a developing player because the highest notes are Fs or Gs above the bass staff. The numbers near the notes are bass viol fingerings and are ignored. Level 3 and 4.

Voxman, Himie. *Advanced Method for Trombone, Vol. I.* Rubank, 1941.

A well-planned method for intermediate development. Lesson plans in the front of the book group scales and arpeggios, duets, articulation studies, special problem etudes and solos into convenient units of study. Each unit can be accomplished easily in a week of practice. Some teachers prefer to substitute other solos for those provided. Level 3.

Voxman, Himie (ed.). *Selected Studies for Trombone.* Rubank, 1952.

An excellent collection of the best studies from several composers. Grouped by keys, the studies provide a means of developing both technique and musicality. Level 5.

Solos

Arnold, Jay (ed.). *Easy Trombone Solos.* AMSCO, 1950.

A large volume, at a relatively low price, of solos that are popular with young students. Level 1.

Arnold, Jay (ed.). *Elementary Trombone Solos.* AMSCO, 1940.

A large volume of solos at a relatively low price. Some of the selections are more appropriate at Level 2 than others. Level 2 and 3.

Barat, J. Ed. *Andante and Allegro.* Southern, Leduc, *et al.*

A very popular contest solo in the early 20th century French style. Has a band accompaniment that can be purchased from Southern Music Co..

Beach, Bennie. *Suite for Trombone.* Associated, 1957.

A contemporary solo which tastefully incorporates subtle elements of jazz. Level 3.

Benson, Warren. *Aubade.* Edward B. Marks, 1959.

A tasteful solo which is technically simple yet musically valid. Top note is one E'. Eighth note rhythm. Level 1.

Berlioz, Hector. *Recitative and Prayer.* Mercury, 1947.

A solo commonly found on many lists. Not technically difficult, but demands mature musicianship. Level 4.

Bernstein, Leonard. *Elegy for Mippy II.* G. Schirmer, 1940.

For unaccompanied trombone and is also available in Smith, *Solos for the Trombone Player.* Level 7.

Blazhevich, Vladislav. *Concert Piece No. 5.* MCA, 1946.

An early 20th-century solo written by a trombonist for trombonists. An excellent contest solo. Level 5.

Castérède, Jacques. *Fantaisie Concertante for Bass Trombone.* Leduc, 1960.

A good concert piece for an accomplished bass trombonist. Level 10.

Castérède, Jacques. *Sonatine.* Leduc, 1958.

A well-written contemporary French piece which effectively demonstrates the trombonist's technique and musical bravado. Has a moderately difficult piano accompaniment. Level 9.

Childs, Barney. *Sonata for Unaccompanied Trombone.* Tritone, 1962.

Not for the uncreative trombonist. Written partially in free notation it must be properly interpreted or it will not be effective musically. The third movement is a do-it-yourself rondo. The themes and variations are provided, the performer assembles the material into a rondo form. Level 10.

Cords, G. *Romanza.* Cundy-Bettoney, 1939.

An excellent study in legato control and phrasing. Level 3.

Corelli, Arcangelo. *Sonatas for 'cello.* International.

Several sonatas are available in performance editions and sold singly by International. All have the same qualities as the Vivaldi 'cello sonatas, except that the Corelli sonatas have a higher *tessitura* and some have double stops which must be arranged for trombone. Some are quite exhausting for a person without a seasoned high register. Most of these sonatas are playable without an F attachment. Level 6.

Creston, Paul. *Fantasy, op. 42 for Trombone and Orchestra.* G. Schirmer, 1951.

A demanding work which exploits technic, range and endurance. The orchestral accompaniment is noted for its unique tone colors. Level 10.

Croce-Spinelli. *Solo de Concours.* Belwin, n. d..

A contest solo which demonstrates both legato control and detached technical facility. Level 4.

Croley, Randell. *Divertissement.* Ensemble, 1968.

A difficult solo, for a musically sophisticated and accomplished bass trombonist. The accompaniment is equally difficult. Level 10.

David, Ferdinand. *Concertino, op. 4.* C. Fischer, International, *et al.*

A popular solo with touring trombone virtuosos of the 19th century. Written in an early 19th-century style. Now a contest solo when appropriate cuts are made. An orchestral accompaniment is available from some rental libraries. Level 6.

Davison, John. *Sonata.* Shawnee, 1966.

A lyric work which is fast becoming a popular recital piece. Level 8.

Galliard, Johann Ernst. *Six Sonatas for Bassoon, Vol. I.* McGinnis & Marx, 1946.

Vol. I contains Sonatas Nos. 1 through 3. Each of these Baroque sonatas has four or more movements and a concert piece can be formed by choosing two movements from a sonata. Available in two versions, one for trombone and another for bassoon and 'cello. The trombonist with an F attachment will probably prefer the bassoon version. (The trombone version has been arranged to eliminate notes below E.) Level 4.

Galliard, Johann Ernst. *Six Sonatas for Bassoon, Vol. 2.* McGinnis & Marx, 1946.

Contains Sonatas Nos. 4 through 6. For further

information see comments about Vol. 1. Level 4.

George, Thom Ritter. *Concerto for Bass Trombone and Orchestra.* Rochester Music, 1964, 1972.

A stylistic bass-trombone solo. Playable by a serious bass trombonist. Alternates between long flowing legato lines and articulated sections in a *giocoso* style. Top note is F'. Many Cs and quite a few pedal Gs and a few pedal Fs. Piano accompaniment is moderately difficult. Orchestral parts are on rental. Level 9.

Green, George. *Suite for Solo Trombone.* New York: Autograph Editions, 1971.

An excellent work in five movements for unaccompanied trombone. The movements; Prelude—Burlesk, Intermezzo, March, Cantilena and Finale; combine for a well constructed full length recital piece. Level 9.

Guilmant, Alexander. *Morceau Symphonique.* Remick, Leduc, *et al.*

A popular contest solo from the Romantic period. High register demands at least a B flat with an optional high C sharp. Level 4.

Handel, George Frederick. *Concerto.* Leduc, 1948.

An arrangement of the oboe concerto which gets a mixed reaction from both players and audience. Level 6.

Hartley, Walter. *Sonata Concertante.* Fema, 1956–58.

Written by a composer who understands trombones and trombonists. Technically demanding with a rather difficult piano accompaniment. Level 10.

Haydn, Franz Joseph. Davis Shuman (ed.). *Adagio.* Witmark, 1946.

An arrangement of the second movement of the Haydn 'cello concerto. Demands smooth legato control. Several alternate lines are provided below the original so that the solo can be played one octave lower if desired. Endurance can be a problem with this solo. Level 4.

Hindemith, Paul. *Sonata.* Schott, 1942.

A physically demanding work with an *extremely* difficult piano accompaniment. Level 9.

Jacobs, Gordon. *Concerto.* Mills, 1956.

A popular concerto, but quite taxing if played in its entirety. The second movement has special endurance problems, particularly when facing the full-length third movement. Moderately difficult piano accompaniment. Orchestral parts are available on rental. Level 9.

Kinyon, John (ed.). *Breeze-Easy Recital Pieces.* Witmark, 1958.

A well-arranged set of folk songs with an easy piano accompaniment. Level 1.

Luening, Otto. *Sonata.* Galaxy, 1953.

A tongue-in-cheek full-length sonata. Technical demands are modest (a few high B flats). Relatively simple piano accompaniment. Level 6.

Milhaud, Darius. *Concertino d'Hiver.* Associated, 1955.

French in quality, a very technical solo which might be more easily played on a smaller bore trombone. Demands delicacy and agility. Orchestral accompaniment is available on rental. Level 10.

Monaco, Richard A. *Sonata.* Autograph Editions, 1969.

An excellent contribution to the modern trombone literature. Well suited to the trombone. The third movement has some difficult ensemble problems between soloist and accompaniment. Top note is a high B flat. Level 7.

Mullins, Gene (ed.). *Twelve Easy Classics.* Summy, 1956.

A well-edited collection of classical and Baroque pieces. Excellent for developing a singing style and a rounded tone. Somewhat high for the average Level 2 student. Level 2.

McCarty, Patrick. *Aria and Rondo for Trombone and Orchestra.* Rochester Music, 1954.

A difficult but rewarding solo either with piano or orchestral accompaniment. The aria has both lyric and declamatory sections. The rondo is difficult, but possible for the accomplished player. Level 9.

McCarty, Patrick. *Sonatina for Bass Trombone and Strings* (Piano). Ensemble, 1962.

A three-movement work which is playable with piano or string orchestra accompaniment. The string parts can be purchased rather than rented as is the usual case with orchestra accompaniments. Though contemporary, the style is partially tonal and not avant garde. Level 7.

McKay, George Frederick. *Sonata.* Remick, 1951.

A work highly suited to the trombone. Has a *tessitura* which tends to rise as the third movement proceeds.

Endurance can be a problem with this solo. Level 9.

Salzedo, Carlos. *Pièce Concertante.* IMC, n. d.

Early 20th-century work. Tonal, somewhat impressionistic, with long lyric lines. Highest note is a D flat. Level 8.

Sanders, Robert. *Sonata in E Flat.* Remick. 1948.

A four-movement work which places musical demands rather than technical demands on the trombonist. The phrasing of long melodic lines and the subtle control of dynamics is quite important in this piece. The accompaniment is only moderately difficult, but the finale with its continuous $\frac{5}{8}$ meter does demand close attention to ensemble. Level 7.

Smith, Henry C. III (arr.). *Solos for the Trombone Player.* G. Schirmer, 1963.

Arranged pieces of Haydn, Handel, Galliard, Rimsky-Korsakov, Bach, Franck, Corelli, Berlioz, *et al.* Includes solos originally written for trombone by Guilmant, Bernstein, *et al.* Useful at several levels of accomplishment. Level 3 through 7.

Stojowski, S. *Fantaisie.* Leduc, 1967.

A popular French contest solo. Excellent for the demonstration of both legato control and technique. Level 8.

Takàcs, Jenö, *Sonata, op. 59.* Mills, 1954.

A contemporary solo for a musically sophisticated trombonist. Level 8.

Telemann, G. P. *Sonata in f minor.* International, 1949, 1960.

Originally written for bassoon. Neither as high nor as taxing as the Vivaldi 'cello sonatas, but is technically more difficult than a few of the easier ones. Level 5.

Paudert, E. *Fantasie Marziale.* Cundy-Bettoney, n. d.

Demands legato control, detached tonguing and the musical handling of a recitative section. Has all the attributes of a contest solo. Level 3.

Vidal, Paul. *Second Concert Piece.* Leduc, 1921.

One of the standard French contest pieces. Excellent for the demonstration of nuance control, moderate high register and technique. Level 7.

Vivaldi, Antonio. *Sonatas for 'Cello.* Editions Salabert, 1916.

This edition is one of several available of these six sonatas. It is recommended because the piano accompaniment is a slightly more florid realization of the figured bass than in other editions. Several movements would require an F attachment or some editing. As with other Baroque sonatas, a concert piece can be formed by choosing two movements of the four of the sonata. Endurance may be a problem—there are no interludes provided by the accompaniment. Level 5.

White, Donald H. *Sonata.* Southern, 1967.

Commissioned by the National Association of College Wind and Percussion Instructors (NACWPI). A fine contribution to the repertoire. Demands technique, legato control and a modest high register. Level 9.

Chapter 32
The Professional Attitude

Although the word *professional* implies that the person performs for money or is a well-schooled person who belongs to a profession, an amateur musician or a student can develop a professional attitude about his playing. The musician who has a professional attitude, or who is professionally routined, is one who is completely dedicated to playing his best whenever he has his instrument in his hands.

A person who is professionally routined is musically reliable. He does not miss entrances, is accurate in the subdivision of the beat, plays in tune and is conscious of the niceties of proper balance and tonal balance. You may be capable of doing all these things, but if you do not play this way everytime, you are not reliable. If you are not reliable, you are not professionally routined.

Your reliability depends on your ability to concentrate without distraction. A momentary lapse in concentration usually results in a missed entrance, an intonation error or a clam. Frederick Fennell's comment to the Eastman Wind Ensemble when a note was cracked was, "It's a state of mind as well as a state of embouchure," *i.e.* the miss may be blamed on your embouchure, but the miss was caused by not thinking about the note properly (maybe not thinking about it all).

This ability to concentrate is a habit that must be cultivated—it is not something you can just decide to do and then do without any difficulty. Sterling Moss, the retired *grand prix* race driver, believes that learning to concentrate totally on a certain job for more than a few seconds takes effort and practice. He says, "It took me *eight* years of intense effort to learn to concentrate so thoroughly that in a three-hour race I would not have to *tell* myself to concentrate, and I would not have one extraneous thought." Musicians may not have to concentrate for three hours without a break like a *grand prix* driver, but many musicians cannot concentrate for even a minute or two without

the distraction of extraneous thoughts.

Musicians are presented with many distractions that make concentration difficult: The person practicing next door; the boring rehearsal; the dance job with a group of incompetent instrumentalists; the unappreciative audience; the muddy football field; the rain, snow and horses of a parade; *etc.* **BUT,** no matter what the distraction, the truly professional musician is concentrating on the musical sounds that he is producing.

A professional attitude does not mean that you think about your breathing, your embouchure, your tongue, *etc.* The person who clutters his mind with concerns about the physical aspects of playing is distracting himself. When concentrating with a professional attitude, you are listening for and projecting the best possible musical sounds to the audience. Any thoughts about the physical aspects of playing are reserved for the concentrated work in the practice room or a split-second check during a performance. Your physical habits must be so set during your private practice that they function almost automatically during rehearsals and concerts.

You must develop your ability to concentrate on the task at hand without a single moment's lapse. You practice concentration whenever you have the instrument in your hand and even though it does not matter whether you do your best or not in some situations, you must continue to develop this professional attitude at all times. Every note from the first warm-up note to the last note of a poor and dull rehearsal must be played with extreme attention to detail. Everything must be played with the complete dedication of a solo in a concert.

Do not expect your ability to concentrate for unending periods of time to be developed by habit or just naturally. It will take constant work for a period of several months before it is possible for you to perform without having your mind notice or think about extraneous things.

Notes

Notes

Notes